# Apache
# over Libya

All proceeds from the sale of this book will be donated to
SSAFA and Combat Stress.

**Combat Stress** is the UK's leading mental health charity for Veterans, providing specialist clinical treatment and welfare support to ex-Service men and women across the UK. Founded at the end of the First World War, it has since helped more than 100,000 Veterans and is today supporting almost 6,000 – more than at any time in its long history.

With demand for its services increasing every year, it is vital that Combat Stress is there to help Veterans rebuild their lives with courage and dignity.

**SSAFA** is the longest serving national tri-Service military charity. For 130 years SSAFA has provided lifelong support to those who are serving or have ever served in our Armed Forces.

Today nearly five million people living in the United Kingdom are estimated to have served in the Armed Forces at some point in their lives. Every year, around 20,000 Servicemen and women leave the services and return to civilian life.

That is why SSAFA's work is so important. We believe that those who have served their country should get the best possible support when they need it.

# Apache
# over Libya

Will Laidlaw

Pen & Sword
**AVIATION**

First published in Great Britain in 2016 by
PEN AND SWORD AVIATION
*an imprint of*
Pen and Sword Books Ltd
47 Church Street
Barnsley
South Yorkshire S70 2AS

ISBN 978 1 47386 762 8

Printed and bound in Malta by
Gutenberg Press Ltd

Typeset in Times by CHIC GRAPHICS

*Pen & Sword Books Ltd incorporates the imprints of*
Archaeology, Atlas, Aviation, Battleground, Discovery,
Family History, History, Maritime, Military, Naval, Politics,
Railways, Select, Social History, Transport, True Crime,
Claymore Press, Frontline Books, Leo Cooper, Praetorian Press,
Remember When, Seaforth Publishing and Wharncliffe.

*For a complete list of Pen and Sword titles please contact*
Pen and Sword Books Limited
47 Church Street, Barnsley, South Yorkshire, S70 2AS, England
E-mail: enquiries@pen-and-sword.co.uk
Website: www.pen-and-sword.co.uk

# Contents

# Glossary

**AAA** (Anti Aircraft Artillery, also known as Triple-A). Typically ZU-23-1 and 2, and ZPU-4, 23mm calibre weapons designed to shoot down aircraft. They have a 400 rounds per minute rate of fire, a muzzle velocity of about 1000m per second and are effective up to 4,500ft and out to 4km. They replaced the older 14.5mm ZPU-1 and 2, which have a slower (approximately 150 rounds per minute) rate of fire and a shorter range. These weapons were prolific in Libya and were often mounted on the back of pickup trucks. AAA mounted on pickup trucks are known as 'technicals'. In Libya they were also used directly against ground forces.

**American lady in the wing**. Better known as 'bitchin' Betty', this calmly enunciating voice tells us when things go wrong. Her real name is Erica Lane and she's from Alabama. The software-triggered voice announcements gain the attention of aircrew and alert them to what is going wrong. She informs us of everything from a missile being launched at us to an engine failure.

**AWACS** (Airborne Warning and Control System). The flying command and control centres, with a large disc-shaped radar in front of the tail. These aircraft provided round-the-clock coordination for all NATO activity in the air.

**AWS** (Area Weapon System). The 30mm gun on the Apache that can fire off-axis and can be controlled by any of the aircraft's sights, including the pilot's helmet, allowing rapid lethal engagements. Each of the 30mm rounds has a High Explosive Dual Purpose warhead, which delivers both a fragmentation and armour-piercing effect.

**Back-seater**. Also known as rear-seater. The Apache has a tandem, dual-control cockpit, with the pilot sitting in the rear seat.

**BDA** (Battle Damage Assessment). The assessment of the effect of their strike conducted by the aircrew after an engagement.

**Bingo**. A fuel state expressed as the fuel required to get you back to Mother with the minimum left in the tank to land. Once your fuel is at bingo you must to return to Mother; there is no spare fuel for any more target time or diversions.

**BM21**. Also known as the 'Grad', the BM21 is a Russian-made multi-launch rocket system mounted on the rear of a truck. Depending on its configuration, 20 to 30 tubes each fire a rocket reaching out to 20km.

**BZ** (Bravo Zulu). A naval signal, originally conveyed by flags, meaning 'well done'. To receive a BZ is high praise, and it is given sparingly.

**Callsign**. All aircraft have a callsign, a name to be recognized by on the radio. 'Machete' is one of the 656 Squadron callsigns. Over Libya we diversified into several different callsigns – 'Prodigy', 'Jilted' and 'Underdog' were among our favourites. They were all official NATO designations and were dropped as soon as the operation was over.

**CAOC** (Combined Air Operations Cell). The CAOC was located in Poggio Renatico, near Bologna in Italy. This is where the NATO air campaign was planned and managed.

**CDE** (Collateral Damage Estimate). Every weapon has CDE implications. When writing the MISREP, aircrew were to describe any CD issues. CD is also considered when conducting BDA.

**CIVCAS**. Civilian Casualties.

**CO** (Commanding Officer). In the Army CO relates specifically to the command of a Regiment.

**CPG** (Co-Pilot Gunner), also known as front-seater. The CPG has control of the sights, sensors and weapons. He is usually the aircraft commander too. Although the Apache has dual controls and can be flown from either cockpit, the front-seater is usually too busy finding and engaging targets to have his hands on the flight controls.

**CSAR** (Combat Search and Rescue). The people who come and pick you up if you end up on the run having been forced to land. For the first three weeks of our work the NATO CSAR was at five hours notice to move. In late June the 56th Rescue Squadron from the United States Air Force joined us on HMS *Ocean*. They sat at thirty minutes notice to move, but well-honed drills meant that they would usually be off the deck in around seven minutes. Consequently, morale went up among the Apache crews.

**CTR** (Conversion To Role). Following CTT (*see below*), newly trained Apache pilots embark on the eight-month CTR teaching them attack helicopter military Tactics, Techniques, and Procedures (TTPs). On completion, a pilot is ready to join a front-line Attack Helicopter Squadron.

**CTT** (Conversion to Type). The eight-month training course teaching already qualified military pilots how to fly and operate the British Apache.

**Delta Hotel**. Direct hit. When a fired munition goes exactly where the gunner wants it to go. Over Libya every one of our Hellfire shots was a Delta Hotel.

**Dunker**. The Under Water Escape Trainer. A module used to practise escape from a ditched helicopter.

**Ellamy**. The name of the UK military operation in Libya in 2011.

**FCR** (Fire Control Radar). Mounted above the main rotor blades the FCR senses objects in the same way as conventional radar. The aircrew can then visually interrogate those objects with the FLIR.

**Feet-wet/feet-dry**. Terms used to describe when the aircraft is over the sea (feet-wet) or over the land (feet-dry).

**FLF** (Free Libyan Forces). Initially, those who took part in the uprising against Gaddafi were known as 'rebels'. As they became more distinctly organized they were recognized as the Free Libyan Forces.

**Flip-flop**. The Air Group planning compartment in HMS *Ocean*. During Operation Ellamy 656 Squadron were allowed sole use of the lower flip-flop. The squadron conducted all its planning and debriefing in the flip-flop.

**FLIR** (Forward Looking Infra Red, but now commonly used for any infrared system). The Apache infrared sighting system can be rotated in azimuth and elevation to provide a wide axis of view and was the most commonly used Apache sighting system in Libya. It is part of the Target Acquisition and Designation System (TADS).

**Flyco** (Flying Control). Where flying is coordinated on a ship, akin to an air traffic control and located on the bridge.

**FMC** (Flight Management Computer). The FMC makes the ten-tonne Apache stable in flight, giving the aerodynamic stability needed to engage targets.

**Fragged.** Once launched from HMS *Ocean*, the Apache would check in with the airborne command and control aircraft and describe its mission number, callsign and timings. If these were unchanged from the original fragmentary order that directed the mission, the commander would simply say, 'launched as fragged'.

**Front-seater**. The front seat pilot, also known as co-pilot gunner. The front-seater is usually the aircraft commander. He controls the sights, sensors and weapons. Dual controls also allow the front-seater to fly the aircraft.

**Hellfire.** An air-to-ground missile used by the Apache. Other platforms such as the Predator drone also fire Hellfire.

**Herrick**. Operation Herrick was the name of the UK military operation in Afghanistan 2002–14.

**H-hour**. This is the time on a mission that the first shot is fired. H-hour is a datum specified as both a time and an activity upon which all subsequent events are anchored.

**HMD** (Helmet Mounted Display). The HMD is a lens attached to the flying helmet and placed over the pilot's right eye. All the information, both infrared and symbology, the pilot needs to fly and fight is projected into his right eye via the HMD, allowing him to get on with the task at hand without needing to search for information. Additionally, on the Apache the position of the pilot's head is tracked, and therefore dynamic data can be presented via the HMD. For example, the position of the pilot's head drives the IR turret around, capturing an image which is then fed into the pilot's HMD in real time.

**IR** (Infrared). This senses the difference in temperature between objects and converts it into a video image. It requires no light and so works both in daylight and in complete darkness. Apache pilots fly using the video image from IR as well as using the FLIR for targeting. They are therefore able to fly and shoot in total darkness.

**Jackspeak**. Royal Navy slang.

**JCHAT**. The live text messaging system used by NATO. This delivers situational awareness across the operating area as users text their SITREPs for all to monitor, without the need for voice radio messages.

**JTAC** (Joint Terminal Attack Controller). A soldier, traditionally on the ground, who controls and orchestrates the airborne and artillery assets in his area of operations and directs them when and where to fire. The JTAC will normally be able to see the target, has a complete understanding of the rules of engagement and controls the airspace used in the strike. In Libya they were based in airborne maritime patrol aircraft.

**Litening Pod**. A precision targeting suite using infrared and laser fitted to a variety of fast jets.

**Looker**. In an Apache patrol the 'looker' observes while the 'shooter' engages a target. The looker relays information to the shooter to assist his wider situational awareness of the target area. The looker is also protection for the patrol, searching for threats while the shooter is focused on the target.

**MANPADS** (Man Portable Air Defence System). Shoulder-launcher missiles that use infrared technology to acquire and track the heat signature of their target. Libya had more MANPADS than any other non-manufacturing country in the world.

**MISREP** (Mission Report). The MISREP is completed after each mission and details what was seen and what was done. It is used by NATO to collate and track mission information.

**Mother**. The ship. Home at sea for all aircraft.

**MPD**. Multi Purpose Display. The screens in the Apache cockpit where all aircraft, navigation, weapons, communications and tactical information are displayed.

**NAAFI**. (Navy, Army, Air Force Institution). The convenience store at military barracks.

**NCO**. Non-Commissioned Officer.

**NEO** (Non-Combatant Evacuation Operation). The military's role in rescuing British nationals and entitled personnel from another country.

**NGS**. Naval Gunfire Support.

**NVG** (Night Vision Goggles). These use the very low levels of light from the moon, or ambient light reflected from cloud, to produce a green video image, allowing the operator to see in the dark. Apache crews use them as an aid to targeting in addition to IR. Pro-Gad had NVG too.

**ORBAT** (Order of Battle). The official list detailing each and every unit assigned to support an operation.

**Parrots and India**. Encrypted electronic codes that are transmitted by military aircrew to identify themselves to other friendly aircraft. Once an Apache launched from HMS *Ocean* the airborne command and control aircraft would interrogate this code to confirm the right aircraft was on the right mission.

**Patch**. The 'married patch', where Service families live in housing provided by the military.

**Phalanx**. A self-defence weapon mounted on the deck of a ship. Its radar finds and then tracks incoming munitions for the weapon to then engage, in the same way as any other radar-guided weapon system. In flying against the Phalanx radar we were able to hone our manoeuvring and defensive flight profiles against a targeting radar. It was also all we had to train with, and we only had one opportunity to try it.

**PKM**. A 7.62mm Russian-designed general-purpose machine gun. In service around the world since the 1960s, the PKM fires 800 rounds per minute and is accurate out to 1,500m.

**Predator/Pred**. A remotely piloted aircraft, also colloquially known as a drone. These have a laser designation system and are also armed with Hellfire. They have an extensive suite of radios and are also able to stream live video images.

**Pro-Gad**. Pro-Gaddafi. All forces loyal to the Gaddafi regime.

**QBOs** (Quick Battle Orders). When a commander needs to make a rapid plan of attack he uses QBOs. These will cover the essential components of the attack such as speed, height, heading and formation style. They rely heavily on a well-trained and competent patrol to intuitively fill in any information gaps.

**QHI** (Qualified Helicopter Instructor). Our helicopter experts, graded B2, B1, A2 and A1. B2 is the most junior qualification, A1 the most senior, B1 is the commonest. The jump from B1 to A2 is a tough exam. QHIs study for months to make the grade. The jump to A1 is herculean and very rarely achieved.

**RF.** Radar Frequency, a type of Hellfire. The Fire Control Radar (FCR) mounted on top of the aircraft finds a target. The pilot checks the target is suitable to shoot and gives the information to the RF missile. The missile acknowledges the target information and displays its readiness to launch via the weapons symbology. The pilot checks everything is ready and points his infrared sight at the target, if he can, so he can see it. When all is ready the pilot pulls the trigger, the RF comes off the rails and heads for the target. This process, from the FCR finding the target to the RF coming off the rails, takes no more than 2.5 seconds. Once the missile is in the air, no pilot guidance is required; the missile does the rest.

**RFI** (Radar Frequency Interferometer). A passive sensor mounted under the FCR that searches for radar-emitting threats.

**Rolex**. A term used to describe delaying an already agreed time. If, for example, the agreed launch time is 21:00hrs and a 20-minute delay is required, a 'Rolex 20' would be requested. The new launch time is then 21:20hrs.

**RPG** (Rocket Propelled Grenade). A shoulder-launched anti-tank weapon with an effective range out to 1km.

**SA-5**. Russian-manufactured radar and missile system. It has huge 35ft-long missiles with 217kg warheads capable of taking down large, high-altitude targets. There were none of these missiles left when we got involved in Libya, but their radars were still working. Able to find and track targets out to 170 miles, the radar could be used to alert other weapons systems and was treated as a significant threat to us.

**SA-6**. A Russian-manufactured anti-aircraft system designed to target jet fighters as well as helicopters. The system comprises a radar vehicle, known amongst NATO pilots by the designation 'Straight Flush', which acquires and then tracks a target at a range of up to 17 miles. A separate vehicle carries up to three missiles, which can reach high altitude jets and low altitude helicopters out to 15 miles.

**SA-7**. A first-generation Russian-made MANPAD. It fires a heat-seeking missile that will typically lock on to the engines of a helicopter. Flares are fired to decoy the missile.

**SA-24**. A very sophisticated Russian-made MANPAD. This heat-seeker will try to ignore the flares and will self-destruct as a last resort.

**SAMbush**. An ambush of surface-to-air missile systems.

**Shooter**. In an Apache patrol the 'shooter' engages a target while the 'looker' observes the area around the target. *See also* 'looker.'

**SITREP** (Situation Report). A brief summary of what has happened. On the way back to HMS *Ocean* a SITREP was always given to the AWACS. This information was immediately relayed to the CAOC and to HMS *Ocean* via JCHAT.

**SKASaC**. Sea King Airborne Surveillance and Control helicopter.

**Stand Easy**. Morning coffee break at sea.

**Starburst**. An illumination round fired from a ship's 4.5in gun. It hangs in the air under a parachute to illuminate targets for the ship to engage. This was required by Royal Navy ships when engaging targets in Libya.

**Symbology**. The Apache displays information on the MPDs and HMD via a system of icons known as symbology. Apache aircrew learn this system from their first day in training.

**Technicals**. Standard commercial pickup trucks with heavy weapons systems mounted on the rear. The weapons were never smaller than high calibre machine guns, but were often anti-aircraft artillery pieces or surface-to-air missiles. Both sides had thousands of technicals.

**Triple-A**. *See* AAA.

**T-72**. A Russian-made Main Battle Tank.

**VCP**. Vehicle Checkpoint.

**VHR** (Very High Readiness). In Afghanistan two Apaches were dedicated to VHR 24 hours a day. Their crews resided in a tent close to the Fight Line ready for immediate notice missions. Their task was simple – react to anything we tell you to do, be it an escort of the Chinook Immediate Response Team or direct support to troops on the ground. When required, a 'shout' comes in by telephone and the crews rush to launch. There are stipulated timings within which the aircraft must be airborne. These are never breached as the aircraft are always off chocks and taxiing within just a few minutes of the 'shout' coming in. Sprinting to the aircraft on receipt of a 'shout' is a feeling that all Herrick Apache crews will remember forever.

**WAFU**. Naval slang for Weapon and Fuel User. The more commonly used amplification however is Wet and F*****g Useless. The term WAFU is only applied to aircrew at sea.

**Wings** (Commander Air or Lieutenant Colonel Air). The colloquial name for the senior officer responsible for all flying activity onboard. He was our go-to man when we needed things fixed, changed, smoothed, thrown over the side or generally made better.

**XO**. Executive Officer. On a ship the XO is the Captain's right-hand man. He is also the discipline officer.

**ZSU 23-4**. Also known as 'Shilka', the ZSU 23-4 is a potent anti-aircraft platform. The '23' stands for its 23mm calibre rounds. The '4' describes the number of gun barrels which fire at 1,000 rounds per minute. The ZSU 23-4 has a radar that finds and tracks its target as well as aiming the gun barrels. All this is mounted on a 20-tonne tracked vehicle for mobility.

# Acknowledgements

There are seventeen principal characters in this story, and almost all are referred to by pseudonym, as is the author himself. Throughout our research and writing we have sought perspective and context from within the 656 Squadron team and the wider Defence community associated with our work over Libya. We are grateful for their contributions, patient editing and support. In particular, we wish to thank Derek Blois for the hours of graphic design on the maps and for allowing us to publish a reproduction of the painting 'Raid on Brega'.

Many of the images herein are Crown Copyright and have been acknowledged as such. The rest were taken by those on board HMS *Ocean*. We thank them for their images. Particular thanks to Neil Atterbury of Four Elements photography for his outstanding work and permission to use his image as part of the jacket design. Special thanks to Simon Mair for reading, re-reading and editing throughout, and to all the team at Pen & Sword, especially Henry Wilson, Matt Jones, Lori Jones, George Chamier and Katie Eaton, who have been so supportive in realizing our ambition to have this book published.

Throughout the summer and autumn of 2011 our families and close friends at home followed our progress through intermittent phone calls and media stories. Waking up on Saturday, 4 June 2011 to Facebook and text messages instructing 'turn on the TV, they're on the news' was the start of a very long worry for them. Their support at the time inspired us, their continued forbearance amazes us.

We also extend our appreciation to the Boeing Company and Augusta Westland for designing and manufacturing the best attack helicopter in the world, Lockheed Martin for the tweaks, weapons and radar, Rolls Royce and Turbomeca for the engines and Selex ES for the defensive aids suite. These groups, and the scientists and engineers who tuned the whole machine, gave us a gunship that took us into harm's way, looked after us while we were there and brought us safely home again. We would not have made it through without such dedicated expertise behind us.

Our greatest debt of gratitude is to the men and women of 656 Squadron and all those who served on board HMS *Ocean* during the summer and autumn of 2011 while we flew missions on Operation Ellamy. Stoic, proud and utterly professional, they kept us going in a very dangerous place.

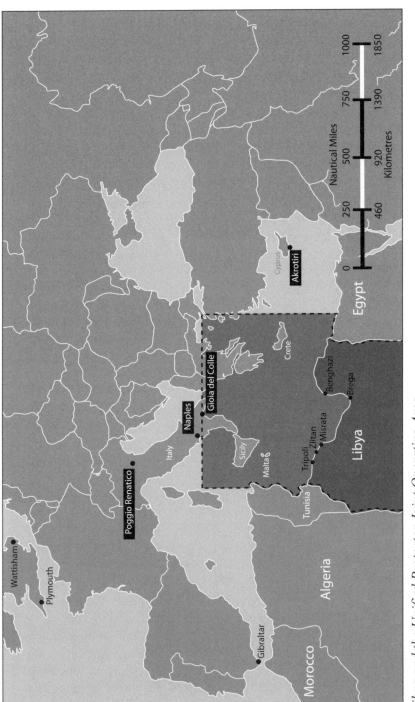

*Libya and the Unified Protector Joint Operating Area*

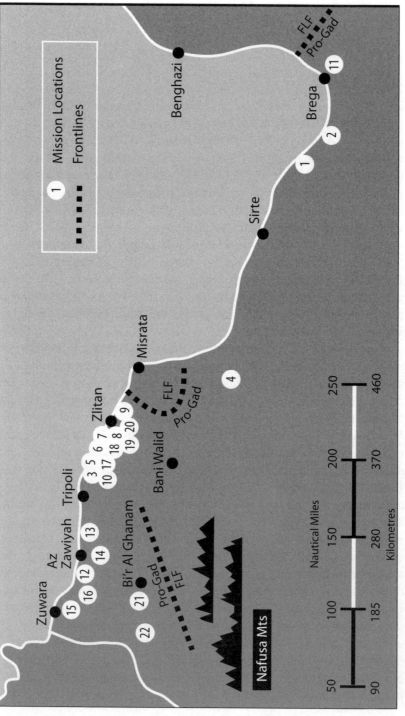

*Libya, showing the three front lines and the 656 Squadron mission locations*

# Prologue

This is the story of a perilous combat experience in the face of deeply unattractive survival odds over Libya in the summer of 2011. Flying ultra low-level over the sea at night into hostile territory became normal life for the Apache crews of 656 Squadron, Army Air Corps. Often engaged by Gaddafi's forces as soon as they were in sight of the coast, they had to fight their way into Libya, complete their mission while evading lethal fire from the ground and then fight their way out again, before searching for a ship in the dark many miles out to sea. Flying well within the reach of Gaddafi's prolific ground-to-air weapons, these men made nightly raids behind enemy lines and got away with their lives. This is the story of eight Army and two Royal Navy pilots who flew against the most potent enemy British aircrew have faced in generations. They defied the odds and survived, playing a fundamental part in the NATO-led campaign. This is the truth about the Apache at sea and in combat over Libya.

This book contains the combined recollection of the men and women who operated the Apache attack helicopter over Libya during the summer of 2011. It is their truth as noted in their own diaries at the time, now collated as the historical record of a six-week training exercise that unexpectedly became a four-month high-intensity combat operation. Spending 155 days at sea, with 130 days on station poised off the coast of Libya, they flew 48 combat sorties firing 99 Hellfire missiles and 4,800 rounds of 30mm cannon, striking 116 targets. Every mission was flown from and to HMS *Ocean*, using procedures they themselves designed for the first Apache maritime operation anywhere in the world. The words herein are theirs, none are embellished or dramatized, nor have they been ghost-written. The story is told by the squadron commander, Will Laidlaw, and has been checked against the remembered experiences of those involved. To ensure the fullest telling of the story, it includes the words of several other squadron members. Every effort has been made to ensure the accuracy of this narrative; it is our truth as we noted at the time and now recall. Any inaccuracy is unintended and we will be happy to correct it in later editions. Some of the protagonists continue to serve in Her Majesty's Armed Forces, while others have since left. In respecting their wishes for anonymity, some pseudonyms have been used.

## Chapter 1

# A New War

'Missile launch, 3 o'clock! . . . Flares! Flares! Flares! . . .
It's coming at us . . .'

**Libya, 9 June 2011**
Rapid tension. Dry mouth. High voice. A new terror, searing fear. The possibility of being shot down over Libya by the most lethal Russian-made anti-helicopter weapon in existence was now a reality. Travelling at 800m per second, the missile was just three seconds from impact.

It was almost midnight and over the Libyan coast, not far from Misrata, two Apache attack helicopters raced in towards their target – a Command and Control node used by Khamis Gaddafi, the dictator's favoured son. As soon as the pair crossed the coast an SA-24 heat-seeking missile was launched from the cover of the sand dunes. Even the most modern military helicopter should not be able to survive an SA-24 hit.

Again, 'Flares! Flares! Flares! . . . Still coming at us . . .'

We had one second left in life. Everything was done, we had strained every sinew to survive, and now, in that last fragment of time, we stared in petrified astonishment as death raced at us. Then a chance was offered. The missile swerved, seduced by our final set of flares, and self-destructed in shards of bright white and orange shrapnel in front of my cockpit. I flinched and instinctively ducked at the explosion.

'Whoa! That doesn't give up does it'? I shouted to Staff Sergeant John Blackwell, my rear seat pilot.

Simultaneously, from the wing aircraft, 'That's not an RPG! Looks high end, I have the launch point, I can see the shooter, ready to suppress.' This was Mark Hall, my wingman, weapons man, Operations Warrant Officer, general expert and now companion in a fight for our lives, coming over the inter-aircraft frequency.

John Blackwell, calm, hands on the controls, kept us heading for our target. His voice cut through the chaos: 'Boss, you're ten seconds from a good launch profile . . .'

Pressing the transmission switch with my left foot, I issued the new plan: 'I have the C2 node, you have the missile firing point, back with you in 45 seconds!'

Only seconds from the firing on the C2 node the surface-to-air missile had interrupted, now I was determined to get the job done, while Mark Hall and his rear-seater, Charlie Tollbrooke, protected the flank. Within 30 seconds I had put two Hellfire missiles into the C2 node and observed a few seconds of panic on the ground, before John brought our Apache hard round to the right.

I transmitted to Mark Hall, 'Targets destroyed, lining up on your right, observing your fall of shot . . .', and we manoeuvred to serve as protection for him as he tipped in, his 30mm disgorging three 20-round bursts to deal with the SA-24 man. It was 9 June 2011, only our third mission into Libya; we had two more months of this.

## Chapter 2

# Forming the Team

Consider this: the aircraft is done in, no longer flyable; you are over the sea at night and just a second from going in. Now, ribs cracking on impact, face thrashed against the controls, teeth smashed and jaw broken, but you're lucky, somehow the canopy was off before you went in and you are conscious. Flesh-ripping ingress of water tears off your flying helmet and fills your mouth. Without air, now submerged, you choke. Entombed in darkness, you are cold-shocked, gasping involuntarily, upside down. In the time it takes to read these words, time has almost run out. All you have left is three seconds to locate your harness and release, undo the three cables still attached to the flying helmet that is hanging off your head, find the hole where the canopy was and force your body, armour, ammunition and weapon through the gap. You could take out the short-term air supply bottle and get another breath, but that would waste time. You've only been under fifteen seconds. You get out. The sinking aircraft is now too deep, you are negatively buoyant. It's too late. You try to swim up, but you can't. You pull the toggle to inflate your lifejacket; the water pressure denies its function. You sink. You're waiting to drown.

*

At the start of this enterprise there were four of us: me, Little Shippers, Big Shippers and Mark Hall. We needed six more pilots to fly the Apache at sea. It wasn't a popular choice. The sea is a brutal place and survival there demands time and luck, neither of which are predictable or likely to be in your favour. Time is measured in seconds, luck controls how badly injured you are, how heavy the aircraft is, how cold the water is, the scores of things that could trap a limb in the cockpit, the chances of getting the doors off before hitting the water. Luck fills the space planning cannot.

The Apache helicopter was designed in the 1970s to replace the Bell

AH-1 Cobra that had seen service in Vietnam. It is fundamentally a land-based helicopter. In the early days the boffins at Hughes played with a maritime design but found it was not required, so stuck to the land project. The original AH64 A model Apache saw its first United States Army service in 1986, two years after Hughes became part of McDonnell Douglas. Notable success in Panama and the first Gulf War followed. In the mid-1990s the British Ministry of Defence ran a commercial competition with the aim of procuring ninety-eight Attack Helicopters for the Army and Royal Navy. With an ever-decreasing Defence budget a compromise was reached, but not on the capability of the platform. Eventually, sixty-seven of the upgraded AH64 D model Apaches were purchased, all with the highly capable Longbow Fire Control Radar. We have even strapped two enormous Rolls Royce engines to the side to give them more power. Since 1997 the Boeing Company has been the firm behind the Apache. The UK procured the aircraft via Augusta Westland, and through this conduit we have the finest attack helicopter in the world. Back in the late '90s there were not enough of these new and highly complex aircraft to spread across two Services, so the Army got the lot, with a promise to train one of its squadrons to fly at sea. The challenge from the start was that the Apache was not designed to operate at sea.

But the British way is to disregard convention and make things work. The earliest embarked trials were carried out in 2004 and 2005, and it fell to 656 Squadron to do the work. They did. The aircraft could land and take off safely; the engineering could be done; the base level concept was proved. Then along came the conflict in Afghanistan. The Squadron put the maritime work on the shelf and became the first British Apache squadron to deploy to Afghanistan, adding another operation to its tally. From 2006 everything the British Army did was about succeeding there. All our training was about Afghanistan, all our equipment was optimized for the arid, talcum sand environment and all our people were brought up to think counter-insurgency thoughts. Nobody could doubt the success of the aircraft. It had a phenomenal impact in support of British and Coalition forces in Helmand. This is where it earned its spurs; six squadrons with lineage in the Auster, Sioux, Scout, Gazelle and Lynx were now flying the Apache and rotating one after another through Operation Herrick, the British name for the military mission in Helmand.

The squadron has an extraordinary operational history. From the Second World War, where the only two recipients of the Distinguished Flying Cross and the Military Cross combined flew in 656, to Malaya,

Borneo, Rhodesia, the Falklands, the Balkans and Afghanistan, the squadron has fought for soldiers alongside sailors and airmen for over seventy years. This squadron's heritage comes not from it finding a niche or somehow being 'the best'; nor is it held in higher regard than any other squadron. It is just because 656 was next on the list to go, and when it did go the squadron performed as any military team would – with determination, spirit and courage, whatever the task and whatever the threat. In the early 2000s the squadron found itself next on the list again and became the first British Army Apache squadron. In 2006, when the UK committed forces to Helmand Province in Afghanistan, the squadron deployed with them. Over the next three years 656 Squadron went there and came back three times, returning for the last time in May 2009. I took command the same month, expecting to deploy with the squadron again the following year.

The scale and importance of the British operation in Afghanistan meant there was no spare capacity for any other activity. Everything was optimized for Helmand, every person, piece of equipment and way of working. Everyone in the Army had to expect to deploy there with only a year or so between coming home and getting on the bus again. The Attack Helicopter Force was no different. Since that first brutal summer with 16 Air Assault Brigade in 2006, its six squadrons had rotated through Helmand, doing five months on the line followed by a year at home, before getting ready to go again. The Apache itself never left. It flew every day and night throughout the province, wherever British soldiers needed its support. Six squadrons worked a well-worn rotation until November 2009, when change was forced upon us. Savings had to be made and we needed to rationalize training and operations, so 656 Squadron was next on the list again. I was training on the firing ranges in Arizona when the CO phoned me.

'The situation has changed.' This is military speak for 'your planning has been overtaken by someone else's decision, so stand by to re-plan'.

'You have a challenge; we are changing your role. No more Afghanistan for 656. You will deliver front-line operational training and I want you to reinvigorate a contingent capability with anything you have left.'

We had only trained for Afghanistan, and I had planned accordingly. Now we were going to run the training and develop ideas for a war that might come next. Our first Apache squadron not being on current operations was unthinkable. The first British Apache squadron, the first one into Afghanistan, the one that flew the Jugroom Fort[1] mission, was closing that part of its operational history and could be beginning another.

In a parochial sense I was disappointed not to be part of the Afghanistan cycle. I had always wanted to be in the Apache programme, and selection for command of a front-line squadron came with the assumption that operations in Afghanistan would be part of the tour. But the situation had changed, we had a lot of work to do and, while others could not, we could see the opportunity in this role. Military operations in Afghanistan would not last forever and we needed to be ready for what came next. Although we were not to know it, 656 squadron was once more about to pioneer a new way in military aviation.

By 2010 there was senior military acknowledgement that, while Afghanistan was the top priority, we needed to be ready for whatever came next. For the majority of the Army what came next was another tour of Afghanistan. Encouraging the consideration of a contingent capability beyond our Afghan responsibility was an uphill challenge. As I searched for support for my part in the project it became abundantly clear that the top priority was the only priority and anything else was to be taken at risk.

So effective was the communication that everything must be optimized for success in Afghanistan that my wish to challenge for scant resources was regarded as trivial, or worse, counter-productive. The 'didn't you get the memo?' attitude was extraordinary. 'What are you doing that for?' was frequently asked. Preparing for something that was not real, that was not currently on our plate, was going to be painful. To me it seemed we were losing our imagination. I was forced to think new thoughts, to talk about operations other than Afghanistan. There were a number of individuals, many of them senior, who recognized the importance of developing a capability for the future, but at this stage of the Herrick campaign they were considerably outnumbered by those who could not afford to think beyond the next Afghan deployment. They had to train, deploy, fight and come home, then repeat. The Afghanistan rotation had harnessed the energy and, in some cases shackled the thoughts, of many who went there. By 2012 a wholesale military reset for the Army embraced contingent operations, but in 2010 in the Attack Helicopter Force it felt like 656 was on its own.

We had not needed to think about how we could work elsewhere in a different scenario, with a different threat. From an attack helicopter perspective it seemed to me that we had become comfortable operating out of the reach of dangerous weapons, where acting with total freedom was the expectation. We had a generation of aircrew who had spent years in Afghanistan and had grown into very experienced and capable operators in most respects; but due to the tempo and nature of that operation other skills had been allowed to wither. The hard-to-learn and easy-to-lose skills involved in defending and fighting the aircraft in a hostile environment, skills we did not need in an Apache in Afghanistan, had become just ten per cent of the training course. These skills were to become ninety per cent of what we needed over Libya. Being ready for whatever came next was wise. Breaking through the layers of 'Afghanistan is the only war' thinking was going to be difficult.

Conflict is unpredictable. It often arrives quietly and by surprise. And all you have to respond with is what comes to hand. You cannot wish more people, planes, ships, helicopters, guns, tanks or whatever out of thin air. Conflict is a come-as-you-are activity. This uncertainty requires agility – warriors in the current war who know that there will be a different war tomorrow. Conflict moves quickly, it is changeable. Conflict finds a new way, a new weapon, a different geography and new recruits. The bellicose persuasion of the human condition will not wait for you to agree with it or realize it needs to be fought. Conflict chooses you. Politicians and soldiers must be ready for it, whatever it may be. When fully committed to one specific conflict there is often little opportunity to consider how to deal with what might come next. In 2010 we had, in a small way, been given the chance to explore this with the Apache and present a case for new and unusual ways of using the aircraft outside its role in Afghanistan.

My priority was training front-line aircrew for Afghanistan. My second task was 'everything else, if you have anything left'. It was clear that if I had anything left it should be taken to provide for Afghanistan, whether it was needed or not. At times it felt like 656 was regarded as a training provider that must be kept in its place. If the squadron started to do anything other than priority number one it was somehow denying a crucial resource that should be taken and used in Helmand.

Our training task was demanding for soldiers and planners, but not overly complex. It had been running for six years. The resources were known, the standards were understood and it was a question of balancing the number of instructors available to teach, the right number of aircraft to conduct the sorties and the willingness of the Great British weather to allow training to be completed. The Apache combat training course, known as Conversion to Role, or CTR, lasts eight months and is as demanding as the preceding eight months learning to fly the machine.

Several years of Afghanistan experience had been reinvested in instructors of exceptional quality, resulting in a CTR syllabus that was Afghanistan-focused and delivered to the highest standard. This is a tough course, but the exacting standards are necessarily high; the ongoing operational context served as a daily reminder of this. Crews in training conducted their planning alongside crews completing their final preparations prior to deploying to Afghanistan. They all attended post-operational conferences together, and the CTR students knew that if they maintained the right standards they too would be in Afghanistan in a matter of months. Combat training has never been better informed or delivered, and the product was well worth the investment.

As long as I did not make too much noise and incur the wrath of the 'Afghanistan is the only war' warriors I could quietly develop the maritime use of the Apache. During the summer of 2010, after my own pre-Afghanistan training in Arizona, I spent three weeks at sea gathering the facts and working out the range of our maritime potential. I needed to understand the unique challenges of conducting helicopter operations at sea, as well as exploring the limitations of putting an Apache on a ship. The immediate problems are obvious to a sailor, but not to a soldier. However big your ship, it will never be big enough. There is very little space. What space there is, is shared. The ship moves all the time – up, down, forwards, sideways. The power supply is different. You have to lash down anything that you want to stay on board, including helicopters. A mistake could mean a fire or a flood or a soul lost to the sea. You will knock your head, knees, hips and elbows on hatches and ladders. You share, a lot. It takes at least a week to know your way round a ship. Meals are measured in minutes. Inspections are frequent and standards are high. Discipline is strong. Sailors speak an entirely different language. Rapid assimilation to this environment is needed to get through the culture shock. Survivor's Jackspeak is essential. If you've only done half a 'dog watch' or you are 'Percy Pongo', you had better learn quickly where to find your port and starboard oars and when it is acceptable to 'double-duff' in the Wardroom. More generally, knowing the difference between wanting a 'goffer' and getting 'goffered' is useful – 'WAFUs' are an easy target!

The sea is a ruthless place. It cares not for mistakes and it is a punisher. Throughout history, mariners have developed and refined procedures that ensure, as much as possible, the safety of a ship and her sailors. Transgression from these procedures could result in fire, flood or unscheduled bathing. The rule is simple: 'the ship you are in is your best life-raft, do everything you can to preserve that.' The challenge I would face in the coming months was how to convince the operators of such multi-layered safety structures to put in that life-raft an aircraft with a narrow undercarriage, high centre of gravity and tonnes of ammunition. Turning off all the lights and flying to and fro by night was a sound and workable idea that would increase capability rather than place it at risk. But first I had to get enough backing among colleagues in the Attack Helicopter Force to entertain such a low priority while the current conflict was in full swing.

Right at the top of the Force, support was there. The Force Commander was as excited as we were by the project, but many of his team and significant numbers of my experienced contemporaries were dedicated to Operation Herrick. Some were supportive, others less so. Whatever their opinion of our maritime enterprise, they had to drive hard to train and deploy squadrons to Afghanistan. Those who cared about the 656 activity acknowledged it might come in useful in the future; those who cared not made it clear. To the naysayers it was simple: we were at war in Afghanistan and must dedicate everything we did to that. To do anything else would be an act of disloyalty to our soldiers in Helmand. If your activity was in any way a distraction from someone else's activity over there, you were doing the wrong thing. Those who feared the technical challenge also remarked that the Apache was a land helicopter and cannot stay upright on a moving, pitching flight deck at sea. It is not made from 'marinized' materials and will literally dissolve as the salt water corrodes it, they said. Additionally, there were concerns over the explosive content of rockets, missiles and 30mm ammunition in the magazine of the ship. The list of why it would not work was long; the challenge was massive.

The Apache was designed for land operations where take-off and landing both take place from a static location such as a field or a short runway. It has a high centre of gravity, due in part to its Fire Control Radar mounted above the main rotor blades, and a narrow undercarriage; these, combined, make it less stable on a pitching and rolling flight deck at sea. To illustrate the problem, take a look at a Sea King front-on and then compare it with an Apache. Someone in the design phase of the Sea King addressed the unstable platform issue by placing the undercarriage wide, and giving it a folding tail section so it can be stowed in tight spaces; they also gave it automatically ranging and folding rotor-blades, also handy for stowing and avoiding the need for engineers to laboriously do that work themselves. Now take a look at the Apache again. It has almost the same dimensions as the Sea King in length, width and height. However, it has none of the sea-going design features that the trusty workhorse of the Royal Navy and the Commando Helicopter Force has. Its tail is rigid, its undercarriage is narrow and its blades have to be folded and ranged by hand, taking a team of eight engineers over an hour to complete. By the end of our Mediterranean mission of 2011 this took just 25 minutes – but still five times longer than the Sea King!

There are a couple of other less than optimal aspects of the Apache for operations at sea which concentrate the minds of the aircrew inside. The aircraft has very poor ditching characteristics. In other words, it doesn't float. The Apache sinks fast, so its occupants will quickly find themselves in a state of negative buoyancy. Once you are negatively buoyant you will sink, no matter what you do to swim upwards. The water pressure becomes too great for the life vest to inflate and the pilot, weighed down by ammunition, survival equipment and body armour, will sink at an increasing rate. We carry a short-term air supply bottle which gives perhaps thirty seconds to a minute of air – enough for another attempt at getting out of the cockpit, but no use if you are already too deep. Getting out in time is the top priority.

Being under water in a helicopter is a horrendous place to be, and many seaborne helicopters have quick mechanically jettisoning doors and floatation gear to assist aircrew should their aircraft have to land or crash into the sea. The Apache was designed to fly over land and take on tanks and well-armed troops. It is bristling with weapons and defensive systems and has no space or, until now, need for floatation aids. The other problem is that the canopy jettison is made from explosive detonation cord. No handy yellow and black lever to pull, whereupon the door falls away. The Apache canopy literally explodes when jettisoned. However, the jettison system has potentially lethal consequences if activated underwater. One of two things will happen. The external water pressure forces the blast debris back into the cockpit, which incapacitates the pilot. Or, if there is any water between the pilot and the canopy, the blast energy is transferred to the pilot, which is likely to be lethal. There is no way of winning once under water; the canopy has to be off before you go in.

For us maritime operators the second page of the Apache Emergency Flight Reference Cards is burned into the memory. It translates thus:

Get the canopy off before you enter the water, you won't survive if you get this wrong. The water ingress will be violent. It will be dark, cold and you will be upside-down. Water will be up your nose and in your eyes and you will be disorientated. Get out fast. Make sure nothing is going to snag you on the way out. Fractions of seconds count.

We all spent time in the Under Water Escape Trainer, or 'dunker', to hone the procedures of escaping a ditched aircraft. A specially designed Apache module is used and aircrew wear the equipment they would be flying with to replicate the tight fit and tricky escape. Even with an emergency short-term air supply bottle to give an extra breath or two, egress, particularly from the front cockpit, is difficult. We all knew that an emergency ditching at night into the sea would lack the composure of the 'dunker'.

Of course the obvious fix to all this is to make the aircraft float. But floatation kit was on no one's scratchpad. It didn't need to float in Afghanistan, so why go to the expense of retrofitting the kit? The calculation was all a reasonable balance of money (not much of that), risk (lots of that, but only if you fly it over water) and operational output (that depends what you want).[2]

In the absence of floatation gear and a more friendly canopy jettison, we would have to get the canopy off prior to entering the water and then fight to get out before the plummeting aircraft took us too deep. With all the additional weight of ammunition and survival equipment attached to our body armour, the egress had to be very quick.

The daily challenges were diverse. I had to enter the debate on why we were developing a capability that did not contribute to operations in Afghanistan as well as facing a conceptual challenge in designing new ways of using the aircraft. It was also a significant engineering project. Then we had the practical 'how to fly it' and 'how to escape it' issues too. The squadron was very busy and I wanted both our tasks to work, but at times it seemed we lacked understanding from our wider community as everyone else was fully committed to the cycle of Afghanistan tours.

Set against criticism that it was needlessly risky, probably not worth it and just a distraction from current operations, I could only agree that it did not warrant the full backing of those not involved. Why should they care? The more career-ravenous around me saw it as an opportunity to exploit – 656 was no longer on the front line, not a proper squadron, the only one of six front-line Apache squadrons not due to feature on the Afghanistan ORBAT. Consequently, this made for some lonely times in 2010. I was just dreaming up ideas, most of them involving a ship – none of which had much relevance to the reality of ongoing conflict in Helmand. Nothing I was doing was contributing to the immediate need, yet I was consuming resources and adding strain to the flying programme. My activities were irrelevant to those who were dealing exclusively with Afghanistan. Some were not content and sought to limit my ambition, others tolerated it as a sideshow to their much more important work. At the time I found this frustrating, but on reflection theirs was a reasonable response. If landlocked Afghanistan was the only war, then training at sea with an Army helicopter was a ridiculous idea. Only a fool would believe such a digression would yield operational utility.

Solving the maritime problems had to be a state of mind as well as an act in itself. We had to embrace the project and deal with all the other obstacles that came our way. We believed in the task and we were determined to make it work. To us this was a challenge worth taking on (and we had no choice). I dealt with the 'what's the point?' debate constantly during my tenure in command, although, not surprisingly, this argument largely went away after Libya. However, in 2010 my biggest concern was how to fly, sustain and then escape the aircraft if it all went wrong over the sea.

My first task was overcoming the technical challenges. There would be no chance of testing the operational utility of the aircraft if we could not maintain, re-arm and refuel it as well as safely move it around the ship from hangar to flight deck. At the same time I had to let go most of my aircrew to reinforce the Afghanistan squadrons, leaving me with a skeleton crew of pilots able to take the maritime development forward, while all the other squadron aircrew were fully committed to teaching CTR. It was all change, all of it resource-driven, and 656 had to settle with everyone else's Afghan leftovers and make do.

When it comes to change and managing people within change, there will always be about twenty per cent who will take on the change and embrace it, whatever it is – the energetic enthusiasts. Similarly, there will always be another twenty per cent who will never embrace it – the pessimists. They have to go. If they are not part of the team, yet have an influence on how it is resourced and operates, they have to be convinced, marginalised or confronted. This can be problematic in an institution where seniority assumes superiority – expert, experienced, qualified or not. If the negative twenty per cent are senior executives in an institution constructed around vertical hierarchies, delicate diplomacy and persuasive advancement of your case is the only way of balancing their voice. In our project a naysayer would occasionally raise an eyebrow and offer criticism, often based on amateurish advice, for example: 'The undercarriage is too narrow, it will fall overboard.'

As a subordinate, I would be duty-bound to answer, 'No it won't, we'll lash it down, just like they do with everything else.'

Then they would counter with a typical 'Yes, but what does it do for Afghanistan?' comment, and I would be left without an answer.

The technical challenge was a relatively straightforward issue of trials, training and practice before going to sea, then running live serials to prove the capability. Much more subtle was the people dimension. With forty per cent already accounted for, the enthusiasts and the pessimists, the middle sixty per cent then had to be persuaded that the cause is worthwhile and that your leadership is worth following. This could only be done with time and action.

In October 2010 we got our chance. HMS *Ark Royal* was available, as was the north coast of Scotland, and seventy soldiers, three aircraft and three weeks in the fifth and last *Ark Royal* gave us the building blocks to make our project happen. Cape Wrath in early winter with sea state seven and driving rain was our first outing! On some days the entire ship's company were taking seasickness tablets, on others the sun shone and we launched. We had both the Shippers with us, Big and Little. If your heritage is Royal Navy and you are on loan to the Army, then 'Shippers' is your name. We had two of them. One was bigger and older than the other: Big Shippers and Little Shippers, everyone knew who they were. It had been a few years since anyone had been to sea in an Apache, and it was down to these two to unravel the mystery and make sense of it all.

A Royal Navy Lieutenant Commander with seven years experience on the Apache, Big Shippers was part of Army Aviation Flying Standards, a powerful man in our world, one who could really make this thing work. Joining at nineteen as a midshipman, Big Shippers had lived a life in Royal Navy and Army aviation. He knew his way around both communities and was highly regarded on land and sea. He was an expert, a genuine, detailed expert. He knew the envelope of the Apache in such technical depth that he became our go-to man with the 'will this work at sea?' questions. As a Standards examiner he also had a formidable reputation. All of us had been under his microscope before, be it in training or during a visit to the Regiment. The stern, analytical manner of the man disguised a wicked wit, which we got to know during the many 'first night madness' sessions when we took a break from operations during the summer of 2011. His flying portfolio was steeped in the skills we needed at sea and he became the crucial link – so crucial, in fact, that his scheduled return to the Royal Navy and the Sea King was delayed until after the summer of 2011. In Big Shippers we had a man who could write the new rules we needed.

The Shippers had to teach one another the deck landing procedure and then deliver the training to the rest of us. We were right at the start of our journey. We had barely any residual knowledge of flying the Apache at sea, just enough instructors with the right skills to redefine the training, and only the minimum of soldiers to make the whole enterprise happen. I leant heavily on Big and Little Shippers as well as the two Regimental instructors who came along to share the burden.

The original aim of the Royal Navy's lending instructors to us was to get the Apache working at sea, but Afghanistan had changed all that. Navy, Royal Marine or RAF, if they were on exchange with us they flew in Afghanistan regardless of their background. Little Shippers had completed flying training just ahead of me in the late 1990s, joined the Commando Helicopter Force and quickly became an instructor on the Sea King. He had already spent five years on the Apache, including a year in Afghanistan. He knew the sea, he knew the Apache and he knew combat. Back in Helmand he had once had to land an Apache after the tail rotor controls had become jammed having been shot by a 12.7mm Taliban bullet. The bullet buckled the armour just beneath his right foot, thumping his leg against the cockpit and seizing the tail rotor controls at the same time. Little Shippers realized he had no control over the tail and had to exit the fight and return to Camp Bastion. Losing the tail rotor is problematic in a helicopter and can often result in an uncontrolled tumble when it comes to landing. He ran the aircraft on to the runway fast like an aeroplane to keep it in a straight line, and the aircraft and the crew sustained no further damage or injury. Fighting and dealing with emergencies at the same time is a high skill; we would all be tested on this in Libya.

Part of reminding one another of how to fly the Apache at sea was demonstrating how to cope with a single engine failure at the worst moment. The aircraft has two engines; if one fails the other can keep it going only if the aircraft has enough airspeed. A single engine failure at low airspeed is a potentially fatal moment at sea. The Shippers had to practise together and then teach us all.

On their first outing, Big Shippers at the controls, they lifted from the flight deck into the 70ft hover on the port side over the sea. With Little Shippers ready, hand on the canopy jettison switch, he demonstrated the single engine flyaway technique.

'Practice single engine failure . . . Go!'

Big Shippers immediately pushed the cyclic lever forward to dive the aircraft, trying to gain airspeed, while lowering the collective lever to preserve the remaining engine and maintain rotor speed. I watched from Flyco as the aircraft dropped rapidly below the flight deck, nose first, toward the sea. A dive is the only way to gain the speed needed to fly away, but the risk is that an inaccurate pilot might not be bold enough and too slow to throw the aircraft seaward. Over land, if this technique is mishandled the aircrew can convert a badly managed engine failure into a run-on landing. Over the sea it can only be converted into a crash, with all the attendant sub-surface dramas already described. Out of sight, beneath the line of the flight deck, Big Shippers gained speed, levelled at about 20ft above the waves and flew away, slowly climbing back into the port circuit. The margins for error are tight at sea.

Safely downwind in the circuit, he then demonstrated the single-engine landing back on to the ship. To maintain straight and level flight the Shippers needed to keep the aircraft airspeed above 40 knots. With the ship heading into wind, and of course moving herself, they could land at a lower relative speed, but this was still much quicker than *Ark* was expecting. As the aircraft approached, the usual yellow-coated flight deck marshallers were ready and, looking aft, getting nervous. The Apache was coming in fast. At a quarter of a mile and about twenty seconds until landing the flight deck teams realized what was about to happen. Big Shippers threw the aircraft on to the flight deck at 25 knots groundspeed, landing on the aft end and using half the deck length to slow down. The sailors on the flight deck, who were expecting a gentle Sea King-like drop on to the deck and a slow walking pace run-on, had to throw themselves out of the way to avoid being mown down. The Shippers kept the aircraft level, brought it to a halt and Big Shippers calmly announced on the radio to Flyco, 'All's well. Can we do that one again to consolidate the technique? No need for marshallers on landing though . . .'

The technical challenges on deck were dealt with in a cautious manner. The most time-consuming and complex skills faced the engineers in adapting their trade, refined by years in Afghanistan, where big open spaces and plentiful spares supported their now extensive corporate knowledge of the aircraft. In a ship there are no large spaces, very few medium-sized spaces and just enough spaces that are almost big enough. The positioning of aircraft in a hangar is a complex jigsaw puzzle, and the scheduling of maintenance must take into account the movement of several aircraft, in addition to those of other aircraft fleets which share the same hangar space. This may appear simple, but a comparison of land and maritime procedures is a useful illustration.

On land it takes five minutes to tow an aircraft from the flight line to the hangar and begin work. At sea it takes up to 45 minutes to fold blades, another 10 minutes to manoeuvre the aircraft on the flight deck and a further 10 minutes to place it on the lift and get it down from the flight deck into the hangar. If the work requires a crane, the other aircraft in the hangar must be moved to make space, taking perhaps another 15 or 20 minutes. Then, after about an hour or so, work can begin. Of course, that assumes that your aircraft move is the priority; if not, you'll have to wait and shift out of the way of the others. The process is then followed in reverse to return the aircraft to the flight deck for use. This requires eight engineers and eight soldiers to complete, with the aircraft being lashed down every time it is not being manoeuvred. While the number of hours flown will likely be lower at sea than on land, the level of preparatory activity will always be higher, with soldiers and engineers working longer in an unfamiliar and unforgiving environment to get an aircraft ready to fly. It just takes more people, and more time. Mistakes can be very costly, either in damage to an aircraft or injury to personnel. With this in mind, and having seen the procedures in action, I needed the right balance of manpower to ensure safe and efficient operations even if the resultant tempo of flying was low. This raised some jeers from the pessimists, who cited my manning needs as a further drain on finite and stretched resources which, of course, should only be used to support Afghanistan.

The *Ark Royal* embarkation was the critical de-risking activity of the Apache maritime story. The work was hard, soldiers had to get used to the confines of the ship, old procedures had to be relearned, new ones had to be developed.

*Ark Royal* came alongside in Portsmouth at the end of October and we stepped ashore. We had relearned the 'how to fly it' and 'how to maintain it' lessons first trialled in 2005. We had fired over 6,000 rounds of 30mm ammunition on the ranges at Cape Wrath, flown many hours at sea at night in formation with and without lights. We had engineered, lived and built our relationship with the Royal Navy. The foundations were strong. I was quietly optimistic that, having proved the machine worked at sea, we could gather some momentum and get some support from the sceptics.

However, just two weeks later *Ark Royal* was decommissioned. The Harriers went too. There would be no jets at sea for at least a decade, and the Royal Navy had just HMS *Illustrious* and HMS *Ocean* left as helicopter carriers. With our maritime future uncertain, Big Shippers and I went to Helmand as guests of 654 Squadron, taking up some of the strain on the aircrew constantly going through the Afghanistan cycle. As guests we were just line-pilots with no other work to do. This was perfect. We spent hours planning what we could do the following year. We knew HMS *Ocean* would have us on board and that we would have almost six weeks at sea if we could get the blessings and the resources. In the meantime, wintering in Helmand with another 4 Regiment squadron was just right for us.

By early January 2011 our tour was almost at its end; 654 had done their bit again and were heading home to disappear on leave. I had one rather pressing problem in 656 – I didn't have enough pilots for the summer trip to the Mediterranean, and with only three months until we were due to embark I needed to solve the issue quickly.

In the year leading up to this point almost all my aircrew had been reallocated to other squadrons and most of those I had left were teaching CTR. I only had four pilots permanently available for maritime work, and this included me. I needed ten.

Little Shippers and Mark Hall were left holding the maritime work together. The squadron Second in Command, Reuben Sands, had done the Afghanistan tour ahead of mine at short notice, even postponing his wedding to step up to the plate. He was on a spot of leave regaining the family time lost over the summer and autumn. Reuben loved flying and was dedicated to it. This powerful rower, often in need of a haircut, knew his stuff. Every time I flew with him he demonstrated he was above the high bar and I had something to learn. A man of principles, of physical presence and of the North-East, Reuben was ready for whatever came next. If he had time in the winter a vintage motorcycle would be renovated in the living room, but mostly it was about flying. He was utterly dependable in the air, a truly multi-dimensional mind able simultaneously to compute, analyse and fight. He would return from leave and embark with us, but in the meantime it was Mark and Little Shippers who led the planning for our summer cruise. Back in Suffolk, they pressed ahead with maritime simulator sorties, ideas of how to shoot fast-moving boats and how to choreograph the technicalities of ship to shore and back to the ship missions. With us four already on the list, Big Shippers agreed to make it five. I needed five more.

Still in Afghanistan, I asked around for volunteers who needed to be unafraid of the dunker and willing to be tested at sea. And, slowly, they emerged. I also had assurances from home that a couple of aircrew would be found from those not on the Afghanistan tour cycle for 2011. In the meantime, I needed to find three pilots from 654. I was asking soldiers who had just spent five months, including Christmas and New Year, in Helmand to give up their summer and spend it in a ship instead. The response was not quick!

I pointed out that 654 would get a good four weeks leave on their return to the UK and then faced a post-tour summer of air testing and admin back in Suffolk as they fell to the bottom of the pile in the Afghanistan cycle. Surely a trip to the Med would be much more interesting? To make my search harder, I specifically needed an Operations Officer. These are not easy to find. It had to be an experienced officer willing to take on all the additional planning a squadron needs to embark as well as to maintain their own flying skills and learn the new ones of flying at sea. There were only two possible candidates and neither needed another summer away from home.

I gave an honest appraisal of the role, the culture shock, the complexity of the Apache at sea and I described the embarkation in outline:

> We'll stop in Gibraltar and run up a rock, we'll stop in Malta and have a run ashore. In between there will be some demanding flying that you'll never do again with this aircraft. It's a one-off chance to do something different. Just make sure you're current in the dunker and remember that going to sea is a come-as-you-are party – what you bring is all you have.

The enquiries slowly started to come in. With only two weeks to go until we flew home, I filled the three empty lines on my list. Nick Stevens stepped up as the Ops Officer. He had done three tours of Afghanistan and was probably ready for the Ops role a year ago. This looked like unusual work, and it appealed to his tendency to see opportunities. With Nick in as Ops I was looking around for some young aircrew to complete the team. I mentioned I was looking for two new pilots, a front-seater and a rear-seater – 'No previous maritime experience necessary, we'll bring you on.' I needed two 'upstarts' to balance the team. I found them in the VHR tent, the two new boys in 654, Jay Lewis and Charlie Tollbrooke. These men had joined to fly the Apache, and after the long march of Sandhurst, the Army Pilot's Course and then the endurance event that is the Apache Conversion, a total of three years training, they were coming to the end of their first Afghan tour.

In his last year of university Charlie had pondered Sandhurst or the City. He did the milk round, spoke to the bankers and the project managers and thought selling money to make money looked rather attractive. He was just days away from the suit and commute when he decided all of that could wait. He'd like to be a gunpilot for a while so he joined the Army. It was a sound choice. He worked his way through the courses diligently, passing each check-ride hurdle without swagger or self-absorption – a man who knows his mind and also knows he will work for what he wishes. Nor is he proud, an essential attribute of the modern officer. He'll wear a hat knitted by the Women's Institute while resting in the dry cold December night VHR tent – those hats are warm and comfortable; and then he'll leap into the role of singularly focused combat operator when the shout comes in for an immediate launch. The first time I flew with him was in Afghanistan, and he called every action exactly right. Charlie Tollbrooke had a future in the Apache.

The younger of the two upstarts, Jay, said no to university and had gone into nursing after leaving school, before opting to go to Sandhurst. His change of careers could not have been more dramatic, but he was suited to both. The modest, good-looking boy from somewhere south had an athletic ability that could have taken him far in the boxing ring but also an essential humanity that carried him well in our line of work. He, too, cleared all the hurdles well and arrived on the front line with a report book that said he was ready in all respects. What both Jay and Charlie had was courage and a spirit of adventure not hampered by 'how we used to do it'. They wanted to get as much out of Service life as they could, and they were willing to give up all their time to get it. To the new breed of Apache pilots six weeks at sea instead of a summer holiday meant more progress, and it was much better than six weeks conducting post-maintenance air testing and the odd parade.

Just two more were needed to make ten. I looked to the home base to provide.

John Blackwell, from 664 Squadron, said, 'Okay, why not?' He had flown the decks before and was already desensitized to the trepidation of over-water activity. But he was only coming along because he was due to leave the Army and therefore not on the Afghanistan plot. John was one of our true blue soldier-turned-pilot men. On his last tour in Helmand he had had to deal with an engine fire in the middle of a fire-fight with the Taliban. He dealt with the engine fire, shut it down and cracked on with one good engine remaining. Not bad from a lad who joined up aged just seventeen. From the recruiting office he went to Winchester and emerged as an Airtrooper. He had no intention of soldiering by manning the radio, refuelling and driving. He wanted to soldier from the air, in a helicopter. As a lance corporal, he started as a door gunner in Iraq in 2003 and went from there into the cockpit. Perseverance got him on the Army Pilots' Course. Determination gained him a pass. The eighteen months of Apache training were the most testing of his career, and two tours of Afghanistan later he wanted to reinvest his energy and experience in our new aircrew. He wanted to be an instructor, and was certainly good enough for the role, but the need was for line pilots back in Afghanistan. John was told he had to complete another turn of that wheel and do another tour over there before being considered for instructor training. In the end, he decided it was time to leave and move home to the North-West. Our 2011 training exercise embarkation was to be the final outing for him.

With three months to go before we embarked I had an outline plan and almost all the aircrew. The ground crew soldiers were already mine, but I had yet to meet the engineering officer. The rest of the engineering team were made up from the 654 Afghanistan team and some of my old *Ark Royal* element. They were coming because they needed the respite, they'd been burned at both ends for too long and a six-week summer saunter around the Med was just the medicine. With ten weeks in Afghanistan done I flew home just in time for the arrival of my second daughter.

By late January 2011 the team that was largely yet to meet each other were at least all in one place, at the home of the Apache in Wattisham, Suffolk. Nick Stevens went straight to work sorting out the squadron for the *Ocean* trip. With his wife still serving on the ground in Helmand, he forwent much of his post-tour leave, preferring work to fill the space where an empty house and fear for her safety would otherwise occupy him.

By the time Nick had put the final aircrew names on the board we were an unusually strong team. Seven of the ten had Afghanistan experience in the past six months, the other three within the past year or so. The talent and experience was high. Once paired up, the average crew had over 4,000 total flying hours at the controls and a year of

Afghanistan behind them. Such high levels of experience were very useful. Before we embarked I thought this would see us complete our training objectives while also allowing us to cope with the new environment. But when war beckoned just a month later it allowed us to cope with the unique complexity of the maritime environment and the intensity of combat. It gave us space to adapt, trial and pursue new ways of working as well as develop the upstarts, deal with the emergencies and stay one step ahead of the opposition.

By the beginning of April 2011 we were ready for the exercise, but somewhere deep in London a question was raised over what the Royal Navy might do if the situation in the Mediterranean got worse. Syria (least likely), Libya (not likely) and Yemen (most likely) were all possibilities for some sort of undisclosed activity, probably an evacuation mission. The Arab Spring, a wave of popular revolutions which started in Tunisia in late 2010, had spread to Egypt by January 2011, and now an uprising was taking place in Libya. Afghanistan was not the only focus in the MoD, and jets had been flying over Libya since late March. Gradually, questions were put to us – 'What sort of defensive aids do you have? How long can you stay at sea?' This was normal planning, staff officers making sure they had the answers when the politicians came asking.

The Defensive Aids Suite, or DAS, was our big ticket in the risk debate. We keep the technology close, but it is well known we have the best in the world, a box of tricks that allows us the time and space to use the offensive capability of the machine to the full. It is a collection of sensors and counter-measures, including chaff and flares. The system finds a threat, be it a radar, a laser or a missile launch, it alerts aircrew to the threat and, in the Apache, deals with it too. The extraordinary technology comes from Selex ES, and without it several of us would not be alive today and these pages would be a very different read.

Of course, the questions sent us into a frenzy of training and preparation. We cut short Easter leave to get everything done. Nick got the whole squadron up to date on their standard military skills such as shooting and first aid. He arranged briefings on the countries of interest and we refined our low-level flying and evading techniques in the simulator. A very confident RAF officer from the Air Warfare Centre came to brief us on the threat to helicopters in the Middle East and North Africa. The jets had been flying over Libya for a few weeks and the research had been done:

If you go feet-dry in the danger zone you'll need to be on the lookout for every MANPAD in existence as well as the triple-A and radar threat. Libya is about as hostile as it gets for helicopters anywhere in the world.

Sobering words from the expert, I thought.

Libya does not manufacture MANPADS, they buy Russian ones and they have more than any other non-manufacturing country in the world, tens of thousands of them. Our man was confident that Libya was no place for helicopters.

Our concerns were distracted by the interest in planning an evacuation mission for another country. The hypothetical questions filtered in from on high: 'What if you had to self-deploy to the Middle East, could you do it, and how long would it take to get there?' Nick and Little Shippers, realizing our lack of global maps, got on Google Earth to knock together a plan on the back of the metaphorical cigarette packet. It all seemed implausible. We got ready for our planned six-week exercise while also thinking about the many 'what-ifs' that could be just around the corner. All we could do was prepare ourselves as best we could and answer the questions as they came in.

While making sure the whole squadron was trained to the basic level, Reuben Sands scraped together enough of the right weapons and body armour to embark with half a chance of being ready by the time we got to the Med. If something kicked off while we were at sea we hoped the home base would be able to furnish our requirements. I made a list of the essential items that would have to be collected if we were to seriously consider launching armed Apaches from *Ocean* in the coming weeks. We still had no clearance to store the most commonly used variants of Hellfire – 'They're only for Afghan, you'll never need them at sea.' And we did not have an endorsed method of launching and recovering two armed aircraft at night – 'That can come later, once you've done some more exercises.' Due to the ditching characteristics of the Apache it was not cleared to low fly over water, the theory being that if an emergency developed we needed to have enough height, and therefore time, to get the canopy off before going into the oggin. But this was a bad height to fly at in combat, one which would put us perfectly on the radar and in range of every weapon from an AK47 to triple-A and all manner of MANPADS. Addressing these issues were large staff effort projects to get cleared; there was no way they could be arranged quickly. The quietly discussed military options in the Middle East and North Africa, it seemed, had come too early for us to be part of. Our understanding of the Apache at sea was not mature enough, and far too much work was required before we would be ready.

We also lacked the right aeronautical information such as maps and satellite imagery, but were told, 'You'll get them if you need them.' When we asked for Sig Saur 9mm personal protection pistols the answer was, 'You're not going to Afghan, you can't have them.' The proactive Regimental Operations Officer ordered them anyway, and we signed them out, tucked them into a box with our A2 Carbines and got them into the ship's armoury before anyone could uncover the heist. There was enough willingness and enthusiasm from within our regiment to see us embark in good order, and I was confident the CO and his team would fight our corner if the flag went up. Some of the Afghan warriors were envious, realizing we were perhaps at the start of something new and exciting, while a few of them mocked our silly games.

*Chapter 3*

# It's Just an Exercise, Home Soon

**26 April 2011. K's Journal**

*The morning Will went away he was up early. This is unusual for him. He's always been a student and he loves his bed. But today he was busy, like he always is when he's off on some exciting trip. I didn't share his excitement. Six weeks of being alone with a newborn baby and a three-year-old and a dog and two hens and a house and bills and cars and monotonous routine counting down to phone calls. I looked out of the bedroom window. One hen, only one left now. I could see the white one, which had been ailing and refused to roost the previous night, was now quite dead. The black one did similar while W was in Afghanistan a couple of months earlier and I'd been rather irritated then, eight months pregnant, dealing with the fallout of another one of his 'Good Life' projects. Behind me slept two tired girls, one delicate and inquisitive the other now established in a 2 hours sleep/30 minutes feed/noise and sewage cycle mothers everywhere are familiar with. Inside I knew six weeks was doable and then the summer together to help build a family.*

*I was tired. W going to Arizona right after our second daughter arrived and just a few weeks after he'd got back from Afghanistan which he'd gone to just after coming back from sea which he'd gone to immediately after another couple of months in Arizona and at sea again, which he'd . . . you get the picture. They don't spend much time at home. It's one exercise or deployment quickly followed by another.*

*When our first daughter was born W was in Baghdad. He'd saved his R & R and made it back just in time for the birth, but a week later he was back in Iraq. The inquisitive, delicate one was eight weeks old by the time he came home. That was the start of this really. He got back from a long stay in Iraq and barely got to know his baby before getting on with the Apache course. Once that course starts it gathers a momentum. You just have to go with it. You give up control when they get into that line of work. Dealing with dead hens when you just want a cuddle, well that's part of the lack of control.*

*So he was off again.*

*Sometimes I can't help feeling that it is all a selfish indulgence. He's excited, I'm struggling. Where's the team in that? We didn't get married to live apart and I didn't get married to live an isolated life on some windy airfield with one bar on my phone reception and miles away from my friends. Him poking off to sea to play with helicopters seemed an utter self-indulgence, and the dead hen was an extra insult. Still, six weeks, just six weeks . . .*

*I made plans to see friends; my parents would come and visit too. It was spring and the Easter weekend had been glorious. We lazed in our hammock in the garden, all four of us, hens free ranging, dog snoozing, with W telling us that the summer would soon be here and we'd have a super time in the Lakes. I also remember him pacing up and down the garden the day before Good Friday, mobile phone pushed against ear and serious faced. 'Just work, someone telling me how they wanted me to deal with risk if it gets . . . well, bigger, and a message of good luck,' he said.*

*He'd also disappeared into work on his only day off. He came back all frustrated and really got me annoyed when he said the sooner he got in the ship the better. 'Thanks,' I said, hurt and tired and about to be alone again.*

*'Sorry, it's just . . . well you know, the ship want us and they want this to succeed, it doesn't always feel like that here.'*

*I knew he was passionate about his project, that he understood it so well and that he'd bashed his head against a brick wall repeatedly along the way dealing with people who, it seemed, would rather see him fail. I knew all of that and was angry for him. I was also angry because he gave up some of our last day together to bash that wall again.*

*Despite all that, there was a slim chance that this Arab Spring may make their grey-line-cruise a little longer. I could just imagine them sailing around the Med looking all tough on the telly to put the pressure on some dictator while I enquired whether we would lose the deposit on our cottage in the Lakes if he didn't get back in time.*

*He was very careful to speak to all the families in the Community Centre about this and I went along to hear what he had to say.*

*'We have not been warned off for operations, but we could end up playing some small part if we are asked to,' he said. All rather vague, but what else could he say?*

*'Where might you go?' an understandably concerned wife enquired.*

*'Not sure, but we will be in a ship and there are four or five countries in the Med with political unrest right now.'*

*'What might you do in any of those countries?' Another concerned wife.*

*'Anything from a specific mission to strike a target to the much more likely show of force or deterrence in support of an evacuation operation,' came the answer.*

*The Welfare Officer said he would keep us all up to date if anything changed. He and W were both at pains to explain that the facts will come from them, not from Facebook or the neighbour or the girl in the NAAFI, or the telly or the newspaper.*

*So, a meeting in the Community Centre where the squadron commander told the families he was off on exercise, but, just in case, he thought he might tell us he was ready for anything . . . we were reassured and perplexed all at once.*

*On Tuesday, 26 April 2011 the Arab Spring, Afghanistan, a NEO (whatever that is), the recession, patch-politics and all the rest was just white noise in my head as I scooped a dead hen into a bag and tearfully asked my neighbour what to do with it. W was off again.*

\*

The day after Easter, the squadron embarked. We were nervous. Nervous because we were flying over the sea again, and nervous because we half expected a diversion somewhere in the Mediterranean. We flew three Apaches in formation from Suffolk, through London following the Thames westward, and then south-west out over the coast to meet HMS *Ocean*. We found her in the Channel, ten miles from her home port of Plymouth. She cut an impressive figure, 21,500 tonnes and 667ft long, battleship grey and stuffed full of sailors and Royal Marines, blue sky behind and sea state two.

With Little Shippers tutoring my approach and saving our embarrassment on the radios, I led the patrol into the starboard wait, and one by one we filtered in to land.

Our three Apaches joined the Lynx and Sea Kings from the Commando Helicopter Force to make up the Tailored Air Group supporting Royal Marines from 40 Commando. This was all about training with the Royal Marines, and making the Apache work at sea. We knew how many flying hours we had (enough), how much ammunition we were allowed to fire (very little, and permission was required from home to fire each time) and where we would get a run ashore (Crete and Malta, with perhaps Gibraltar on the way home). Six weeks and we would be done. We numbered only nine aircrew, with the tenth, Josh 'JB' Charles, still completing his Apache refresher training ashore and scheduled to fly out and join us in Crete in a few weeks.

On board *Ocean* it was the usual Army meets Navy meets Royal Marines standoff. All Royal wanted to do was get ashore; all we wanted to do was avoid getting caught on the wrong side of the thousands of rules yet to be learned; and all the Ship's Company wanted was to have their ship back. The scene in the wardroom said it all. There were two and a half corners with seating fixed around the walls, the rest being the bar. The largest, most comfortable corner, the one where the biscuits got put out at 'stand easy', belonged to the Ship's Company. They sat in a tight group, all known to one another, understood seats, pecking order and all. No one else was allowed in. We had invaded, they were disappointed. The other corner, the one with all the car magazines and the best view of the telly, was dominated by Royal. He didn't care who anyone else was, he was Royal and that was that. Sleeves up, guns and ink, they were the tough guys. The half corner and the bar (standing room only) was left to the Air Group, which included us. Everyone sneered at the WAFUs. It didn't matter which Service the aircrew were from; they were aircrew, enough said.

The tribes were set. All three groups were busy enough with their own work, and establishing a convivial relationship didn't matter. Royal could roll up his sleeves and push weights around in the gym. The Ship's Company could carry on thinking they were the only people who knew how to break into the beer fridge. And the aircrew, who had worked out how to break into the beer fridge on day two, could sneak a quick post-night-flying drink as long as no one from the Ship's Company was there to find out.

The usual land grabs on spare compartments were made and they were then reallocated. Computers were in short supply, so they were reallocated too. The hangar was stuffed full of Apache, Lynx and Sea King helicopters, and the engineers from all three embarked squadrons had a real-time game of 3D Tetris to manage the priorities under the fixed crane as well as the up-lift and down-lift and the whole flight deck spotting of the aircraft. Soldiers and sailors rushed about folding blades, moving aircraft, refuelling, de-fuelling, arming and de-arming, while the engineers worked on the deck and in the hangar. *Ocean* wasn't full, but she had a lot of aircrew, soldiers and engineers who were new to her and to the sea. Her crew were right to be aghast at the newcomers. We were shabby, ignorant and slow and we had to grasp maritime philosophy quickly if we were to remain welcome beyond the normal two-week tolerance period.

The man charged with bringing all this together and making aviation sense of it was 'Wings'. As luck would have it, Wings in HMS *Ocean* was a Royal Marine. He had flown Cobra AH-1 with the United States Marine Corps, run the aviation show in Helmand, spent years at sea and understood all the tribes. He had grown up in Glasgow in the seventies and eighties, run the gauntlet of the bully boys in his green school blazer and carried a savvy intuition and ability to resolve any human fault lines with him to Lympstone. Hugely welcoming, with impeccable manners, the man with the smile and the answers ran the hangar, the flight deck and everything that flew. He was our critical link to the ship, an aviator on the Ships' Company.

On my team the uncluttering of the flight deck and the management of the engineers fell to Doug Reid and his 25 Army Air Corps ground crew soldiers and to Charlotte 'CJ' Joyce with her 35 Aviation Technicians of the REME.

Doug had been in the squadron almost a year and he'd been thrashed, mostly by me. He arrived straight out of Sandhurst, full of enthusiasm, mild eccentricity and big talk about how he was all set for Afghanistan. I had met him in Arizona the previous summer and after listening to him tell me about himself and where he wanted to go, I asked him if he knew the difference between a ship and a boat.

'You can fit a boat on a ship, but you can't fit a ship on a boat,' was his reply.

'Outstanding, you're in! We're going to sea, not Afghanistan, and I have no idea what we'll do when we get there, but trust me we'll have a laugh.'

I gave him all I knew on the maritime role. He had served to the rank of corporal before commissioning and knew the Army and soldiers well enough. But he was new to aviation, and I had spent the last ten months scrutinising his team and encouraging the senior NCOs to bring on the new boy in whatever way they thought best. His programme lacked the structure of the Afghanistan squadrons and he had to battle hard to keep me from getting into his business. He had the bulk of the squadron soldiers directly under his leadership, and every stress and pain they felt had to be managed by him. Six weeks in *Ocean* in the Med looked like a pretty tough working holiday, not one that many of his team would volunteer for.

In the hangar CJ had a different set of issues. She had enough engineers and they were very experienced on the aircraft, but again *Ocean* was new and they had the culture shock of Army meets Navy to get over. Hers was an excellent team. This embarkation was supposed to be a respite from the Afghanistan rotation and the high tempo that forms the baseline of the Attack Helicopter Force. The embarkation would be hard work, but at least it was different to what they normally did. At the end of the summer they would rejoin the Afghanistan cycle, hopefully a little refreshed. CJ herself was in her last eight months in the Army. She had spent six years as an officer in the REME, completing a tour of Afghanistan, and now it was time to move to Cumbria, get going with her smallholding and perhaps do a little lecturing in engineering if time allowed. Coming to sea was her last task and she had postponed some of her resettlement courses to fit it in.

During the early May Bank Holiday, *Ocean* turned to port, presenting us with a geography lesson that Africa is indeed very close to Europe as we entered the Mediterranean through the Strait of Gibraltar. After the early training sorties and charge south through Biscay we had a brief period of maintenance before completing the rest of our flying training and then getting into the exercise proper – escorting Royal as he gets ashore and then supporting him once he's on the beach. This is the stuff of helicopters in amphibious operations, and we were embarked to prove we could do it with the Apache. The plan was to fly formation sorties, practise our own procedures and then get to Cyprus, where we would conduct all manner of joined-up training with Sea King and Lynx, with Royal in boats and helicopters hitting the beach and fighting. This was all training and part of the Royal Navy's demonstration that it had an agile amphibious capability. As well as being part of that, I needed to prove we could fire all our weapons; the exercise planners had identified an opportunity to do this in early June, after the important validation of Royal, boats, helicopters and big ship manoeuvres had been ticked.

At the 10.00 a.m. stand-easy on the day after the Royal Wedding I got chatting with Wings. A calm intensity settled into his conversation: 'How about we organize a Hellfire range south of Gib? It would de-risk the training requirement in case we run out of opportunities later?'

This was a surprise. We did want to fire Hellfire at sea, but we had not even begun to think about it. Why now? We hadn't talked about this before, it was not in the programme. We could do it but we needed an explosives safety man – an Ammunition Technical Officer, known to all as 'ATO'. We didn't have one because we didn't need one for another few weeks. Anyway it was a Bank Holiday, so what was the rush?

Wings had the answers. He knew a man who knew a man who knew an ATO in Germany, as it happened. 'The Army are on side, so is the Navy. We'll fly him out to Gib, send the Lynx over to pick him up and get him on the ship. Fire, fire, fire. All happy, he goes home, big training objective done. Sit back.'

He made the logistical challenge sound easy, but he wanted this and he could make it happen.

This was our final objective. If we could load, launch, fly, fight, land back on the ship and do it all again, we would be ready for combat. The whole ship would be ready. We would become an option. Perhaps staff capacity back in England would be made available to cover some of our other clearances like low-level flight over water and landing armed aircraft facing fore and aft at night.

It was all a good idea, although the haste was somewhat mysterious. I briefly thought I should let the Attack Helicopter Force HQ know, but then I thought they might ask for detail I didn't have, or even ask me to wait until later. In any case, they could say 'no'. I didn't want 'no', so I went for the retrospective line – 'It was a Bank Holiday, all rather busy, on the weekend, it was an opportunity, Army HQ were okay with it, it worked'.

'Just tell us next time!' was the response when I did tell them. They were on side. Still, it was mysterious.

Mark Hall got on with the planning. A Hellfire sea range had not been done before and the template he produced was enormous. Clearing the range of all vessels would not be possible; instead, we would have to wait to get the work done until nothing was in the way. Firing missiles and 30mm at sea requires the whole ship to work together. Weapons engineers and soldiers prepare the missiles in the magazine, they then get brought to the flight deck. REME and Air Corps soldiers prepare the aircraft and upload the ammunition. The ship steers a navigational track to clear the range. A Lynx helicopter is launched to drop targets into the water and check all is clear. Finally the aircrew brief, the ship settles on a flying course and everything is set up to launch.

Over, fortunately, sea state two, around lunch time on 3 May, the first of nine Hellfire was fired. We all had a go. We all hit our targets. *Ocean* and the Apache could arm, launch, strike, return, re-arm, launch, strike and return again. This was an unconscious dress rehearsal. The Royal Navy and the Ministry of Defence very quickly got the pictures of an Apache launching missiles with the sea as a backdrop, on the news and in the papers. One month to the day later, I fired the first Hellfire into Libya. Only in retrospect have I considered that 3 May was perhaps the first shot of psychological pressure being applied to Gaddafi: pictures of an Apache firing Hellfire into the same sea that washes his own shores. The threat of attack helicopters visiting Libya had begun.

By early May a No Fly Zone had been in force over Libya for six weeks. Disaster in Benghazi had been averted, but Libya was divided. Benghazi and the east were rebel-held. Everything else was contested, with three separate front lines all static in stalemate. Misrata, in the centre, had become a symbol of Libyan suffering. Gaddafi thrashed the population day and night. The telly kept on transmitting. What else could be done? The NEO was over. There were no more plans to dock ships or land planes. Nothing *Ocean* had on board would be needed. But several hundred Royal Marines were embarked, as well as Lynx, Sea King and Apache helicopters. We could intercept suspicious shipping, board and inspect the cargo. Perhaps they would need armed overwatch. We thought about this and worked out a rudimentary method of operating with Royal. Then we worked out a way of directing the Apache on to seaborne targets found on the radar of the Mark 7 Sea King. Again we ran up a method and had a quick airborne experiment. It all worked. We just needed someone else to need it, and if they didn't it wouldn't matter: we were developing good ideas for the future anyway. In the meantime, we carried on with the amphibious exercise, supporting Royal on manoeuvres.

After three weeks at sea, and well into the Mediterranean, *Ocean* drew up alongside HMS *Albion* in Chania, Crete for a couple of days' re-stow and shore leave. *Albion*, along with HMS *Liverpool*, had sailed early to position as a contingency option. *Liverpool* had carried on and was now poised off the coast of Libya, spending much of her time at Action Stations and firing her 4.5in gun in response to the rockets that came out to meet her.

Going alongside in Crete meant our first opportunity to set foot on dry land since England, and no one was going to waste the chance. We were about to be indoctrinated into the legendary 'First Night Madness'. Down on 6 deck in the Air Group accommodation Doug Reid was contemplating whether a cravat was needed or if the relaxed aesthetic of the open collar was right for an evening ashore, when Big Shippers emerged from his cabin completely sanitized. No watch, no phone, no wallet; he wore sandals, shorts and a polo shirt.

'Mate, what am I doing wrong?' Doug mocked him, flicking imaginary dust from his shoulder.

'Well, gentlemen, you pay for the taxi and I'll tell you how to get though First Night Madness.' Then Big Shippers told us how it would unfold:

We've been in a ship for a little while, and there is the shore. The ship is tied to the shore and we may proceed ashore. Here are the Golden Rules of First Night Madness:

1. First nighters is for one night, but may be repeated until the ship sails, except for those that fail to observe rule 5.
2. 6Ps – prior planning prevents and all that. Rendezvous in the wardroom first for a few drinks before boarding the liberty boat. This ensures you are the best looking and most amusing person ashore.
3. Dress to survive – attire should be flexible to allow smooth transition from dinner in harbour-side taverna, sipping cocktails in 5-star hotels, dancing like your dad in a club, entertaining on cruise ships and breakfast of pizza and beer overlooking the Mediterranean. Maroon moleskin trousers, Ralph Lauren shirt and sports jacket are NOT appropriate for first night madness.
4. Sanitize – only take what you can afford to lose: cash and ID card. Never, ever take your mobile, 'nuff said. Phones are bad, they make you call home and then apologise pathetically long after she has hung up because you don't know its four in the morning back at home in Somerset.
5. Know your limits – exceeding them might limit your port visit to one night only and may require a parade on the flight deck in the blazing sun with a hangover.
6. Doubles only – there's not much time, bourbon or chips.

We did proceed ashore. It was messy. We'll leave that in Chania.

The following morning, the entire Ship's Company, Royal and Air Group – all 690 of us – were on the flight deck giving the XO a very hard listening-to. First nighters had been strong. Rumours of the night spread quickly. Some individuals were in trouble, some were in jail. Fortunately, someone else had let their hair down just an inch more than we had, the heat was all theirs and we were in the clear. There was no second nighters, and on the third night we let slip and sailed east for Cyprus.

Before *Ocean* left Chania our tenth pilot arrived. Josh 'JB' Charles strode up the gangway, returning to an old friend. Recently refreshed after a break from the aircraft, he had been part of 656 at its Apache beginnings, flown the decks and been among the first into Helmand right at the start with 16 Air Assault Brigade in 2006. He was the senior citizen rock star of the team and had lived the Army man and boy. Having joined at seventeen as a soldier and dashed around Germany in the 1980s in a tank, he decided to give flying a go as a corporal. It worked and he discovered his talent. JB cantered through the ranks, proved himself as 656's first Apache instructor and was later given the daunting role of Regimental chief flying instructor in the first Apache regiment. He had had a brief break and now it was time to come back. He shoehorned an Apache refresher course into his Easter leave and flew out to Crete to join the ship. He arrived, just after first nighters, duffle bag on shoulder, laptop under arm, and announced with a wide smile, 'This is going to be fun, again.' An A1 graded instructor, the only A1 in the Attack Helicopter Force, JB was absolutely sound and knew both the aircraft and flying to an extraordinary level.

Complete, we sailed east and prepared for exercises in support of Royal. We would be home in a month.

## Chapter 4

# We're Not Going to Albania

On 24 May the senior men in *Ocean* and I were invited to HMS *Albion*, the fleet flagship and the command and planning vessel, to discuss the next phase of the exercise – a morning to be spent listening to planners talk about diplomatic clearances, the availability of firing ranges and, hopefully, the carrot of a run ashore in Malta or Gibraltar on the way home.

I climbed out on to the flight deck along with the Captain and the Air Group Commander. We flew in a Lynx, a high-powered passenger list, and me. We could see *Albion* from the flight deck of *Ocean*, and beyond her *Sutherland* escorted us, all heading east. The flight lasted all of three minutes, neatly touching down on *Albion* to be met, it seemed, by everyone with a badge and a rank. The Royal Navy exchanged deference, paying exquisite attention to their traditions, and stepped inside. I followed. As I got through the double airlock doors Chris James, our Apache planner in Albion, grabbed me.

'Steady on, sailor. They have business with the Commodore. You shall come with me.' He gestured with mock theatricality and slid down a ladder. 'Come on, this is good, really good.'

He hurried along the passageway towards his planning space, turning his head and speaking fast and quietly: 'Got some interesting news and some very interesting news. Which first?' He was excited. Perhaps he'd organized another Hellfire range, I thought. That would be good, more live firing at sea to get the procedures as good as we could.

'Well, let's remain calm and start nice and easy with the entry-level *interesting* news,' I replied with jovial sarcasm.

We got to the planning area and Chris rushed past the Apache compartment. I stopped to enter, but Chris beckoned me onwards. He was now standing outside the Intelligence compartment. 'Step into our shack, old boy.' He punched in the simplex code and pushed open the heavy steel door. Inside stood the Commodore's senior Intelligence analyst and the Chief of Staff.

Chris introduced me: 'This is Will Laidlaw, he's our Apache man in Ocean.'

Things now started to get serious. The senior man took over the conversation: 'Okay, all the usual caveats. This is a Secret space and this information is very sensitive . . .' He drew back a curtain on the bulkhead, uncovering a map. 'I know you've heard talk of Libya. Well, here it is!'

Politics was on the march. The Commodore had been asked to generate a plan to get involved in Libya after the big political and military hitters in Paris and London decided more needed to happen. Chris James had to show what the Apache might offer. That morning, while he presented his estimate to the Commodore, the ticker-tape newsreel at the foot of Sky News read, 'British Government to send Apache helicopters to Libya.' The decision had already been made.

The Chief of Staff described how the Secretary of State for Defence had agreed with the Prime Minister and President Sarkozy of France that helicopters would be used in the attack role in Libya. This was shocking, obvious and logical all at once. I had been warmed up to this, not least by the suspicious urgency of the early May Hellfire range off Gibraltar. The now constant media speculation was fed into *Ocean* through television, email and telephone calls home. On the telly a smorgasbord of experts, not a flying hour or a trigger-pull to their name, lent their opinions, presumably trousering a tidy fee as they did so. We'd been discussing the 'what ifs' in the wardroom amongst ourselves. Libya had been a plausible target for a few weeks.

'There's a ministerial submission which sets out your boundaries, the dos and don'ts, and risk.' The senior man took over again. He was focused on the mission. He pointed at Brega in the east. This was where we were going.

'Both the regime and the rebels need Brega to secure oil and fresh water. It's a stalemate. You may remember the news footage of rebels and pro-Gaddafi fighters skirmishing up and down a road, gaining and losing, gaining and losing. This is that road. It runs from Benghazi in the north-east around the coast, past Brega and on toward Misrata.' His finger traced the map. 'You can see it then continues all the way up to Misrata and onwards to Tripoli. Control the road, control troop movement and logistics. Control Brega, control oil and water for the eastern side of Libya . . . We'll get to Misrata later.'

I drew a slow, deliberate breath, nodding in recognition. The road to Tripoli would start at Brega.

I had been expecting a conversation about options in Libya, but this was one-way. I wasn't being asked if it was feasible or what sort of activity the Apache could contribute to. That had been done. The decision had been made. We were going to Libya. The purpose of this conversation was to tell me where, when and how.

The senior man continued:

As for targets, there's everything you would expect from a modern Army at war. Tanks, artillery, armoured personnel carriers and logistics vehicles, but also a lot of 'technicals' – pickup trucks with large calibre weapons mounted on the rear. In Brega the armour is all up on the front line. We don't have boots on the ground so we won't go mixing it right up there – too much possibility of fratricide. We have placed a Restricted Fire Line a few kilometres into the pro-Gaddafi side. You will operate on the pro-Gaddafi side of that. This means we know you are definitely hitting regime equipment. Also, hitting him back from the front line will severely disrupt his supply chain and get on top of morale.

I had to give vent to the voice in my head: 'Always behind enemy lines. We can do that.' I looked at Chris: 'It's going to have to be as fast as we can go and low-level flying, very low-level.'

'Yes,' he replied. 'We have a call with the Air Warfare Centre scheduled for later today. We'll get their view on the flight profile, but from what I'm seeing I agree. Very low, dynamic manoeuvring, fast decisions.'

The senior man continued:

There are over 20,000 MANPADS in Libya. They top out at 11,000 feet and the jets are at least another 10,000 feet above that. You are the only NATO asset they can reach. Not even the Predator drones are going low enough to get shot. The triple-A is big too. Again, the jets can't get caught, they're out of range. Pro-Gad is going to try and get you, he can't catch anything else.

'Pro-Gad'. A new phrase, the new enemy. It would work its way into almost every conversation for the rest of that summer.

The Chief of Staff joined in:

Your overarching mission is to have a cognitive effect on the regime. We're not going to win a war with a handful of Apaches, but they have a formidable reputation. You are feared the world over. You only need to go to Libya occasionally to reinforce that reputation with the target audience in Tripoli. That's where the effect needs to be – right in the minds of the regime. The NATO aim for attack helicopters, driven by London and Paris, is to intensify the pressure on the regime. It is risky, it is dangerous and we'll do our best to mitigate that for you. Part of that is keeping you in the NATO air campaign so we can have jets watching over and the Pred looking for targets.

Psychological pressure; creating more problems for Gaddafi than his troops could answer; relieving the pressure on the rebels and, perhaps, creating some openings for them to exploit. This was our mission. We didn't need to be hitting targets day and night to achieve this. We didn't need to fly past Tripoli on a sunny afternoon to demonstrate the power of the newcomer in the war. I wanted to fight at night, as dark as possible. Night and Hellfire, the message would be clear enough. I envisaged flying two or three sorties a week. The NATO planners would allocate us the targets. Chris and his team were heading off to Italy to join them and make sure our missions were helicopter-shaped.

The part where I was invited to speak was in answer to the question 'So, tell us what you need?'

I was happy with the proposition, not least because I knew that Chris would never let a bad plan stick. He'd handed command of 656 to me two years earlier and been a keen supporter of our development of the maritime capability. He was also an Apache original, having trained in the USA, instructed on the UK conversion course and then taken 656 to Afghanistan twice. He was a details man, too, and he knew the Apache in combat as well as anyone anywhere. And he could talk a lot.

Just as I was about to list Hellfire variants, more 30mm and rockets as well as more chaff and flare as top of my list, Chris went into monologue overdrive:

I have gone through all the right channels and requested both Afghanistan variants of Hellfire, as many as they can give us, 30,000 rounds of 30mm and as many rockets as they have. Chaff and flare are on the list too. You'll get another aircraft in two days time, with a fifth arriving in about a week. We just have some clearances with regard to storing Hellfire and rockets to finish off. It's about the total explosive content of the magazine, something the Navy are dealing with. Any odds and ends your team need the engineers can bring out with the aircraft, but move fast, they'll be on their way to Brize Norton first thing in the morning.

'Well, that just about covers it then!' I replied. 'You've been thinking about this, haven't you!' I was about to take delivery of more ammunition than we fire in a year in Afghanistan and, judging by the descriptions of the sort of targets available in Libya, we were likely to use most of it.

Chris and I went up to the Wardroom to talk the detail. His monologue continued:

We have just three days to get everything done in Cyprus and then you will head for Libya and I must get across to the NATO air planning place in Italy. Lieutenant Colonel Jack Davis is already there. He's been up in London with the CO and they've decided to put a team in Italy where the air campaign is being planned. He's short of people so I'm heading over there after we've put you through your paces.

When Chris is talking about plans there is little point interrupting. I listened.

I have organized a mission rehearsal exercise for the next three days. We can put each of you through a day and a night live firing range at sea. After that we'll switch to mission specific training. I've arranged a night-time low-level raid for a simulated strike against targets on land. I'll do my usual judgemental training scenarios and test your crews on their fast decision-making and understanding of the ROE.[3]

He set out the plan for our only opportunity for tailored training. We would normally have preferred a month of training, putting each crew through a graduated series of sorties and range work. There was no time for this. One sortie on the range by day and another by night was all we had on the trigger. Then, the big one-shot only per crew sortie against simulated targets ashore. Three sorties each, and just three days to get it all done. We would need all our aircraft serviceable day and night. Live ammunition meant all the ground crew would be working flat out for the daytime ranges and then late into the night for the evening sorties. Aircrew, operations soldiers, flight deck teams and the REME were all going to work all hours just to get us ready for the operation. And we had to reach a very high quality line if the Commodore was going to be happy with our ability to cope with the risk we were preparing for in Libya. Chris continued:

> You need to practise the low-level, no-lights formation flying over the sea running into dynamic concurrent attack profiles against pop-up targets. I'll set up one deliberate target to test the planning and coordination. Once that is struck you'll return to *Ocean* and wait on deck on alert for a time-sensitive opportunity target. That one will test on the hoof planning and coordination as well as ROE and command decisions. I'll make it as tricky as I can and we'll debrief over the phone each night.

I had everything I needed – times, dates, outline targets and a one-shot training opportunity to prepare the team. Now it was time to tell them.

With the Task Group travelling in convoy for Cyprus, *Ocean* and *Albion* were still together and it was only another three-minute Lynx flight back to Mother. I headed for the wardroom to catch lunch and found Nick Stevens picking over the last of the salad. He was alone.

'Where's everyone else?' I asked.

'We've got one aircraft to ground run and the rest are building Hellfire targets with Mr Hall. He's going to run another range south of Cyprus, if we get permission. Should do day and night RF and 30mm. We have loose dates for the end of the month. I don't suppose there will be any live firing when we get to Albania.' Nick was his usual picture of calm. 'How was your session with the big planners?'

I had my serious face on. I had news to tell. Big, fearsome, exciting news. 'We're not going to Albania . . . we're going to Libya.' These words have lingered in my head ever since. The speculation was over, now we were getting into the fight. We all wanted a part in this. I laid out the facts: 'We need to get the aircrew, Doug and Charlotte together. We only have a few days to do everything. They want us in Libya at the end of next week. We'll be in Cyprus tomorrow, then three days with Chris smashing us though a rehearsal exercise and then we're off. There's no time to get anything wrong, and a raft of senior officers are coming out to tell us how it is.'

He nodded, slow and deliberate and, adding a smile to the calm. 'Six days. Libya in six days? Busy. Yes, busy, but doable!'

'Let's have a cup of tea and I'll fill you in on the detail.' We went on to the quarterdeck and in the early afternoon heat and noise of a Royal Navy ship at sea I explained the situation. 'This is really big. I'm surprised. Very risky. I know we're up for it and we're good enough, but this is dangerous stuff. There are thousands of MANPADS, thousands. We're the only thing flying that's in range. Some Gaddafi fast jet got shot down in April by one.'

Nick was ahead in his thoughts. 'Where are we going? Is Royal going on the ground?'

'No. No boots on the ground, no policy shift there. Royal's getting off, he's not coming. It's us, just us and the SKASaCs. They want us to do strikes against targets NATO will give us. All part of the air campaign. All new.'

'When do we get the target?'

'Targets, targets. Not a one-off. Lots. Chris is joining the Apache planning team in NATO in Italy at the weekend. He's our man, with Jack Davis. They'll shape it, make sense of all that badges and watches and flying suits stuff they love, and give us the mission in soldier talk.'

The conceptual work was over. Conflict, unexpected conflict, had chosen us. We had less than a week to get ammunition, another Apache, swap people in and out, and get into the low-level, no-lights formation over the sea to practise firing and defensive flying. Wild times were upon us. Privately I wondered if we would all survive.

In *Ocean* we had a planning space know as the flip-flop. There was an upper and a lower flip-flop, a steep ladder separating the two. We had the lower, no one used the upper. The lower flip-flop was our planning, debriefing and general working space. Weapons, morphine, secret computers and phones and usually more people than there was room. The team gathered in the flip-flop. I arrived last and launched straight into the detail.

'Here's what I know. We are going to launch Apache strike missions into Libya . . .'

In a four-minute brief the atmosphere went from silent nodding to smiles and serious faces. The proposition was unprecedented, seductively dangerous and way beyond our expectations. Overwatch of a boarding party checking out some knackered fishing boat, or even a NEO, had seemed likely, but a proper low-level charge into the brutal might of Gaddafi's army was breathtaking. We all knew what this meant to us:

that thousands of shoulder-launched missiles would be coming out, that the triple-A would meet us, that every man with half a chance at fame would take a shot. We were heading right into the middle of it all.

I didn't want anyone to know we were coming. Any warning, however vague, might give pro-Gad the percentage point he needed to kill us. I wanted all of this to be a secret. I wanted the first realization of our involvement to come when our first missile hit. But that wasn't the mission. Adding helicopters to the campaign was about putting psychological pressure, also known as 'cognitive effect', on the regime. Just as a picture of an Apache firing missiles at sea in early May was a signal, speculation surrounding our deployment ricocheted around the internet, telly and print media. Five days in late May made nervous reading for families at home: 'Apache Attack Helicopters to be Sent into Libya by Britain' (*Guardian*, 23 May 2011), 'Libya Apache Deployment Approved by David Cameron' (BBC, 27 May 2011) and 'Libya: Apache Attack Helicopters to be Deployed within 24 Hours' (*Daily Telegraph*, 27 May 2011).

Then confirmation, and we shut down communications from the ship. Too much talk might compromise a mission. We had to revert to well managed Royal Navy messaging to families, the ship controlling the message content. Some people grumbled about it, but they weren't about to fly into Libya. In my last call home in late May I told my wife that we were all good and had everything, that I wasn't able to speculate, but she should watch the news. I also told her that the Ops Officer at the Regiment would pop round and tell her what he could when he could.

Our families were expecting us home in two weeks; now that wasn't going to happen. Instead, they got it from Facebook and the news that the summer was cancelled and we were getting involved in some incredibly dangerous conflict. Those meetings in the Community Centre back in April were proving to be important. The Welfare Officer had all the contacts he needed. We made sure he knew how we would contact him, how we would tell him what was going on, but we all knew the first message would be a headline on Sky, ITN or the BBC. He would then have to react. With the ship in a tight communications posture, but with journalists embarked, I knew our families would wake up one morning to worrisome news.

At 1435 hours on Saturday, 28 May the Captain piped the official news to *Ocean*. Our mission was 'to provide Attack Helicopter capability and supporting assets to Operation Unified Protector in order to intensify military pressure upon the Gaddafi regime'.

On *Ocean* speculation was replaced by certainty and preparation for combat. Now embarked with only those who needed to be part of the mission, the 400 or so souls in the ship went into operational mode. This meant 'Defence Watches' – a shift system of eight hours on duty and eight hours off, in perpetual rotation. Some departments did six hours on, six hours off. A ship's company can operate 24 hours a day on this system, fully alert, ready for combat, ready to defend, conduct re-supply, launch and recover aviation. They did this for up to a month at a time, only stopping when the ship came into port. HMS *Ocean* was about to go to war, again.

Back in the UK, the CO had been rushing between London, Suffolk and Hampshire for over a week, shaping the mission, our way of working and the risk appetite, and thinking about what to do if the worst was to happen. By the time it became clear that he should be with us in the Med he had three hours to get home, pack and be at the airport. Expecting to deploy for a couple of weeks to get everything set up, he packed light and told his wife he'd back in a few days. Lieutenant Colonel John Upton had been in command of a squadron in Afghanistan only a year earlier and been promoted, before a top adviser's job settled him into his new rank and prepared him for Regimental Command. He had begun his career in tanks, switched to flying and had every operational medal on offer since the early nineties. Approaching forty, he still played competitive rugby and hockey and fancied his chances in the Station triathlon, which was rapidly approaching. An accomplished equestrian in his youth, this tremendous-haired son of a cavalryman Band Sergeant Major demanded accuracy and judgement from his people. He flew out to Cyprus to get on board and be the interface between us in the squadron and the scrutiny of everyone else. In the final reckoning, before each mission was launched, he would be the dispassionate arbiter; the man who talked us through the risk, thought about the alternatives and sold the whole thing back to NATO.

I had only known the CO for a couple of months. He had arrived while I was in Afghanistan, and his predecessor, a staunch supporter of the maritime, was off into the staff machine. Like him, John Upton had an open mind; he was ready to understand and to keep his regiment agile enough to manage its Afghan commitments while having a go at developing this new and unusual opportunity. He was an ideas man and a doer; he got into the detail of our work and made it his place to understand it all.

With John Upton on board in *Ocean* and Jack Davis heading up the team in the Combined Air Operations Centre (CAOC), we had the dispassionate risk appreciation where it was needed – at the planning place and at the action end. All I had to do was understand the target and fly.

The ranges and the rehearsal exercise were carried out with only a few minor stumbles, not least Reuben and JB effectively denying the rest of us the opportunity to fire. We had tied five floating targets together so that we could keep them all in one place. JB was first up. He arrived on the range, found the targets, actioned a Hellfire and pulled the trigger; it went where he wanted it to go, hitting the middle target, but drove all five to the bottom of the sea. 'Sorry about that. Do you think it's good luck?' was his offer. The rest of us had all fired on the range off Gibraltar earlier in the month. Wings had done what he said he would do – 'de-risk it for later, in case we don't get the opportunity again . . .'

We all fired rockets and 30mm by day and night into the sea and we checked all our chaff and flare dispensers were working. As a method of testing the very perishable skill of unlocking from a radar using chaff and manoeuvre, Mark Hall decided we should fly against the ship's Phalanx radar. The plan, drawn on a scrap of paper over a cup of tea, was to fly towards the ship, have the Warfare Officer activate the radar, get locked on and evade. We all did it, we all got locked on, we all evaded. This was not just a simple confidence boost; in the coming weeks it could be the difference between crashing and continuing to fight. Gaddafi had radar-guided missiles waiting for us. Within a month our lives would depend on our flying skill and the effectiveness of the Apache defensive systems, as we rushed to unlock from the regime radars before they got missiles in the air.

Then we had the night-flying profile to master. Getting down to 100ft, no lights, formation flying over the sea at the darkest part of the night took nerve. We forced ourselves into this deeply uncomfortable place, certain that trouble would keep the canopy on if we ditched, but knowing that we had to do it if we were to get into Libya and out again. We flew low-level concurrent attack profiles. Targets appeared quickly and disappeared as fast. We manoeuvred hard, bought seconds to think, practise an engagement and duck away again. With just one attempt each at the exercise serials, the pressure was high. I had just two nights to be sure the whole squadron could compete, that it was efficient, agile and safe. At 3.00 a.m. on 29 May 2011, with the last aircraft on deck, crews debriefed and Chris James happy on the phone, I reported to the CO and then to the Commodore that we were good to go. *Ocean* turned south-west.

At that hour, with the middle watch about to become the morning watch, only those who had to be awake were moving to their duties, or their beds. In the wardroom we broke open the last of the Speckled Hen and wondered if we had done enough to see us through. Nothing in our collective experience of military aviation in combat could give us the assurance we wanted. A new place of danger was waiting somewhere near 32°28'20.65" North and 14°39'23.18" East, and *Ocean* pushed steadily towards our launch. We listened to whoever wanted to play their phone and drank the fridge.

We had four days until the fight started, and we also had half a dozen journalists and their MoD minder onboard. The military has long been wary of the media. Journalists want a front-line interpretation of the political intent. They want to report how politics becomes reality in war. They also want names and faces to give their stories a human touch. We, on the other hand, want to avoid political associations, and instead of telling them whether we will deliver the political results we tell them we are working hard in difficult circumstances but that we will prevail, and so on. They, in turn, are bored by our rehearsed lines. Fighters have forever been confused between what politicians say we do and what we think we do, and we tend to blunder about awkwardly as journalists pick the low-hanging fruit of the military/political communications divide.

Of course, the combat operator doesn't get involved with political intent. The operator just wants to get on with it and do the work. The people who do care are the journalists and politicians, and people who want to be politicians, and the gossips in the pub. Journalists and politicians care greatly about how they beat one another with their respective versions of the truth, and soldiers' comments are played with until the editor's buzz-word bingo shapes a stick with which to beat the politician. Both sides are trying to sing louder, but the soldier in the middle just wants to get back to work.

Media speculation over Libya in May and June 2011 went like this: 'stalemate, desperation, helicopters, escalation, they will crash, British airmen (they didn't know we were soldiers) will die, NATO is failing'. Even *Private Eye*[4] and those venerable military thinkers Richard Madeley and Judy Finnigan had an opinion.[5] A former Ambassador to Libya, Oliver Miles, also lent the view of his 'military friends' saying this wasn't a good idea.[6] Of course, there was risk, and danger. Whatever the political motivation, London made big, brave decisions that put careers, and our lives, on the line. Our team knew the size of the task and its dangers. The journalists who came along with us got to appreciate it too. And they were as bored as we were with the Dettol-scrubbed official line. They wanted to see the story for real rather than the version we wanted to sell. And they were eager to get on and get their work done. They were bored. They did not come aboard to run up a tab in the wardroom and sit waiting on the quarterdeck while no one spoke to them. I didn't like it either. They wanted interviews.

During the two-day passage to Libya I slowly, somewhat awkwardly, introduced myself during tea-drinking diversions on the quarterdeck: 'I'm Will. Sorry it seems a bit boring. We're quite busy. I need to get my plan straight and then we can talk perhaps.' My best efforts at casual chat were staccato at best. I was very concerned at what was coming, all the known hell Gaddafi had ready, all the warning we had given him. I wondered what surprise we might have left on our side. I felt we were running out of time, that the whole thing was known and that we might cross the coast and be ripped up on the first night. I wrote a last letter to my wife and told Doug and Nick where to find it 'if things unravel for me'.

Whatever my own private fears, my duty was to make the whole enterprise work. At the same time I had to let the media in. I got chatting on the quarterdeck more often. An agreement was struck: we would tell them on the day about an hour before the mission briefing and I would conduct TV and print interviews after the mission was over. This was good enough, but I also insisted on my anonymity, fearing having to explain myself to the wicked Colonel in some post-shoot-down prison.

As we steamed for Libya, Chris James flew to Poggio Renatico in Italy to join the planners in the CAOC. His journey wasn't quite how he wished it would be. Having conducted the debrief of the final serial of the rehearsal exercise with me over the phone in the early hours of 29 May, a power cut meant he had to prise open the washing machine mid-cycle, liberate his uniform and pay a double fare to his taxi driver to get him to the airport on time. His connecting flight to London went to plan and he arrived in Bologna in time for lunch – except he missed lunch because he was the lonely figure standing in front of the empty luggage carousel in sandals, shorts, polo shirt and sunglasses, Wilbur Smith novel in hand, phone and credit card in pocket. He was looking forward to picking up a bag stuffed with wet, half-washed uniform, but it hadn't made the journey. Instead, he had to make his way to the CAOC as he was, just arrived from Ayia Napa with two days of stubble. On arrival at the NATO nerve centre he was straight into a meeting with the three-star General running the operation! Two days later, his bag of stinking, wet, mouldy uniform arrived and his summer began.

He joined his old friend Jack Davis, who had deployed at 36 hours' notice. Together their task was to get us missions that made sense, then shape them with their expertise. A mission, the target, the risk and the rules of engagement were always shaped in the planning, so that its final analysis, that last piece of dispassionate consideration, should be arrived at without issue. Our planning options were well shaped for us, first by the team in Poggio. Jack headed up the team and Chris was the Apache expert in a team of planners all well versed in how to use attack aviation. These were not just Army aviators; there were Royal Navy and Royal Air Force officers in the team, and it was their job to assist in integrating this fundamentally land-centric platform into an air campaign, but with the additional consideration of operating it from the sea. The new platform, the Apache, came with needs which would have to be coordinated with the other fifty strike sorties launched each day.

That process of integration and target selection would begin up to two days before a mission, and we would only be exposed to it in outline the day prior to launch and then again in detail on the afternoon of that evening's mission. Our team in Poggio went through a ruthless process of negotiation, planning, targeting and legal discussion before handing off a mature enough plan to us at sea. On the day, they would be rushing about finalizing the legal context of the target, which would be confirmed as late as possible in order to preserve its validity. They would then wait until the mission had launched, struck and returned before discussing by phone what had happened and how this might influence subsequent missions. They had very long days, often frustrating, occasionally satisfying, unsung, unacknowledged and largely unrewarded. It taught me about how plans were made, how groups of people think and about the danger of not addressing preconceived ideas early. And there were plenty of those ideas doing the rounds in the minds of people who didn't fly helicopters.

However difficult a group is to break into, you must have first-class thinkers from your team in the place where the plan is made. They are likely to have to break into a culture without the necessary time to do so naturally. They may have to overcome obstacles to grasping how the place works and to being understood how they work themselves. They are likely to find it difficult, perhaps unsatisfying. But they must be there if the plan is to have any chance of being fit for purpose and if the soldier flying in combat tonight is going to have a chance of doing so without coming unstuck. The team were constantly advising, at times cajoling, and occasionally explaining what is and what is not suitable for attack helicopters. Eventually, late in the afternoon on mission day, a target or, more usually, targets, would be confirmed and allocated to us.

When talk of bringing the Apache into the campaign became reality it brought with it more risk – risk to the lives of us flying soldiers, and reputational risk to the NATO air campaign, specifically the British contribution. The team in Poggio had the delicate balance of giving us enough freedom to get the task done with sufficient latitude to choose our own way both in planning and in the air, but also appropriate constraints to prevent us wandering away from the precision of the target selection and the protection allocated to our mission in the form of anti-enemy air defence aircraft and other offensive aircraft. Jets would have to be on hand at our most vulnerable times to somehow alleviate our danger.

Each Apache mission would be tightly coordinated with packages of protective jets. Fast movers tens of thousands of feet above us turned red into green on a PowerPoint slide and lowered risk from *high* to *medium*. Then CAOC planners could call it a 'Go'.

The air campaign had the might of the most advanced weaponry that any nation could bring to bear, yet to the pundits Gaddafi showed no sign of stepping down after three months of intensive operations. The easy targets were long gone, and regime forces had wised up to the tactics that would keep them alive. Several contributing nations were wavering, and the loss of a helicopter and crew might have just tipped the balance in favour of a pull-out. NATO would have failed as a modern and relevant organization. The challenge was to find targets within the bounds of the ministerial submission that were relevant and would have an effect on the campaign, but without sending the aircraft into certain disaster.

On the first day of June I had a telephone conversation with Chris. He talked about the ROE and the Legal Adviser, an RAF Squadron Leader, who knew the task inside out. He mentioned the frantic pace and the meticulous detail that was considered for each target selection; then he told me where we would go for our first mission:

The jets have had a go at this one, but is too small. It's a radar mounted on top of a mast about 80ft above the ground, and so far the bombs dropped on it have hit the ground beside it rather than the radar itself. It's barely a metre across. After that we want you to go to a vehicle checkpoint. Pro-Gad is controlling the road, we want you to disrupt that.

'What's the threat?' I asked.

'We're not expecting much if anything at the radar and you should be able to deal with that feet-wet. The VCP might be different. All sorts of stuff is moving through it so anything portable could be in play. There are no big air defence installations around, so you should not expect any of that. We need to be cautious with the ROE, be sure the targets are suitable and people are pro-Gad soldiers and you'll be good to go.'

A little after lunch on Thursday, 2 June, the Commodore's targeteer briefed us: 'We have confirmed two targets for tomorrow night. The first is a coastal radar, the second is a pro-Gad vehicle checkpoint.'

PowerPoint slides of aerial reconnaissance photographs showed a radar mast with several associated buildings only a few hundred metres from the beach and miles from any town. The second slide showed the road, that road, the one that linked the whole coast of Libya, with a clearly armed checkpoint. Both targets were at the southern end of the Gulf of Sirte, near Brega.

She continued, 'It's up to you how you do it, but you need to back-brief the CAOC later today with the plan. They want attack headings, weapons, heights, the whole profile. They want some screenshots of your route too.'

The plan had to be made in detail. New radio procedures, new flying techniques, a whole world of threat, all had to be considered and understood. John Blackwell and I would be the lead, with Nick Stevens and Little Shippers as the wing. The flight to the target would be simple – straight in off the sea, one Apache firing, the other looking for threats. How to actually hit the target was less obvious.

'We could hit the base of the radar mast. That would do it,' I suggested.

'Back yourself. Go for the top, hit the radar itself, it'll go all over the place,' Nick interrupted.

'It'll have to be perfect. The slightest wobble on the cross-hairs, the missile goes a fraction off, it will miss.' I knew the first trigger pull of the mission had to be good.

This had become a challenge. An unspectacular Hellfire into the base of a mast might buckle the structure, sever cables and render it useless, but it would still look like a radar. Hitting the radar itself would be spectacular. The media message would be big and bright and carry a long way. Missing would leave me feeling rather embarrassed.

'Then what? What if it misses?'

'I won't miss. But if that does happen, we'll clear the area and Staff Blackwell will land beside the mast, I'll get out, climb the thing, batter it with my Gerber knife, climb down again, get back in and we'll all make best speed for the second target . . . And we won't talk about it again.'

'Good first shot then! No pressure, although the redacted guntape of you giving a radar an actual kicking will look great on Sky.' Nick was pleased his idea had caught on and he was also happy to turn up the pressure!

## Chapter 5

# Feet-Dry in the Danger Zone

As *Ocean* made best speed for Libya, how not to die occupied my mind. It kept me working hard by day, with occasional dry retching over the aft railings on the quarterdeck. And it loomed dark over me in my cabin by night. This was real. We were about to launch big, slow-moving helicopters low-level into a war, with thousands of MANPADS, triple-A systems and various other nasty helicopter-catching weapons waiting for us on the coast. I was going to be in the front seat of the front aircraft on the first mission. All I could do to edge out the odds of perishing was plan and check, plan and check. In a quiet moment, on the quarterdeck, I asked the CO what we would do if the worst did happen.

'We'll fly the following night,' was his answer. He didn't need to think about it. 'And if it's you that's gone,' he added, 'I'll fly the following night.'

We were thinking the same thing; nothing more needed to be said on the subject.

Life was suddenly very serious. With two days to go I had to ask the aircrew to provide me with a few hundred words of sterile narrative on themselves to be used as a media release should the worst happen. Writing your own obituary takes you almost into bad luck territory, and I was unsurprised that most of them were agitated by the task. Washing it down with a bit of banter helped. 'You did not invent lasso-dancing!', 'I didn't know you went to a convent school' and even 'I didn't know you went to school' – all these bounced off the bulkheads. With the writing done, we all walked out on to the flight deck and, one by one, looked as strong as we could for the camera in front of an Apache – one of these pictures might accompany the words 'Pilot Shot down in Libya' or 'Pilot Missing in the Mediterranean'. But we all got it done, locked it down and moved on.

The whole squadron was working flat out. If they weren't at work, they were at rest ready to start work. The aircrew had been in a night routine since mid-May, and we kept to it. From the start it was clear that our missions would be flown at night. We had gradually reset our body clocks to sleep from 5.00 a.m. until just after lunch. This gave us the afternoon to plan and every hour of darkness to fly. With all ten of us in this routine, no one was spare to fly the odd morning air test or answer questions; but the simple fact was there were only five crews and they were needed, all five of them, every night. Two crews would be on the mission, the third crew would be in the Ops Room and the fourth and fifth crews had to check, fly and run up all the aircraft systems in the late afternoon. They were also the stand-by crews to fly as top cover for any rescue mission if anything went wrong on the night. Much thought had gone into pairing up the crews. Consideration was given to maritime and combat experience, but most of all to temperament. It was vital that a crew could cooperate under high levels of stress. There had to be a strong professional relationship, and everything rested on this. We had done the initial crewing assessment in April, but it was updated again for Libya. We now set the crews for war; thereafter we did everything together as crews – planning, flying, maintenance, manning the Operations Room, the lot.

I flew front seat with John Blackwell in the rear seat. Nick was front seat with Little Shippers as rear seat. Big Shippers and Jay Lewis paired up just as they had over the winter in Afghanistan, with Big Shippers, unusually, commanding from the rear seat. Mark Hall sat in the front with Charlie Tollbrooke on the sticks; and Reuben Sands was front-seater, with JB's thousands of flying hours piloting from the rear seat.

The balance had to be on the safe handling of the aircraft low-level over the sea at night. Where a rear-seater was qualified in both seats (most were) and he was the more experienced pilot, I opted to keep him on the sticks – this was where the critical flying would come from. Exactly half of the aircrew were qualified in both seats and could have flown from either seat and commanded missions as well as their own aircraft. I was spoilt for experience and had to make some tough choices. Over Libya fast decisive action would be needed from the front-seaters, but it was the rear seat pilots who performed the immediate life-saving manoeuvres. Given the perils of night and the Mediterranean, I was convinced accuracy on the flying controls would make the difference between coming unstuck and mission survival. The ability to fall back on experience was crucial. Handling the huge bison of an aircraft at speed, low-level, while evading incoming fire and having enough situational awareness to avoid pylons, wires, buildings, the other aircraft or tipping a rotor blade into the desert or the sea – all this required high skill. Then there was the possibility of an in-flight emergency and the need for safe control of an aircraft while diagnosing that emergency in a hostile place. The natural hazards and the possibility of mechanical failures were exacerbated by the unknown magnitude of the threat. Each crew was balanced for skill and decision-making. They all knew they had the skill to take on the targets. What none of us knew was how hostile pro-Gad was going to be in response.

The threat to us from the ground consisted of a whole new and terrifying list of things we talked about in training but hadn't needed to consider on operations for years. We were used to air superiority, troops on the ground and an enemy we knew we could overmatch. This was very different, there was so much that we did not know. Flicking through some recent photos of the Libyan conflict taken from Google, our trusty source of ground intelligence, Charlie Tollbrooke cantered through the possibilities:

> First up, the triple-A threat, ZPU-23-1, 2, ZU 23-2 and ZPU 4. One, two or four barrels. The old ZPUs have a 14.5mm round, fire at 150 rounds per minute and are effective out to about 3,000 to 5,000ft. The replacement ZPUs are much neater, a 23mm round and good out to 2–4km. The Intelligence Officer estimates around 20,000 of these in the country. Everyone has one, usually mounted on the back of a pick-up truck, known as a 'technical'. It will get you, but they have to see you to aim it. This is standard for all the other triple-A in theatre. They probably have Night Vision Goggles too.

With the triple-A covered, he moved on to the high-end heat-seeking missile threat:

> MANPADS. SA-7, 14, 16, 18 and the newest and most brilliant SA-24 are all on show. There are thousands of them. You probably won't know anything about it until the American lady in the wing tells you one is in the air. Flares, flares, flares, gentlemen!

Charlie clicked to photos of the MANPADS. We had all seen the videos on YouTube of the MiG23 shot down in March, probably by an SA-18 or 24. The high-end double-digit infrared (IR) threat was a plague in Libya. The photos didn't matter, the ensuing conversation about what profile to fly and what our DAS could do to help against missiles with counter-counter-measures was the important thing. These conversations are always private and I will not record them here – we knew what to do if we met such a missile one dark night.

> Now for the radar threat. ZSU 23-4, quick radar tracks the guns, four of them, 23mm, hence the name, but you all knew that. It will reach you at 5km, but inside 3km is best for him. A 3-second burst will send 200 rounds per barrel at about 1,000m a second to the azimuth and elevation the radar tells it. If you are there, then it will do you.

'How many of these?' I asked.

> Several hundred apparently, and not too many have been hit so far, probably because it's a 20-tonne vehicle and they turn the radar off and hide. It hasn't been out much because it can't reach the jets, although it has been seen firing horizontally in the ground war. It's a helicopter-catcher and with such a quick radar, which I forgot to say, will track you out to 20km providing there isn't much clutter to confuse it, perfect for positioning on the coast to watch us coming in. We should expect it. But this is a risky one for both sides. ZSU turns on his radar to track us and the jets will pick up his energy. If he's on for long enough he'll get shwacked. If we're on his radar for long enough, and we get in range of the gun, we'll get shwacked, by him.

'How long is long enough?' Me again.

> A couple of seconds. That's why it's risky. He'll have to turn his radar on, track us and then switch it off to avoid the attention of a jet. If we get in range he'll probably turn it on long enough to get one of us, but the other aircraft or the jet will almost certainly get him. Not a good career choice just now. But still, he'll undo our evening in a very bad way too.

My notebook was filling up. 'Happy days, we'll draw lots for that mission. What else?'

> SA-8, the Gecko. Mobile radar and missiles. Big problem. Very savvy operators. Very few systems, but they move around and

are reckoned to be in the urban areas in point defence. They occasionally switch on and then off and quickly hide. Tripoli most likely. Nothing else known. Of course you all know it will lock on and launch in seconds and the missile does the thinking after that.

'Not so keen on that mid-afternoon Tripoli fly-past now.' Nick raised a laugh.

'Not before the weekend, old boy. Crawl, walk, run and all,' I said, needing the whole session to be over. We were going into all of that in 48 hours and I wanted to work out the possibilities and our reaction to the hostility if it was waiting for us.

The severity of these systems was staggering. We were used to the odd AK47 or PKM heavy machine gun chancer. Exceptionally, in our recent operational experience an isolated triple-A incident might concentrate the mind. Now the threat was like being the sole pawn in the middle of a 3-D chess match. Whatever height, speed or profile we flew, something could hit us. The Apache and the skill of the aircrew was all that could make the difference between living and dying.

Throughout the planning I never had any concerns over what we would do once we arrived at a target. Our judgemental training has always been first rate, we understood the Rules of Engagement and their application; Chris James had done that assurance in Cyprus and he had done the same for every Apache pilot deploying to Afghanistan for the previous two years. We were well drilled on the decision-making process, we had watched hours of guntape and discussed complicated scenarios.

I knew the crews would make the right trigger decisions in the interest of the operation and its legal basis ('can I shoot?'), and also the right moral decisions ('should I shoot?'). Our collective worry was how to deal with the unprecedented threats. Heat-seeking missiles, radars locking on and triple-A were going to be there to meet us. We would be flying within their range and they were quite able to shoot us down. The almost 900 miles of Gaddafi-controlled coastline would be picketed by scouts, all there to report the sound of helicopters. Just inland from the scouts, the MANPAD and triple-A teams would stay hidden until a shot was possible. As soon as helicopters were in range they would fill the sky. PKM-man and AK-man were also part of the ambush. We faced independent missile systems, large calibre anti-aircraft fire and heavy machine guns just to get into the country. This was our expectation on crossing the coast – and, of course, we would face it all over again when it was time to leave and return to Mother.

Actual time over Libya was known as 'Vulnerable time' for all aircraft, shortened to 'Vul'. Within the Vul there were distinct periods when the risk of being shot down increased. Crossing the coast and at the target area were always regarded as the riskiest points on any mission. This was when the jets would be ready to assist; quite how was never clearly explained, but they had to be up above when we were down there. Concern over the Apache Vul window led to long discussions over risk and how to deal with it. As a matter of course, jets that could detect, jam or shoot radar systems were on hand. Without them it was a 'No Go'. Later, fast jets such as F-16s and Tornados were added, as well as drones with eyes on the target to hand over to us. All of this lowered our risk and meant it was a 'Go'. As the operation went on, I decided to refine Apache risk management down to the nine things that could kill us over Libya. These included SA-24, PKM man- and radar-guided missiles, as well as the physical environment and hazards such as pylons and wires. I would consider whether we might encounter the threat, then demonstrate what we could do about it both in planning and in action. It was not scientific and relied completely on military judgement. The only thing on the list that a jet could assist with was the radar-launched and -guided missile, but only after a missile was on its way at the first Apache.

When it came to the other threats out there, jets stacked 5 miles up above us were just going to watch the crash site and tell the CAOC what they could see. This didn't make us safer, it just made planning more complicated. Insistence on the use of a drone was reasonable for missions where the CAOC wanted to see the targets before we engaged. This gave them control, a long lens, the ability to make a decision. Precision targeting was vital and they needed to iron out every possibility of a mistake. It also allowed us to hold off until the target was good to go. This made it safer for us, but being paired with the Pred became an anchor. 'No Pred, No Go' saw several missions scrapped later in the operation.

A deluge of information arrived from the CAOC. All of it in jet lingo and all of it in need of translation. There were new maps and satellite imagery to be examined, radio frequencies to be programmed and airspace coordination to be understood and transposed into our planning systems. Everything was done from first principles as though we were the first people to do this job – which we were. This is the first and most lasting lesson of contingent operations. There is no handover, no one there to tell you what to expect. You don't get a familiarization trip or a well thumbed map and list of contacts. Safe places and hostile places are not yet known. Everything is new and it is up to you to find the best way to stay alive and the right way to win.

I read through the communications document. It was a thick forty-pager written by wiggly amp experts, who clearly understood numbers and radios but not much about delivering simple information in an easily understood format. This was critical stuff and we had to get it right, but I had no chance of understanding it. John Blackwell was our radios man so I had a quiet chat with him.

'You understand the radios don't you, Staff?' I casually asked, handing him the NATO communications list and procedures.

'Yes. First there are the V-UHFs, two of them . . .' He launched into his I've-just-done-a-Standards-check-and-I-know-everything lecture.

I interrupted: 'You could give me wiggly amps and algorithms and cypher and blah, blah, blah, but there are not enough years left in our careers for me to take it all in. You see, Staff, inside those radios are millions of tiny men. Some days they work well together and the radios work. On other days they don't work well and radios don't work either.'

'Er . . . yes, okay.'

'Just take all this NATO comms voodoo and make it into a picture that I can understand in the dark, low-level, no light, getting shot at.'

He took the document from me. 'Don't worry, I won't tell Big Shippers about the massive gap in your understanding of the aircraft!'

In the last 24 hours before the mission we had everything in place. *Ocean* lay over a hundred miles from Libya, able to head either west or south to launch a mission, keeping Gaddafi guessing. In the flip-flop the Ops team of six soldiers had been working 12-hour watches to ensure all the NATO data had been entered into the mission planning systems. Every detail from the daily changing Airspace Control Order had to be plotted. This happened while the aircrew were in rest, and by the time we had received our orders and targets for a mission, there was minimal input required. Soldiers with an average age of just twenty-four were trusted to programme mission-critical information with the minimum of supervision. This was their job and they were good at it. We knew they could be trusted to get it right first time. An incorrect keystroke could misplot a hazard, a mast, a front line; or a frequency could be wrong and we would be alone in the dark in a fight with no one to hear us. Trust generated belief and created one coherent planning team.

So the plan was made, checked and rechecked. The threat was discussed and our 'actions-on' rehearsed. We ran through every conceivable variation of threat and our response, including what to do if we had to make a forced landing in Libya. We each had hundreds of rounds of ammunition for our A2 Carbines and Sig Saur pistols. We had GPS, radios, locator beacons, night vision and escape maps stuffed into our life vests and grab bags. Extra batteries and a few bottles of water filled any spare room. This equipment, along with our body armour, added an extra 15kg per man. Not a big deal on the move on the ground, but a significant issue if the forced landing was into the sea. Our final concern was who would come and get us if we had to make that forced landing.

Combat helicopter pilots have to consider the chance of being shot down. There is no ejector seat. If the aircraft is unflyable everyone inside accompanies it to the ground, or into the sea. If the aircraft has been taken by the incoming, the aircrew might also have been injured. In the Apache, where the aircrew are in separate tandem cockpits, self-aid replaces first aid. Then, having been unable to conceal a 58ft long, 8-tonne crash landing, the aircrew are now into escape-and-evasion mode. If they are in the sea, then getting to the surface is the aim. Once there, it's time to inflate the individual life raft and wait. If they are on the ground a running shooting match is the most likely outcome.

If we went into the sea and it was sufficiently far from shore a ship could come and scoop us up. If we went in over land we were on our own. The NATO Combat Search and Rescue (CSAR) was held at five hours notice to move. This meant that from the point of being notified of downed aircrew the CSAR could take up to five hours to launch. We could reasonably assume that during those five hours our landing site would be compromised and daylight would be upon us. We would be running, probably running and shooting, behind enemy lines. We would have to choose where to go – try and make it to a safer rebel-held place or go deeper into pro-Gad territory. Getting to the rebel side meant crossing the front line and meeting ever-increasing numbers of regime soldiers. Time would favour pro-Gad. Bad luck in the incoming meant at least 24 hours on the run in the 'danger zone'. We had to accept this, and we did, but Wings got on in the background and began to organize a better option. The rescue situation would improve, but not for three weeks.

Our limits and our risks were reasonably well understood. The first mission was to be an 'easy-on' – a crawl, no tricky targets, just a straightforward 'get in, shoot, go feet-dry for a few minutes and leave'. No dramas, not an area of high pro-Gad concentration, but enough to get us into the operation and get a message out in the media. NATO chose the time and the place, and not even the embarked and trusted journalists were told of the mission until an hour before we briefed. Even then, they weren't told where we were going until the aircraft lifted from the flight deck.

I got up early on mission day. I was well rested, but anxious to get on with it. I didn't feel like eating, but fresh air would help. Lunch was finished anyway and the empty wardroom revealed a ship hard at work. The eight-hours-about shifts were well established. There was no sitting around drinking tea and reading last month's newspaper. It was work or sleep for the 310 sailors of the ship's company. I made a cup of tea and negotiated the airlock on to the quarterdeck. The hot, damp Mediterranean air surprised me. It had been more than a week since I'd been outside with the sun up and I had to half shut my eyes to deal with the intense blue and white burning my retina. As I got used to the light I looked around me. The quarterdeck was empty. A wooden bench, the sort you might see in a garden, was pushed up against the aft railings, an incongruous piece of furniture at sea. I made my way over, sat facing aft and the wake, and closed my eyes looking for peace. The deep rumble of the engines resonated through my body, the sunlight pushed against my eyelids and the heavy, humid air shut out escape. There is nowhere in a ship to escape.

I needed to get the mission going. That afternoon, in the flip-flop, we finalized the plan and discussed the variables, I wrote some notes to brief later and we waited for dark. Just before supper on Friday, 3 June I stood up in front of a packed aircrew briefing room and said, 'These are Orders for an Apache strike mission into Libya . . .' Behind me the slide projected on to the wall read 'Machete 1&2, Time on Target 2245hrs'.

In the airless, sweating, half-dark room forty soldiers and sailors listened as the ship's Principal Warfare Officer briefed *Ocean*'s manoeuvre plan, Wings detailed the flight deck activity and the Intelligence Officer described the situation on the ground and what might be out there to meet us. Then it was my turn. I described in detail what our formation would look like – the heights and speeds, how, where and with what each target would be struck, our 'actions-on' and our plan of escape if we went in. The whole thing took forty minutes, and the four of us who had lived the plan for the last three days just wanted out on to the flight deck and on with the low-level night charge into Libya. The wait was excruciating, but we were now just minutes from the off.

At 1800hrs *Ocean* went into communication shutdown, effectively switching off all unclassified messaging to the outside world. With the brief complete and all agreed it was a 'Go', the aircrew had their own private moments of preparation. Down on 6 deck John Blackwell got himself ready for the mission. He had already wrestled through the pain of writing a last letter to his family, just as he had done in 2003 in Iraq and again in Afghanistan more recently. All that remained was to prepare for the fight. He emptied his pockets. A photograph of his family and a St Christopher chain, given to him by his mother, were the last things out. He tucked the photograph into a drawer and slipped the St Christopher back into his pocket. Everything else was stripped out. No identifying objects, nothing that would link him to his work, in case the worst was to happen. Then he filled his pockets with morphine syrettes and tourniquets. Finally he folded his Libya escape map into a thigh pocket and left his cabin.

An hour before take-off we met in the flip-flop. Our personal weapons were laid out, mission data cartridges were signed for and maps were checked. A last pat-down confirmed no personal items were being carried, then we loaded up and made our way up towards the flight deck. On the way we donned our load-carrying vests and body armour, checked our personal ammunition, signed for the aircraft and then stepped out through the airlock on to the hot, dark flight deck.

Reuben and JB had already got both aircraft up on auxiliary power with all systems run up and working perfectly. I walked around the outside of the aircraft for a final check that all was well. Our aircraft sat, offset to port, on the forward spots, eight Hellfire and the gun pointing out to sea – Wings and Big Shippers had arranged the armed at night clearances just in time.

We climbed into our cockpits, stowed our carbines and ammo bags and strapped in. On the left side of my armoured seat I plugged the microphone lead into my flying helmet and, with a separate lead, connected the sensors on my flying helmet. On my right I attached the Helmet Mounted Display (HMD), swivelled the optical lens over my right eye and began to settle that eye into absorbing the forty-plus pieces of information and symbology now being projected into my head. Four button pushes of the Multi Purpose Display (MPD) activated the sensors confirming that the aircraft knew where my head was. This now allowed me to slave either sights or the gun to my head, effectively making those systems point where I was looking if I required it.

With both hands following a rehearsed routine of shortcut fixed buttons, I flicked through the scores of pages on the MPDs checking the flight instruments were calibrated, the radios were tuned to the right frequencies, the weapons were correctly configured and the target information was right. Reuben and JB had done it already; all we had to do was watch the clock and wait until it was time to launch.

The clock counted down to eight minutes to launch. It was time to get the engines up and the rotors turning. *Ocean* and her aircraft made no radio transmissions prior to launch. All flight deck communications were done by light and hand signals and we kept to a prearranged timeline for all our activity. Old fashioned pencil, paper and runner communicated any deviation. A brief flash of the strobes and a thumbs-up from the marshaller, and both aircraft began to rumble, engines up to full power. The steady high frequency hum of the flight deck was replaced by the aggressive roar of two armed aircraft readying for action. As the roar settled and my left eye interrogated the engine systems page, confirming oil temperature, hydraulic pressure and torque settings were good, I noticed in my right eye that *Ocean* was changing course. The coordination between Wings in Flyco, just 20m away overlooking the flight deck, and the Officer of the Watch, was working. They were on the timeline. Engines up meant only five minutes to launch, and *Ocean* turned on to a flying course and headed into the wind.

I briefed John on our immediate actions if we had a drama on take-off: 'Safe single engine speed is 44 knots. If we get an engine failure you'll jettison the Hellfire, I'll bang out the canopy, you dive the aircraft to gain speed.'

'Got it. Ready when you are, boss,' he replied.

'Okay, we're all set.' I flicked a handheld torch on and off, signalling to the marshaller that we were ready to lift, ready to go to war.

The marshaller looked fore and aft, pointed at me with his wands and signalled the aircraft to leave the deck.

'FMC in.' I engaged the flight stabilization system, announcing to John that our final check was done and he was clear to get us up and away.

He called, 'Lifting now' and gently raised the collective lever while steadily pushing the left pedal, countering the torque reaction and keeping the aircraft straight. We became light on the wheels, and, with the torque rising towards 80 per cent, we left the deck.

My left hand hovered over the canopy jettison switch. Each eye was focusing on different information. My left eye interrogated the engine systems page on the MPD, hunting for any change from the norm, while my right eye interpreted the HMD symbology of our movement. All was good, time to get going. I guided John through the take-off sequence just as we had been taught, initially in the simulator, and had practised for the previous five weeks.

'Engines all good, keep coming up, good . . . come left of the deck . . . more . . . keep climbing . . . clear of the deck, transition.'

And John pushed the cyclic forward and we went from a 70ft hover over the sea into forward flight, rapidly gaining that crucial safe single engine speed. Twenty seconds behind us Little Shippers and Nick Stevens were doing the same. Within a minute they were in formation and we turned south.

John had dealt with my comms bewilderment and given me a single-page diagram of who to speak to and on what frequency. He had simplified the whole massive document perfectly. I got on the Strike net and spoke to the AWACS controlling all NATO aircraft over Libya,

'Matrix, Machete launched as fragged.'

Tonight Matrix was British: 'Machete, parrots and India sweet. Continue.' Matrix had us on his radar; the identification code we were transmitting was correct we were clear to proceed to our target.

Everything was done. We were on time, on course and in communication. I armed the counter-measures that would be used to decoy radars and incoming missiles, setting the flares to automatic dispense. John got us down to 100ft and we charged headlong towards the fearful unknown of Libya.

On my left MPD I flicked to the situational display. It showed a thin green line from the Apache icon at the bottom of the screen to the target in the middle. Beneath the Apache icon a text box read '18 nautical miles, 9 minutes 50 seconds to run'. Over my left eye I brought down a single Night Vision Goggle (NVG) tube attached to my helmet. The left eye now had two jobs: look inside at the MPDs and look outside through the NVG. The right eye continued interpreting the HMD symbology with infrared video superimposed from the FLIR mounted on the nose of the aircraft 3ft in front and 2ft below me. I now had my left eye looking for normal light and an NVG intensifying what little ambient light there was. This, with the HMD projecting the infrared end of the electromagnetic spectrum into my right eye, meant that if it had a light or a temperature we would see it. Above the rotor blades the Fire Control Radar searched for targets and beneath it the Radar Frequency Interferometer passively searched for any radars searching for us. We were fully armed, protected, all-seeing and very hostile to anyone who wanted to take us on.

I lowered my seat to the bottom of its limit, keeping as much of my body as possible within the armoured sanctuary surrounding the cockpit. In a fight I would rely on the FLIR to see out. In the rear seat John had no such safety. To fly, he had to look outside and to do this he needed good all-round vision outside the cockpit, so his seat was most of the way up. His NVG and HMD infrared were used to position the aircraft relative to the target and to keep an eye on our wingman. An extra piece of armour on the side of his seat slid forward to give some lateral protection. In combat the incoming would be from below and the layers of armour between the underside of the aircraft and the aircrew were designed to keep bullets and blast out. John's job was to handle the aircraft whatever hell came from the ground, and this meant he would have to be able to see the ground and everything around him.

With six minutes to run we were still eleven nautical miles from the coastal radar target. I slaved the FLIR to the target coordinates and zoomed in the magnification, visually interrogating the coordinates. Its coastal location and our low height provided a perfectly silhouetted warm radar head. Even at this range it was already visible on infrared.

I described the picture to John: 'Target visual, still 20km to run. It's a great FLIR night!'

The conditions were perfect. A hot day had warmed the radar and it stood out against the relatively cool night sky. I knew Nick and Little Shippers would be looking at the same thing, so there was no need for a radio call. Looking outside and down I could see the gentle waves of sea state two just below us. It was perfect. Two Apaches, racing low-level over the sea, to a target in Libya. This was an extraordinary situation; we were about to join a new war. With the looming coast of Libya ahead and the clarity of the target, I knew we would be able to conduct the first part of the strike mission feet-wet. Staying over the sea meant I knew where the threat was, and that we would not overfly it and stand the chance of being ambushed.

'All good, should get the missile off at long range and stay feet-wet. You okay?' I said to John as I noticed a flashing green light reflecting off the canopy.

'Yeah, good. Really dry mouth, lip-light on my microphone causing the light, sorry. Little bit of nerves.'

'It's all good, mate, all good. I better not miss or you'll have to land, remember. I'd like to see your nerves then!'

I could deal with my worries by sitting low in the cockpit and keeping busy with the target countdown. John had to stay sitting up, eyes out, staring at Libya and wondering which of the thousands of bad things might happen first. Rear seat, hands on the flying controls – in combat that is where the courage is.

With four minutes to the target I actioned the missiles and counted down the range until we were less than 10km to go. With the situational display reading just under three minutes from the target I squeezed the right-hand trigger and placed the laser on the target. I was just seconds away from firing.

I was now dedicated to the shot. I searched all around the target with the FLIR. South of the radar by 400m was a dirt road. A track ran from the road to the radar. There was no movement, no vehicles and no people. Around the radar were three low buildings, clearly part of the radar site. They were damaged, presumably by previous strikes that had missed the radar itself. The radar was in good condition, the mast was straight and the radar on top was clean and facing north, out to sea.

'There it is . . . No one about, no vehicles. Just one good-looking radar . . . and us.' I described the target scene to John, who had now selected my video image on his right-hand MPD so that he could see my FLIR image and symbology too. He was now at a critical stage of flying. He had to maintain his awareness of the sea under us, the target in front of us, our proximity to both and the other aircraft and make sure he set the aircraft up so I could fire a missile.

Then, on our inter-aircraft net: 'Target is good, no civilians, no movement. Call ready.'

Nick replied straight away: 'Ready!'

With my right-hand middle finger pulling the laser trigger and my right thumb steering the crosshair, I placed the laser on the centre of the radar. A quick glance in at the right MPD, now showing the weapons page, and I checked that the missile was ready. Through the symbology in my right eye I noted it had locked on to the laser energy. The aircraft was perfectly set up to fire. Everything was ready, so I counted down the trigger pull.

My left-hand trigger finger lifted the heavy trigger-guard and then settled lightly on the lever. 'Three, two, one . . . firing!' Left trigger squeezed. A half-second delay and then a rushing whoosh and intense orange sparks accompanied the missile as it accelerated off the left-hand rail, climbed, gathered the laser energy and raced toward the target. My right hand held the laser dead centre on the radar, the missile seeker head tracking its reflected energy.

'Good missile.' John confirmed all post-firing checks were fine.

Then silence and the laser. Silence. No one spoke, radios hushed. Outside, darkness and a soaring missile ripping a trail toward war. Ten seconds later the missile hammered into the radar at over 700 miles an hour, its warhead punching through the delicate skin, followed a fraction of a second later by its fragmenting sleeve shredding the whole radar head. White-hot explosive fragments and debris sprayed out and showered to the ground. The first of ninety-nine Apache Hellfire had arrived in Libya.

To be sure, and perhaps part in response to the surging adrenaline, I fired a second Hellfire into the base of the mast before John pulled the aircraft away to the right. Still feet-wet, he set us up for another run-in as Nick and Little Shippers covered our break with a burst of 30mm. I brought the FLIR back on to the radar to check the damage. The radar had been completely destroyed, its buckled frame holding up a useless skeletal head. We were in; the first job was done.

'Good BDA, target destroyed. RV at holding point two, prepare to move to target two.' I told Nick to fly to a prearranged point over the sea and set up to run-in to the second target 10km to the east.

This target was a pro-Gad vehicle checkpoint on the main highway linking Brega to Misrata, the single continuous link between all the coastal towns in Libya. Pro-Gad owned the road and everything on it. To maintain control they needed checkpoints, but these were isolated, manned with few soldiers and open to attack. Safely behind their own front line they were clear of the rebels, but NATO could reach them from the air. With reconnaissance overflight confirming positions and military equipment, the CAOC was able to allocate this VCP to us to strike.

With my eyes inside the cockpit, I was busy reorganizing the MPDs and linking the navigation track to the VCP: 'Tell him to follow us, trail left. We'll give it a wide orbit to see what it looks like.' I asked John to relay the information to Nick and Little Shippers and set off.

It was likely that the VCP soldiers had seen our Hellfire in the air and heard the strike on the radar site. It was possible that a coastal scout had alerted them. It was also possible that they were there to attempt to shoot us down. Whatever had alerted them, they were ready. As soon as we got within earshot the seven men on the VCP began rushing for their weapons, but they appeared leaderless. There was much hurrying about, but nothing actually happened. I held off shooting because although I could see weapons and soldiers, no one was looking hostile. After a few moments of uncertainty a pickup truck arrived from the direction of the radar site. A man got out of the truck and took command. Hostilities ensued.

Two men ran to a ramshackle sun shelter and drove a previously unseen technical out on to the road. On its flatbed sat a ZU-23-2. The anti-aircraft weapon was perfectly mounted and bright white in my infrared right eye. Excellent concealment, I thought to myself – no jet or Pred would ever see it on a fly-past. Only from our low angle could it be seen under its shelter. The men parked, jumped on the rear of the truck and began revolving the ZU-23-2. The leader and two more soldiers crouched beside the technical. Seconds later, sporadic flashes came spitting from the barrel as it ranged 23mm rounds around the clear night sky in our direction. The night flashed from white to black, white to black as the triple-A felt for us in the dark. No need for a stand-off any more; it was time to engage.

'Weapon system on the truck!' I transmitted. Then to John, 'Get into constraints.'

I actioned the gun and squeezed the laser trigger to get a range and trajectory for the 30mm, while John tried to bring us on to the target. The technical was 70° out to the right, a very difficult shot. John tried to make the firing angle less acute, but pro-Gad interrupted with another burst of anti-aircraft fire from the ZU-23-2 in our direction. In self defence I squeezed the laser and gun triggers simultaneously, landing a quick burst in the vicinity of the technical but not deterring its action.

'Your target!' I burst on the net to Nick, as John began weaving to evade the incoming fire.

Little Shippers had his aircraft in perfect balance, with the technical directly to his 12 o'clock, giving Nick in the front seat an ideal 30mm firing solution. Laying his laser on to the technical, he fired four 20-round bursts of lethal 30mm, ripping up the ground around it, hitting the vehicle, destroying the ZU-23-2 and killing both the gunners. The three others threw themselves to the ground as the technical caught fire.

As the ammunition inside the vehicle started to heat and explode they ran, fell, dived, crawled and eventually sprinted out into the desert. I tracked them with my FLIR, gun actioned. Powered by adrenaline and fear for their lives, the lucky three kept running at impressive speed, legs high and arms pumping. I wanted to kill the leader – it was he who had directed his men to try and kill me – but I knew not to pull the trigger. It was far better to let pro-Gad military leadership, however junior, go free and tell his colleagues and commanders what had happened. If we were to have an effect in Libya it was going to be through witnessed lethal precision. This was the first time NATO and the regime had exchanged shots, had a fight. Up until now it had been whack-a-mole – jet on target, big height, no sound. No face-to-face fighting or fear. To cause problems for Gaddafi and the regime we needed his foot soldiers to be talking about us, we needed noise and we needed survivors.

With the runners heading out into the desert I returned my FLIR to the VCP. The technical was cooking off ammunition alarmingly, sending projectiles and shrapnel sideways and vertically. The fire burned so intensely that I was able to use the day camera sight to record the damage. All hell had visited and no one remained at the VCP. Our mission was complete, and as the receding noise of rotor blades sounded in the survivors' ears we turned for the sea once more.

'We're done here. Turning north for Mother, my lead.' I guided the patrol back out to sea. Once clear of the coast and out of range of Libya, I set the navigation to track *Ocean*'s recovery point. While we were airborne she had moved to the prearranged pickup point and was now readying to receive us back on deck. John and Little Shippers pulled in the power, increased our speed, and we found *Ocean* in just six minutes. With plenty of fuel and a cautious approach we landed in turn, sticking rigidly to the new armed, night-landing procedures Wings and Big Shippers had designed.

With both aircraft on deck and lashed down, John and Little Shippers brought back the engines, and the rotors slowed to a full stop. With all switches set, weapons triple-safe and saying, 'All done, switching off,' John turned off our battery. I sat, helmet still on, eyes closed, in silence. Brief, perfect silence. We'd gone there, had a fight and come back. Relief and the elation of survival and success settled on me. I knew the others would be feeling it too.

The ground crew soldiers removed the remaining Hellfire. Once they had finished, the lead lance corporal tapped on the canopy, startling my eyes open: 'Sir, there's an empty 30mm case from the gun, do you want a souvenir?' I nodded, no words needed. He handed me the empty case and I tucked it into my pocket.

I climbed down on to the flight deck. The engineers and the ground crew were already getting to work, folding the blades and moving the aircraft into the hangar. *Ocean* headed north for safer waters and half a dozen journalists wanted to hear about what had happened. First, I needed to debrief with all the aircrew and write the Mission Report

(MISREP). We went down to the flip-flop and played back the guntape.

Guntape debriefs are usually private meetings between the owner of the trigger pull and his senior commander. Killing and then replaying the killing, examining the weapon effect and describing the fight are deeply personal moments. However, the intensity of the scrutiny could not be avoided, and the Commodore and even the Padre came down to the flip-flop to listen tn the debrief. All the aircrew were there too. This time the guntape debrief had to be much wider. In a new war everyone has to know what happened first. To the aircrew it might give them their one chance at winning later. Both Nick and I both felt uneasy, with the Padre present, describing the precision of Hellfire, the fragmenting effect of 30mm and killing. Guntape debriefs are analytical and dispassionate. Their purpose is to review the facts, and check the ROE and the gunnery; they can take up to two hours. They are about logic and reason, but they also acknowledge the moral responsibility of having killed. We had risked our lives, been shot at and taken lives. All these things weighed heavily with us and, as they always do, they would take a long time to settle in our heads afterwards. Killing never leaves your mind, it can't be unseen, and you will always remember it. Its memory visits your dreams and sometimes in the daytime too. That night we had to kill to stay alive and we knew there would be more in the coming days.

With the Commodore and the Captain fully briefed, we were left alone to finish the MISREP. Spirits were up, we'd gone to Libya, fought, come back, targets hit. But there was a demon in the guntape. I phoned Chris at the CAOC and described the mission. The ZU-23-2 was the fear. It was so well hidden that no jet or drone would ever have found it. The pro-Gad gunners were quick and accurate in bringing it into play and they kept firing while our 30mm was landing all around them. These were well trained and motivated soldiers, their standard was high. This was troubling, and we were unhappy about it. It did not matter that the weapons were hidden from the jets. We expected a fight. What took the edge off the elation of going to Libya and back was the professionalism of the incoming fire. Pro-Gad was ready for helicopters.

With the MISREP done and the guntape edited, the Ops team emailed it out. I had one more duty that night – honouring my arrangement with the half dozen or so embarked journalists. I put away my concerns and went to talk to them. I had the tricky problem of needing to give an interview while preserving my anonymity. We agreed that I would sit in the cockpit, helmet on and with the camera angle over my right shoulder. Geraint Vincent from ITN did the prompting, and the footage was pooled and subsequently used by Sky, the BBC and ITN. Just before we started I slapped a badge on to the velcro on my right arm, our well-known Apache image set in a circle, as seen on the arms of all our crews in the UK and Afghanistan. Written around the outside of the circle was 'Apache Maritime Strike'. The cameraman saw the badge and asked if I wanted it in shot.

'Yes, absolutely!' I encouraged him. 'This is our thing; it's what we do. We want people to know that.'

This was our new role in combat, a new way of working. Eighteen months of development had brought us to this point, and I was very happy to show the naysayers. The 'easy-on' mission had put the Apache at sea firmly in focus, and the huge media interest was going to expose it in every newspaper and news broadcast in the coming days.

After the telly interview I had a sit-down chat with Kim Sengupta and John Ingham. They were writing articles for the big British newspapers and had come on board to get the details of the first mission. By this time it was almost 3.00 a.m. and I was sat drinking tea with the journalists and their MoD media minder; meanwhile, the rest of the aircrew were deep in the catacombs of *Ocean* enjoying a beer. After half an hour of very careful discussion I was free to find the team. In the empty wardroom a note was left on the table. It read, 'We're in 7NA2 – the Seniors Mess. Mr Hall is getting a round in, history in the making! Nick.'

This wasn't celebration, it was relief and exhilaration. Before we had finished our beer the grainy green image of two Apaches – dark silhouettes against the clear night sky, lifting from the flight deck of *Ocean* – was on Sky News. We sat, mesmerised for a moment, watching our ghostly selves fly into the black. The footage then cut to the distant bright green light of exploding Hellfire. John flicked to the BBC news and the same footage was being broadcast. Within an hour the redacted guntape of our Hellfire hitting the radar was added to the piece, which was shown constantly for the next 48 hours by everyone from Al Jazeera to Sky and covered on every news website with an interest in the Arab Spring.

*Chapter 6*

# The Seventh Son and the Revolution

The first sparks of revolution in Libya were struck by families of the 1,270 men murdered in the 1996 Abu Salim prison riot. Muammar Gaddafi, looking west at Tunisia and east at Egypt, needed to reassert his control and had their leaders and legal representatives arrested. Civil unrest had always been easy to quash, with an ever-present secret police and thousands of fearful informants. The certainty of incarceration and brutalization for those found guilty made political resistance hazardous. While popular revolution overturned the status quo left and right, Libya looked set to continue its police state existence. The regime was strong, its networks were all pervasive and its bizarre leadership was tolerated.

In 2003 Libya was the only country to buy the 'if you have a nuclear weapons ambition we'll come and get you' threat. Iraq said they didn't have any, got invaded, and apparently didn't have any. Iran looked too tricky and North Korea was pointless. But Libya gave up their programme and Britain shook hands with the regime, effectively endorsing Muammar and his boys. Acquiescing to the West's demands allowed them to remain in power unchallenged. All looked good for the wicked Colonel.

Then the 2011 ripple of democratic aspirations gave the West an advantage. Western leaders could now base their political aims on a local desire for democratic change. Democracy, its promotion and its demand by the people, is instantly respectable, whereas hand-shaking in a tent with a despot is much less attractive. Democratic protest makes for good front-page pictures; the tent scene, not so much.

Huge posters with photographs of the Abu Salim victims hung high behind the bitter grief of their families in Benghazi in early 2011. As they had done for fifteen years, the families and survivors held vigils and protested. Typically, the regime shut these demonstrations down. But the people had had enough and they fought back against the police and the army. Moreover, the picture was no longer local. The international community was interested, and their cameras brought to our attention the desperate humiliation of a people beaten up by its own government.

Encouraged by successful revolts in Tunisia and Egypt, the people stood their ground. The regime took aim and began firing. In Tunisia the military had refused to take orders from the government, effectively rendering the state impotent in quashing the uprising. The people won. Although violent, the protests in Egypt quickly led to political concessions and the eventual resignation of the government. The people won again. The Benghazi protesters hoped for similar success, but neither dynamic was present in Libya. The army started shooting, arrests were made and people disappeared. But the people had had enough and they kept fighting. By mid-February 2011 Libya was in full revolt.

With thousands of contract workers from all over the world caught up in the turmoil, several nations mounted evacuation operations, plucking their people from the desert and the harbours. Even China flew in. North Korea, fearful that talk of revolt would come home and germinate, made her citizens sit it out. Britain got the RAF and the Royal Navy to go in, pick up our people and bring them home. With civil war ramping up, economic production faltered and the everyday necessities of life became scarce. The side that could last the longest as time trickled through the hourglass would win. Libya was besieging itself.

The political opposition set up in Benghazi, and Libya's second city became the regime's primary target. At the same time, the central coastal city of Misrata became a rebel stronghold. Gaddafi mobilized his military and the fighting began. NATO got involved, promising the UN a No Fly Zone to take 'all necessary measures' to protect civilians under Article VII of the UN Charter. In the UN Security Council ten 'yes' votes and zero 'noes' were recorded. Germany, India and Brazil abstained. Notably, China and Russia abstained too. Their decision not to veto UN Security Council Resolution (UNSCR) 1973 effectively allowed the NATO mission to shift to regime change – 'all necessary measures' had a wide interpretation. Good news for France, Britain and the USA, who all wanted rid of Gaddafi. The morality of the decision to protect the people of Libya appeared to be coincidental. But politics isn't about morality. At the heart of politics lies power. If power, its reinforcement, its culture and the promotion of its likeness reflects high moral values then that is a good thing. But it is not the main consideration – that is power itself.

UNSCR 1973 was passed on 17 March, and two days later a French jet destroyed a regime tank, thus beginning an intervention that would end with Gaddafi's pitiless death, blown up, captured by a rampaging mob, sodomised with a bayonet and shot on 20 October. The NATO mission was called Operation Unified Protector. The British contribution was Operation Ellamy.

Enforcing a No Fly Zone was easy work. Once the regime's air defence systems were taken down the jets could fly without threat. Targets were found, analysed and destroyed. The regime's military were hit whenever they showed themselves and the siege continued. But Gaddafi had long been a survivor, and the regime adapted. They hid in hospitals and schools, knowing NATO would not strike there. Gaddafi's soldiers did the same. They hid their armour, used technicals and travelled in buses. The rebels' much wished-for breakthrough did not happen. They were ordinary citizens with guns; they had no military structure or tactics and they were being hammered by the regime. They were determined but disorganized, and thousands died as Gaddafi took his chance to extinguish the fires of revolt with as much force as he could muster.

Then stalemate took hold. The anticipation of April led to nothing, and May brought the rebels and NATO no closer to winning. Politicians looked around for what else they could throw at the problem, and we were chosen. An introductory mission near Brega, big media exposure and resolute words from Paris and London made us part of the campaign. We were there to cause problems, get in Gaddafi's mind, prove NATO was willing to take risks and was unwavering. I was told to have a 'cognitive effect' on the regime by striking wherever NATO saw it best to use us, by making noise and menacing the regime, by taking down the targets others were unable to hit. And by not getting shot down.

Muammar's seventh and youngest son, Khamis Gaddafi, was a career soldier. Schooled in the West and with military training in Russia, he was a genuine operator. His father had put him in charge of the elite 32 Brigade, based west of Tripoli at the Al Maya barracks. When the revolution began they mobilized to crush the resistance in Misrata, an easy task with their tonnes of heavy metal and thousands of shells. They lodged the 10,000-strong formation in the area of Zlitan, about 30 miles west of Misrata on the central coastal belt. Another 20 miles further west sits Al Khums, home to the Libyan Special Forces (SF). Khamis' brigade was elite in its own right, and the pairing with the SF worked well. He had tanks, armoured fighting vehicles, artillery and technicals. And he had the very best anti-aircraft weapons. ZSU 23-4, SA-7, SA-7b, SA-18 and SA-24 were all part of his arsenal, and everyone was driving around in pickup trucks with a ZU-23 stuck on the back. The SF had fast boats and small-team patrols capable of getting behind the rebel front line and causing mayhem.

Together they surrounded and cut off Misrata in late February, then waited for the city to die. Their modus operandi was straightforward. They hid in farm buildings on the outskirts of the city. Periodically they would break cover, fire a barrage of artillery into the city and sneak back into hiding before NATO could find them. They blocked the roads, and anyone attempting to leave the city was arrested; when the jails filled up, regime snipers kept the population contained. At the same time the SF would dart up and down the coast, inserting patrols to sever rebel communications, kill them in their safe places and create the fear of being surrounded in a forlorn and helpless siege.

With fifty miles of depth to hide in, Khamis' forces were well dispersed; there was no need to concentrate men on the front line where they would be vulnerable to both a rebel breakout and NATO jets. Misrata was being squeezed. Thousands lay injured in hospitals with scarce medical supplies. The Royal Navy halted any meaningful pro-Gad maritime operations, thus allowing a fragile opportunity to link with Benghazi. But this link was precarious and supplies were always well below the requirement. Overloaded ships would dock at night, often under artillery attack, offload rebels and equipment, load up with wounded and then head back to Benghazi. The slow, poorly coordinated sea lane was Misrata's only lifeline, but it was not enough to keep the city from gradually, agonizingly, slipping into hell. Khamis had time on his side and he was steadily strangling the city. Day by day, barrage after barrage was edging Misrata towards defeat.

NATO kept up the air strikes and the Royal Navy patrolled the coastal zone, even lending gunfire on several occasions. But Khamis still looked strong. The rebels needed to take the fight to 32 Brigade and move the front line away from the city. If they could advance west Khamis would have fewer places to hide and NATO could find and strike them. If they moved the front line away from the city the siege would be lifted, supplies would move quicker, the wounded would get the help they needed and more rebels could join the fight. But time favoured Khamis. The longer the impasse continued the weaker NATO looked. At the same time Misrata was suffocating and Khamis was looking at a shiny new medal, higher rank and a bigger palace.

*Chapter 7*

# The Zlitan Raids

The night after the first mission, 6,000 hours of flying skill in the hands of JB lined up the perfect Hellfire and Reuben Sands put it straight into a BM-21 multi-launch rocket system dug in next to a house outside Brega. NATO had considered the target three times before and rejected it as too risky due to the proximity of the building. Chris James had convinced them we could do it without damaging the building. When the Hellfire hit, the truck and weapons were destroyed, leaving the house untouched. The Targets people in Italy sat up. The Apache was now a compelling option in an air campaign that was at risk of stalling.

In the second week of June, after our two missions near Brega, *Ocean* lay 80 nautical miles north of Zlitan and 656 Squadron were planning to hit the command and control (C2) heart of the Khamis operation. Our part in the battle for Misrata was to disrupt Khamis where he thought he was safe and deny him the ability to move freely around Zlitan and Al Khums. The rebels could deal with the toe-to-toe fight on the front line, and we were going to create gaps for them exploit and push through. We knew Khamis was dangerous, but we had no idea he was ready and waiting to take us on.

At 6.00 p.m. local time on 8 June 2011 Sky News reported that HMS *Ocean* was off the coast of Misrata, ready to strike, and I had a security problem with big red attention-getters. Two unexpected strikes near Brega had kept pro-Gad guessing, but they were low-threat missions. Heading into the dark heart of 32 Brigade was a different proposition and I wanted as much surprise as I could get. With our location compromised, Khamis put his artillery away and sent his scouts and MANPAD teams to the coast. Pro-Gad was looking north, expecting the Apache. The following night, we went in.

Mission number three was simple enough – a C2 node made up of buildings and a radio mast. The target was coastal, but we would have to go feet-dry into the centre of 32 Brigade's operation. John and I took mission lead, with Mark Hall and Charlie Tollbrooke, on their first mission, as wing. Running in against Khamis was about to give us our first brush with the most deadly anti-helicopter weapon on the modern battlefield.

With the target several miles from the low tide mark, we had to get into Libya first, turn on to an attack heading and then tip into the strike. We looked at the map and the satellite imagery and chose the uninhabited expanse of sand dunes five nautical miles north-east of Zlitan to go in feet-dry. No one would be there to hear us cross the coast and we could intercept our attack heading, get the missiles off and get away before Khamis had got his boots on. After that we would head east and take a look at a suspected vehicle checkpoint, rattle pro-Gad some more, then track out the 20 nautics for Mother.

But the pro-Gad scouts were already out. They were hidden and waiting all along the coast, and we were expected. We launched just before midnight on Thursday, 9 June, pointed south and arrived over Libya nine minutes later.

Six seconds after that the American lady in the wing announced, 'Missile launch 3 o'clock!'

'Flares! Right, 3 o'clock low!' Charlie shouted.

Out over the side of the aircraft all four aircrew could see the missile now arcing up through the darkness, its motor burning brightly, racing directly towards them. Time slowed down to a crawl while the world around them accelerated to light speed. They braced for the impact.

From our lead aircraft, just ahead and positioning for our final run in to the target, John transmitted 'Flares! Flares! Flares!' in a decisive tone, followed by the briefest of pauses and then 'Missile seen!' – confirming what Mark and Charlie already knew and adding to the noise inside their cockpit as the aircraft's self-defence system reacted to the missile ripping through the night towards them.

Both aircraft pushed out a rapid release of flares, briefly blinding the aircrew and identifying the aircraft like low-level shooting stars to the assembled ambush of pro-Gad chancers. We were now relying entirely on the technology inside the Apache to save us. There was fear and anger, confusion and chaos, and a missile doing Mach 2.3 towards us.

Charlie stared at the missile as though at his own mortality. Suspended there in the darkness, low through his right hand canopy, an intensely bright white flame streaked through the blackness and arced towards him. The brightness of the rocket motor and the dazzling plume in its wake captivated him. The way the missile moves is disturbing. It seems agitated, aggressive and determined. The fear is here, everywhere; there is no escape. No one is able to speak.

More flares. And the cockpit is illuminated with a double lightning flash as the white-hot flares project themselves into the night and fall away below. But on the missile comes, marauding on its demonic course to intercept the aircraft.

Another pattern of flares erupt, rushing forward into the darkness. The rotor disk above illuminates as the burning flares fall away out of sight. The missile swerves away as if seduced by the flares and then menacingly tips towards us one more time. The flares are bright enough and the missile is close enough for Charlie to see its shape, its white body and the black markings on its mid-section. Then it whips past within metres and explodes, leaving both aircraft untouched. Six seconds over Libya on their first mission and Mark and Charlie had met with and survived the SA-24. The ambush was perfect, but the missile bought the flares and now it was our turn to fight back.

While the first two missions had been novel work, this was a whole new and terrifying threat that changed our entire outlook on the operation. The long discussions in the flip-flop about what might happen and how we would deal with it were no longer just conversations and plans. Now, 40 miles from safety, low over Libya, four of us had arrived at the point where theory meets reality. We could turn and run or we could stay and fight. Running was the right thing to do. Khamis had missed, we had survived, and returning to Mother to fight another day would still be a small victory. The other option – fighting – would make us feel better, but not much more. Perhaps the shooter would be killed and denied the ability to try again, but we would come closer to being shot down in the process.

Getting stuck into a fight when triple-A or MANPADS were coming out of the dark was the wrong thing to do. It was a high stakes risk – winning would be the only satisfactory result, and getting hit would be a disaster. The thought of crashing, surviving and then finding ourselves on the run right in the middle of 32 Brigade was fearsome. Capture would be very hard to evade, and the rescue crews somewhere in Europe were still on five hours' notice to move, leaving us very much on our own for the rest of the night and all of the following day. Anyway, who is going to try and rescue downed aircrew when the most sophisticated anti-helicopter weapon in the world is at large? Whether it was a crash landing or simply being shot out of the sky, the regime would make the most of how it defeated NATO's last gasp. The helicopter option had failed, NATO could not now win, the rebels would be defeated and Gaddafi would hold on to power.

We chose the second option; we chose to fight.

Mark and Charlie immediately closed in on the SA-24 firing point in the dunes. While the missile was coming at them Mark had glanced at the firing point, flicked his left thumb across the 'store' button on the sights and sensors grip and sent the coordinates of SA-24 man to the FLIR, the gun and all his Hellfire; all of it done in a fraction of a second. The infrared drew them to a man rushing about on his own, appearing to hide the weapon and picking up another. Mark sent an instant burst of 30mm to suppress another attack.

John and I put two Hellfire in quick succession into the C2 node, delivering panic to pro-Gad right where he thought he was orchestrating hell, and we then joined our wing in destroying SA-24 man. Just as we had killed the triple-A shooters outside Brega the previous week, it was important to us to deal with this shooter too. A man who shoots and misses can reassess, try again or come back tomorrow with some friends and do better. He must be stopped, and we had to make it so if we were to survive the campaign.

With the initial target dealt with and the ambush defeated, I brought the patrol back out over the sea to safety. The irony of flying two Apaches low-level over the sea in order to check our systems were still good to continue was striking. Only a few weeks earlier we had regarded the sea as the most dangerous place to be in this aircraft. Now, when compared to the hostility from the dunes, the sea was a sanctuary, a place to regroup, calm down and to make a new plan.

The Zlitan raids of June 2011 brought home right to our core the dangers of flying in combat. We flew ten sorties into the middle of 32 Brigade in the first half of the month, with no reasonable chance of rescue if the worst were to happen. We varied our routes and times, massed fire on to targets, darted away and never crossed the coast in the same place twice. For their part, Khamis' soldiers were adapting too. They adopted a tactic of firing flares into the air when helicopters were heard. This did two things for them: it alerted others of danger, much like lighting a signal fire, and provided illumination for them to use their NVG to locate and engage us. The scene was played out every night in the Zlitan area: we arrived, flares went up and the shooting started.

With the moon waxing gibbous and about to give pro-Gad more chance to see us than we wanted, a last mission was planned before a few nights alongside in Sicily. NATO had recognized a pattern of activity from the Al Khums-based pro-Gad SF. They were avoiding land movement by dashing up and down the coast in speedboats, conducting re-supply and disruption operations in and around the front line. While Khamis was operating well on land, keeping his weapons hidden most of the time, the regime planners had forgotten that NATO also had a watchful presence at sea. The public face of this capability was the French aircraft carrier *Charles de Gaulle* and the British destroyer HMS *Liverpool*, as well as frigates HMS *Iron Duke* and HMS *Sutherland*. These, and other less visible assets, could observe and listen without being seen themselves. They could follow and report, establish the SF routine and hand the evidence over to the NATO planners and their legal advisers.

On 11 June Chris James called from the CAOC with an unusual proposition for a mission:

We want you to go on deck alert, like VHR in Afghanistan, and work for the Commodore if other maritime assets find the SF speedboats. The legal advice is that we need to be sure where they came from, that the pattern is consistent. Once that is established you can be launched to strike. The SKASaC will be up and they can give you a steer to the boats. Once you're done, get back to *Ocean* for a re-arm and a refuel and we'll send you against whatever else the Pred can find on land.

The 857 Naval Air Squadron Sea King Airborne Surveillance and Control helicopter (SKASaC) could sit a long way from the coast and hoover up the entire sea and ground picture with its radar. With this all-seeing electronic eye it could track anything that moved and then steer another sea or airborne asset to intercept. The SKASaC crews flew night and day over the Med, providing electronic intelligence for the Commodore and shaping NATO options for maritime strike activities. Coupling the already vigilant surface and sub-surface maritime assets with the SKASaC, and ultimately cueing the Apache to strike, kept the watchers unseen and silent to the regime. Conducting the strike at night over the sea, where the pro-Gad SF had chosen to work, meant we stayed feet-wet and unseen too. It was a compelling task. These SF operators had been terrorizing the rebel front line for months, as well as mounting raids against the city of Misrata itself. They laid mines in the sea and left partially submerged boats laden with explosives to hamper humanitarian efforts. They were also guilty of stuffing mannequins with explosives, clothing them and dropping them into the sea as improvised explosive devices aimed at hitting NATO or aid agency vessels.

Striking pro-Gad SF would be a big blow to the regime's military planners. The improvised explosive mannequins were an alarming tactic – no mariner will ever leave a body in the water and these devices were designed to exploit that code of the sea. Preventing this activity and denying pro-Gad the use of their coastal waters for manoeuvre would either confine them to Al Khums or force them to travel by land, thus risking a NATO airstrike. Fast-moving small boats at sea in the dark presented a challenging target for NATO; the aircraft would have to get low and slow, so only attack helicopters would do.

In the CAOC Jack Davis and Chris James had cleared two VCPs close to the front line as the primary targets for the mission, and they requested that we be ready to launch two hours before the scheduled Vul time in case the pro-Gad speedboats were at work. The Commodore and his team in the ship, who now included the CO, ran up the plan, liaised with every other asset out there and handed us a neat pack ready for our final detail. This process happened for every mission. The CAOC team rushed about making things happen in a confusing and fast-jet-oriented environment. The Commodore's team in *Ocean* worked very long hours to assist in developing the understanding of the plan by getting various maritime assets involved. The CO would spend the early morning in discussion with James and Jack in Italy, while the Commodore's targeteer got everything she could with a sensor to provide more detail of the route and the targets.

And we aircrew would come well rested and fresh to the briefing room at circa 1400hrs each day to receive the proposition for the next mission. Throughout the afternoon discussions continued while the crews planned. I would discuss the legal elements with the CO and the lawyer in Italy and finally we would settle on the way to approach the mission.

That night the plan was simple. Be ready and react, just as we did every day and night in Afghanistan with the quick reaction VHR pair. We were all well practised at launching quickly with little information, receiving target coordinates while airborne and then arriving on scene and deciding how to fix the problem. This was the stuff of the Apache in Helmand and it is a core skill in all our aircrew. This time we would do it at sea against boats, but the fighting philosophy was no different.

Throughout the afternoon of 12 June the two VCPs were very active, with regular rocket and artillery strikes heading across the front line and into Misrata. The jets and the Pred had been busy, and we waited in anticipation of the evening launch. Late that afternoon I had a telephone conversation with our legal adviser in the CAOC. She gave me the full legal basis of the VCP strike, as she did for every target, but this time she also presented me with her analysis of the potential speedboat strike. The pattern of life, the origin of the boats and the activity they got up to while they were out would all be considered by the CAOC, and we would only be released when they were sure the targets were good to strike. This mission-by-mission assurance from the CAOC told us what we needed to do to make a just and precise trigger pull. With this final and most up-to-date piece of crucial information I briefed the mission in what was now refined to a 30-minute session. We were set, *Ocean* was in her silent timeline and Nick Stevens and Little Shippers got ready to launch in Machete 2 while John Blackwell and I prepared Machete 1.

During my final checks, as I signed out my morphine and personal weapons, Chris James was once again on the phone from Italy:

All set, and we have a Pred too. He's limited on fuel and he doesn't have any Hellfire left. So, if the speedboat task gets done early enough you'll be getting targets from him over land. Oh, and no pressure but the Attack Helicopter Force Commander has just arrived here and he's on the shop floor watching all the feeds right now.

Ha! The big boss was watching live from Italy and we were doing something new and unusual. Oddly, the news barely broke into my mission bubble; I was completely focused on how we would react to a rapid launch.

I didn't have to wait long to find out. Within five minutes of both aircraft completing their weapons and FLIR checks I noticed the compass header in my right eye rapidly shifting as *Ocean* heaved on to a new course. It could only be actions for a flying course. We were on a silent timeline as usual, so no radio transmissions were made, but I knew Nick and Little Shippers in the aircraft to my front would be anticipating a launch. Thirty seconds later Doug was tapping on the canopy: 'Launch, boats! Here's the coordinates!' He stuffed a piece of paper with the last known position of the pro-Gad speedboats into my right hand and ran forward along the flight deck to deliver the same news to Nick.

The nil-light flight deck spun into launch mode. Our engines came up to a roar, rotors turned and the ground crew removed the last of the lashings. Within three minutes of Doug's news we lifted from the deck and slipped away into the low-level dark of the Mediterranean night. The next few minutes were about speed in getting to the point of need, finding the boats and accuracy in doing what needed to be done on the trigger.

As soon as I checked in with Matrix a steady, precise Midwest accent updated the coordinates and told me to raise the SKASaC, Viking, on our own discrete Apache mission frequency and continue on our way. The plan was running very neatly.

'Viking, this is Machete, ready for your SITREP.'

'Machete, head 230° and 15 nautics for target, two fast surface movers as briefed', came the assured reply.

John brought the patrol on to the heading, tipped the nose forward and raised the collective, charging hard towards the fight. In the front seat I flicked on the FCR and began searching the sea for the movers.

'Now 234° and 12 nautics,' called Viking, counting us down. 'Now 245° and 8 nautics . . . now 251° and 6 nautics . . .'

Both Nick and I were searching hard. We were closing on the speedboats, which were steadily crossing our south-westerly track from left to right. This meant they were heading up to Al Khums. Nick beat me to it.

'Got it! Two movers, bearing of 265° and 5 miles, stand by for data . . .' Nick had found the speedboats. Viking, able to detect everything that moved in the sky, in the sea and on the land, confirmed we had the correct target. We were clear to engage.

I called to Nick and Little Shippers, 'You shooter, me looker, your QBOs.' He had found them first while I was still getting my sights into the area. It was his turn to lead the patrol, give the quick battle orders and do the shooting.

When it came, less than 40 seconds later, the 30mm was devastating. The two speedboats were racing, six men to a boat, one behind the other, parallel to and a couple of miles from the shore. Nick closed to a point where he was sure his first rounds would hit, no adjustment needed, and threw four sharp 20-round bursts at the rear boat. Every round hit, stopping the boat dead, no survivors. The lead boat immediately turned south-west and headed for the shore, but Nick already had his sights predicting its path. Another four rapid bursts of 30mm, anticipating the track and speed of the boat, came from his gun. Again they tore through the boat and its occupants, and all pro-Gad SF activity at sea ceased. The pro-Gad SF speedboat teams, previously operating with impunity, were now out of business and Gaddafi's grip around the throat of Misrata had been loosened a little.

I scanned the scene with my infrared. The first boat burned intensely, indicating fuel and ammunition on board. The sea around the wreck was cold and empty; her former occupants were beneath its gentle swell. The second boat was partially submerged and listing heavily to the stern. Around her, in the water, I could make out three areas of heat. As I zoomed the infrared to observe closer, the heat spots were becoming less defined. We circled closer to identify the heat, and they faded all the while. Those men who went into the water had done so mortally wounded, and they were now succumbing to their injuries, limbless and haemorrhaging in the sea.

I watched their final ghastly, fearful and lonely expiration, waves washing over and darkness surrounding. The horror of the violence and our action in war was once again clear, as it is every time we use lethal force. Their plight in the sea beside their stricken vessel was hopeless, and we had nothing to offer that might ease their passing.

'Okay, my lead for Mother,' I transmitted, and we turned north-east, hoping for an early end to the evening's mission. I relayed to Matrix what we had left behind and let the flying suits in Italy wonder what it might be like to be dying in the sea.

Our cockpits were silent during the 5-minute transit back to *Ocean*, minds half on the task of landing and half on the horror of the speedboat strike. The well-honed procedure of joining to land was dealt with like a drill, and John and Little Shippers lined up from a long way out for a straight-in long final approach to Wing's clockwork deck. I wanted the night to be over, to be able to debrief the strike and deal with the guntape, but no such opportunity came our way. As soon as we were both down on the deck and the lashings were on, the CO urgently tapped on my canopy and gave me a sheet of paper.

'ZSU 23-4! Here! Image too slow on the network, but it looks like this.' He had drawn a quick diagram. 'A copse, the ZSU is right in the middle. There's a building, here, close by, about 50 metres away. CAOC says the ZSU is good to strike with Hellfire. Pred is on task to give you a laser handover. He's low on fuel so you need to get going!'

This was precise, no unnecessary words. He gave me all I needed and let me get on with the job.

I got on the radio to Nick on the spot to my front: 'Urgent task, only take ammo until you're refuelled, then we're off. ZSU, Pred handover, limited time window, got to get moving.'

'Ready in 30 seconds,' came the reply, and I saw the soldier removing the high-pressure fuel nozzle from the starboard side of his aircraft.

Then, looking up at Flyco where I knew Wings was in the know and coordinating the deck and the ship, I called on the radio, 'Machete ready'.

Flyco cleared us both in turn to depart and within seconds we were again on our way into the darkness. I had Charlie's threat brief whizzing around in my head:

ZSU, radar finds its target. It lays all four barrels on to the azimuth and elevation and fills the space with 800 bullets with each 3-second burst, reaching out to 5 kilometres.

Here we were rushing to go toe-to-toe with the one of the most feared anti-helicopter weapons ever made. The coordination between the Pred and me had to be quick, and I had to identify and engage the ZSU before it was brave enough to turn its radar on and engage me. I had no chance of knowing whether it was hiding and hoping to avoid detection or whether it was an active part of Khamis' plan to bring down a NATO helicopter.

The most likely sign of its intent was us getting hit; then it would be all over for John and me, leaving Nick and Little Shippers to deal with the aftermath. This scenario was my own personal fear throughout the summer – an aircraft being taken down by the regime, behind their lines, low fuel and limited rescue opportunities constraining the consequence management. If one aircraft went down we hoped the other one of the pair would be able to assist. As the surviving on-scene aircraft, their job would be to hold pro-Gad back from our wreckage while, if we had survived the shoot-down, we made an escape, and then attempt to coordinate a hasty rescue; but the recovery option was still on five hours' notice to move. Meanwhile, the Attack Helicopter Force Commander, Jack and Chris would be watching live on Pred TV from Italy.

Now once more low-level over the sea, I rushed through the radio calls to establish our new mission with Matrix. The CAOC and the CO had arranged our passage, and as soon as I made contact Matrix pushed me once again to our own Apache frequency, telling me the Pred was waiting. I reached up into the sky to gather the facts: 'Hello, Nomad three-five, this is Machete, send SITREP.' Fifteen thousand feet above Libya the remotely piloted Pred had its eyes on the target. Its pilot could have been sitting anywhere in the world, but tonight he was in

Creech Air Force Base, about 50 miles north-west of Las Vegas in the USA.

'Machete, got you loud and clear, I have eyes on the ZSU, no other movement, call ready for talk on.'

I glanced at the two multi-purpose displays in my cockpit and, using the fixed buttons around the outside of the screens, I rushed through the weapons page and selected Nomad's laser frequency while simultaneously checking the navigation figures. The aircraft did the calculations for me – I could be in the right place to fire in seven minutes.

'All copied, on scene in seven minutes. Are you able to give me a laser handover?'

'Affirm. You're gonna need to hurry, I only got nine minutes fuel left and then I'm off.'

John and Little Shippers raised the collectives and bled every last knot out of our heavily laden gunships in the charge towards the ZSU.

With the Pred inside his last three minutes of fuel I settled the FLIR on to the coordinates the CO had given me. At long range I could vaguely make out a copse in a field with a single-storey farm building about 50m to its right. If the ZSU was in the copse I needed a laser handover from the Pred to get my sight on to it. John set the aircraft on a steady heading, no angle of bank, no change in height. With everything set, all I needed was confirmation of the target and then I could go into the firing sequence.

'Ready laser,' I called, noticing our range rapidly closing with the copse. Silence. 'Ready your laser,' I called again, expecting Nomad to shine his laser on the ZSU so my FLIR, searching for his code, could identify the target. Still silence.

I could make out the copse but I needed that final confirmation from the Nomad's laser. There were similar bunches of trees in almost every field, some with buildings close by. I had to be sure. But Nomad was silent: no laser and we were getting closer to the shore, dangerously close, well within ZSU 23-4 range. With no laser spot handover I broke the patrol away. John banked hard left, calling Little Shippers to follow.

'Too close, with no confirmation,' I transmitted to Nick.

Little Shippers interrupted on the inter-aircraft frequency, 'He might be thinking you want to fire on his laser, tell him exactly what you want.'

John continued the turn and we immediately re-set for an attack. I got back on the net.

'Nomad, this is Machete, can you identify the target with your laser?

I do not intend to fire using your laser, I just need you to identify it for me.'

Both aircraft were now well inside the crucial 5km range and I was very nervous in the knowledge that all ZSU man needed to do was switch on his radar and he could rinse us out of the sky in three seconds.

'Roger, laser on, call when you have the target.' All was calm in Nevada, but I was getting frantic over Libya. His laser brought my sight right into the middle of the copse, exactly as the CO had described.

From the rear seat John called to me, 'Ready when you are!'

I let Nomad know the handover was complete: 'Got it, my target, your laser off, engaging in ten seconds.' Then I actioned the Hellfire with my left thumb and pulled the right-hand trigger, sending a constant pulse of my own laser to the ZSU and back to my missile. There was no time to re-plan or think. The common language misunderstanding and lost seconds in translating my needs had put both aircraft well inside the engagement zone for the ZSU; it was now only about self-preservation.

I transmitted to Nomad and Machete 2, 'Firing!'

The Hellfire symbology in my right eye showed the missile was locked on and ready to launch, and with my right hand laser providing the guidance I pulled the left-hand trigger, sending the missile towards the copse. A few seconds later the copse erupted in fire and shrapnel, but to my horror a rectangular, car-sized silhouette appeared, apparently untouched by the strike, just in front of the trees. In my wide-open infrared right eye it seemed to me that the ZSU was still there and that the Hellfire had gone long and missed. I immediately pulled the left-hand trigger again, sending another Hellfire into the object.

Whatever the second object was, it was not a ZSU. The missile impact lifted it high into the air, sending it end-over-end across the field before landing, bouncing and rolling to a halt.

'Nomad, what can you see?' I called up again.

'Machete, that looked beautiful to me! Good strike on the ZSU with the first missile. Not sure what that was with the second one. I'm off, out of fuel, out.'

And that was it. One ZSU 23-4 down and some other nameless object too.

Perplexed but pleased to be alive and ready to get away from all the unknowns around us on the ground, I got on the radio to Nick and Little Shippers: 'Machete complete, regroup at waypoint five, my lead.'

This was pro-Gad territory and I needed to return to the sanctuary of the sea to plan our next move. As we manoeuvred away from the coast,

Mark Hall and Will Laidlaw in the dunker, early 2010. Laidlaw is still making his way out of the front seat, while Hall has already got to the surface

Apaches arrive on board. The view from Flyco, 26 April 2011

Approaching HMS *Ocean*. Just an exercise – deck landing training in the Mediterranean, May 2011

An Apache approaches the flight deck at dusk, May 2011

Approaching HMS *Ocean*

Deck landing training. Behind the Apache is a Sea King Mk7 Airborne Surveillance and Control helicopter (SKASaC) from 857 Naval Air Squadron. They were able to find targets and give us highly accurate steers as well as guide us over the sea on the way out to Libya or on our return to HMS *Ocean* (*Published by the Ministry of Defence © Crown Copyright, 2011*)

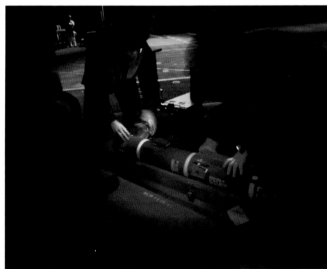

Sea King Mk7 Airborne Surveillance and Control helicopter (SKASaC) from 857 Naval Air Squadron lands after a maritime surveillance sortie. It always felt close when an aircraft landed on the spot to your front.

Hellfire being prepared on the flight deck (*Published by the Ministry of Defence © Crown Copyright, 2011*)

The ground crew load another Hellfire to the wing-stub, Summer 2011 (*Published by the Ministry of Defence © Crown Copyright, 2011*)

The start of 'cognitive effect'. An Apache from 656 Squadron fires a Hellfire missile at sea, 3 May 2011 (*Published by the Ministry of Defence © Crown Copyright, 2011*)

An Apache fires its 30mm cannon on a high seas range. The spent shells can be seen ejecting from underneath the gun. At the target end the high explosive warhead has a hand grenade-like effect. Crews preferred the 2-second, 20-round burst (*Published by the Ministry of Defence © Crown Copyright, 2011*)

Check firing personal weapons in the Mediterranean, June 2011

Screenshot from the BBC news channel, 4 June 2011. In the early hours of 4 June Will Laidlaw gave an interview which was transmitted widely. The first mission had gone in, the aircraft took us into danger, looked after us while we were there and brought us home. The whole team had worked and brought the newcomer into the operation flawlessly.

An Apache approaches to land on the deck of HMS *Ocean* at the conclusion of a pre-mission airtest

An Apache sits ready on deck at night, as seen through the infrared right eye Helmet Mounted Display

HH60G Pave Hawk from the 56th Rescue Squadron. 'That Others May Live' (*Published by the Ministry of Defence © Crown Copyright, 2011*)

Royal Fleet Auxiliary vessel *Fort Rosalie* conducts a Replenishment at Sea (RAS) with HMS *Ocean*, summer 2011. Fuel, ammunition and people were exchanged, as well as food and engineering spares.

Our fifth Apache, ZJ179, arrives on the back of Royal Fleet Auxiliary vessel *Fort Rosalie*, 11 June 2011. Will Laidlaw and John Blackwell went across and flew it back to HMS *Ocean* (*Published by the Ministry of Defence © Crown Copyright, 2011*)

Hellfire re-supply at sea, July 2011 (*Published by the Ministry of Defence © Crown Copyright, 2011*)

An Apache is placed on the lift in the hangar of HMS *Ocean*. Blades folded, it was a tight fit  (*Published by the Ministry of Defence © Crown Copyright, 2011*)

Sunset, engineering complete, airtesting complete, weapons loaded – two Apaches are ready for the mission  (*Published by the Ministry of Defence © Crown Copyright, 2011*)

An Apache departs HMS *Ocean* on a training sortie, Summer 2011  (*Published by the Ministry of Defence © Crown Copyright, 2011*)

An Apache comes alongside for another deck landing, Summer 2011

HH60G Pave Hawks mission ready on deck. 'That Others May Live'

HMS *Ocean* with her aviation assets on deck. An Mk7 Lynx from 847 Naval air Squadron sits on zero spot, three Apaches from 656 Squadron sit on 1, 2 and 3 spots, a Sea King Mk7 Airborne Surveillance and Control helicopter (SKASaC) is on 4 spot and two HH60G Pave Hawks from the 56th Rescue Squadron sit on 5 and 6 spots. The spare HH60G is on the aft starboard spot and another Apache and SKASaC sit next to the superstructure. (*Published by the Ministry of Defence © Crown Copyright, 2011*)

*The Raid on Brega*, painted by Derek Blois. The image captures Jilted 1 and 2, feet-dry, south of the town, being engaged by AAA, while feet-wet in the foreground Underdog 1 fires flares to decoy a SA-24 heat-seeking missile as Underdog 2 engages the firing point with Hellfire. (*From an original painting by Derek Blois and reproduced with kind permission*)

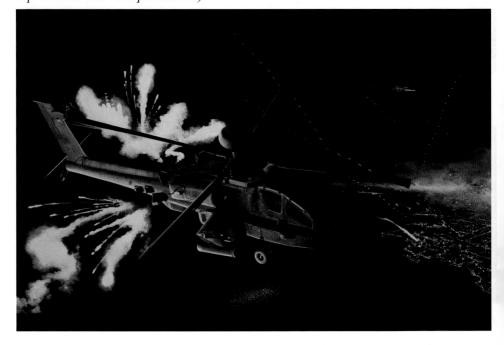

## Guntape Stills

All guntape stills are taken from defenceheadquarters on YouTube. As such, the following twelve images are Crown Copyright

 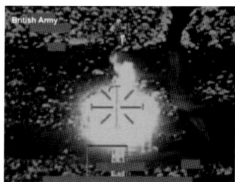

The first target, the first Hellfire on the night of 3 June 2011.

A Hellfire missile destroys a building during the week of the 27.

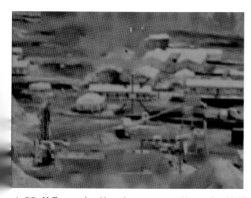 

A Hellfire missile about to strike a building. Delta-Hotel, the building is destroyed.

The communications node at Okba Airfield is destroyed.

A technical is targeted near Okba Airfield on 6 August. Pro-Gad soldiers can be seen running away. Once they are clear a Hellfire missile destroys their equipment.

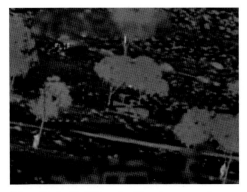

The 99th Hellfire is lined up against a technical. Pro-Gad soldiers can be seen hiding at the foot of the trees in the foreground. The missile destroys the technical, leaving the soldiers unharmed.

over the huge empty space of the Med at night, Nick was mocking me on the radio. 'Hay bale?' he enquired.

At the same time a flare launched from the ground less than a mile to the east, in the vicinity of the target VCPs given to us by Chris. Anxiety, relief and mild confusion were replaced by hostility from the ground once more. This was the primary combat indictor that bad things were about to happen, and both aircraft went to guns. We had no surprise left. The unseen pro-Gad on the ground would have heard the 30mm going into the sea half an hour earlier and seen and heard my Hellfire just up the road where they knew their ZSU was positioned. If a MANPAD was going to be launched, now was the time.

I slaved my FLIR to the VCP. The linear checkpoint was strung out for 800m along an east-west road linking Zlitan with Misrata, and it was rushing with pro-Gad. Some were hiding, others hurriedly moved equipment about, all keeping to the cover of trees and ditches. Everything about the scene was military. This was the gateway to the regime front line outside Misrata, and vanguard units from 32 Brigade manned it. If they had a ZSU 23-4 on their flank they were highly likely to have SA-24s all over the place, particularly working alongside the scouting screen on the coast. The flare going up was them getting ready. We needed to be fast and decisive to complete the mission and get away untouched.

From a point just over the beach I issued the quick battle orders and we turned our weapons on the VCP and its scouting screen.

The sustained and persistent use of attack helicopters, from the initial strike against the speedboats to this onslaught against front-line troops, had spread panic on the ground. In between the 30mm and Hellfire detonations the low altitude thunder of our rotor blades hidden in the night sky ranged in and out of earshot. Listening pods flying miles above Libya recorded the troops' confusion and lack of coordination. When SA-24s and NVG were requested the reply was too slow and they didn't know where to aim them. The weight of fire we sent into the VCP prevented any meaningful retaliation and left Khamis with a huge gap in the front line.

The initial assessment of that night's work was positive. The rebels moved forward, up to 5km. Pro-Gad had taken a hit, their coastal SF option was closed and the front-line troops were temporarily in disarray. Sadly, this progress did not last; by sheer weight of troop numbers and a well-organized supply chain Khamis was able to restore his stranglehold on Misrata. We, too, were unable the take advantage. The moon was up and we had to wait a week until the night conditions were suitable for us to go again. We took heart in the small advance, however transient, but at the same time realized that the task was vast and we were no quick fix for the problem.

*

Each month when the moon was at its fullest pro-Gad could use his NVG to target us. This tipped our risk equation too far in his favour and we sought to avoid flying on those nights. To take advantage of the break from missions *Ocean* returned to port to re-stock, conduct maintenance and give her crew some respite from defence watches.

After three weeks on the line *Ocean* pulled in alongside in Sicily, over a month since we had last stepped ashore in Crete. First nighters was about to be launched once more. One of the peculiar things about fighting a war from a ship is that you can go to sleep at the end of a combat mission and then wake up in a harbour in a different country, in a very different world. This time, when we woke, the concrete that we found ourselves attached to was the industrial port of Augusta.

A high-tempo programme of maintenance was scheduled for the ship. For 656, aircraft maintenance continued too. For the aircrew it was a chance to reflect on what we had done and to consider how we could do it better and safer. Jack Davis and Chris James brought the Attack Helicopter Force Commander over from Italy. The lawyer and the senior RAF officer in the CAOC came too. We pored over the guntape, read the initial SA-24 analysis and discussed the best way to fly in the coming weeks. It was great to see some friendly faces and share some stories, and these visits were vital face-to-face links with the planning centre. But what we all wanted was to step ashore and put combat aside for a night or two.

Finally, it was time to sanitize and take a trip down the gangway. The team went out and kept to their night routine, remaining energetic well beyond breakfast. A spontaneous lock-in at an old town jazz club continued till dawn, then half the aircrew were invited for pizza and to watch the sunrise over the Mediterranean. We justified it to ourselves by claiming that we were in a night routine and therefore needed to remain nocturnal – no point in jet-lagging ourselves just for a few days. It was such a good night that we inadvertently repeated the itinerary the following night. Much thanks are due to the brothers who ran the club, who were not only wonderful hosts but, coincidentally, had grown up in Libya whilst their father was serving in the Italian military.

At the end of the second first nighters, with weary heads, we travelled back by taxi to the ship. As we approached the dock, the driver, who spoke no English, having listened to JB's persistent monologue, leaned over to us, pointed to JB and exclaimed, 'Il Radio!'Henceforth JB had a new nickname.

After a couple of nights off the line *Ocean* made her way back towards Libya, and having lived through one turn of the wheel we were anxious about our return. But morale was on the up because Wings had worked more magic; on board had arrived the 56th Rescue Squadron and three HH-60G Pave Hawks packed with well experienced rescue crews and a 'brother aviators never get left behind' attitude to their work. The extraordinary pararescuemen carried their motto, 'That Others May Live', with a calm, determined modesty. Five hours notice to move was replaced by seven minutes, and we knew they would come and get us no matter what. The following week brought them close to a call-out on several occasions as we encountered some extraordinary resistance from the ground.

The SA-24 of mission three was no isolated instance. Only a week after the first MANPAD shot against us, Reuben Sands and JB, with Big Shippers and Jay Lewis as wing, were leading a patrol on their way back from an inland strike west of Zlitan when SA-24 shot number two arced out of the monochrome nothing.

Big Shippers and Jay were the front aircraft of the pair, with a mile or so split between them. To their right lay the flat rural hinterland and in the distance the partial lights of Misrata. Zlitan was on their left, well lit and innocent-looking, as though war was a distant thought. In the front seat Jay was willing the sea on and their safety with it, knowing that these last few miles to the coast were their most vulnerable. But theirs had been an inland mission; they had crossed the coast, further north, an hour earlier and Khamis knew they would have to cross it again within the hour, low on fuel and ammunition. With a well-connected communications network he would also know where they had overflown, and if he was quick he could predict where they might attempt to exit Libya on their way back to *Ocean*. And on this night he got it right.

With the lights of Zlitan ahead and the safety of the sea beyond, the two Apaches pulled in the power and pressed hard for the coast. Pro-Gad on the ground could hear them and an SA-24 team with NVG would be able to see them too.

While interrogating the infrared and symbology in his right eye Jay sensed a streak of light low to his right in the black space below. They had been spotted and an illumination round was launched from a mortar, signalling pro-Gad's intent. The now familiar pattern of anti-helicopter operations was in full swing.

Jay announced to Big Shippers, 'Illum round, watch for the tracer . . .'

They watched the illum round rise, searching around it for the inevitable triple-A or machine gun fire. But the illum did not rise vertically as usual, but appeared more direct, perhaps at 45°, and it travelled quickly. Then it appeared to stop, pause, turn and rush at them.

A fraction of a second later, in Jay's cockpit, the American lady announced, 'Missile launch, 3 o'clock!'

A second later, JB transmitted from the other aircraft, 'Missile seen! Your right.'

Jay and Big Shippers both now realized the illum round was in fact a heat-seeking missile, and it was heading for them. Milliseconds of comprehension in brilliant intense light, hands scrambling for the counter-measures, releasing both chaff and flares, Jay and Big Shippers could only watch and wait. The flares pumped out and away but still the missile kept its course, now straight and level, directly, it seemed, for the cockpit. This was it, the moment when you realize you are defeated, the part when you die. This was the end. Then one last release of flares with the missile metres from impact sent it dipping below the aircraft, close enough for Jay to recognize its markings and guidance fins, and into the ground.

'It's gone!' Jay shouted simultaneously on the radio and through the intercom to Big Shippers.

Big Shippers banked sharply to the north-east and took the patrol away from danger, before making the quick plan to deal with the shooter. 'Use the FCR, have a scan, could have been vehicle-mounted,' he directed Jay.

Within a few seconds the FCR presented them with an array of possibilities. Linking the FLIR to the FCR, Jay visually examined the most likely firing point.

'Got it! Vehicle, something hot on the flatbed, runners moving away . . . Two Ks! Come right, actioning missile . . .' Between two palm trees sat a technical; they were still dangerously close, close enough for a PKM shot and well within MANPAD range. On the rear of the technical a multi-tubed missile system sat pointing upwards with one tell-tale warm tube.

'That's it, coming into constraints . . .' Big Shippers steadied the aircraft and brought their own Hellfire seeker in line with Jay's now constant laser.

'Good messages, good range.' Jay rushed through the last of his checks and pulled the left-hand trigger, sending the Hellfire into the technical, now less than 2,000m from them.

The missile went straight to the target, taking just five seconds, and shredded both the vehicle and the missile system it was carrying. The palm trees rippled with the shockwave and then sagged, dormant and bent by the blast. Nothing moved, no one fired up at the aircraft and all was dark. SA-24 number two had been defeated, the defensive aids suite had carried us safe through once more. The flares were working – but if you play the game enough times, eventually one will get through.

*

The Apache maritime strike team from 656 Squadron had gone from media fanfare through three weeks of hard fighting. We had got away with our lives. Our wit and imagination, along with the defensive aids suite, had kept us alive, but the operation promised more of the same. During those first few weeks we encountered new aircraft emergencies, including a simultaneous double GPS failure of both aircraft in flight over the sea at night. A fifth aircraft arrived aboard the Royal Fleet Auxiliary vessel *Fort Rosalie*, and *Ocean* clocked up her thousandth deck landing since leaving the wall in Devonport on 25 April. The Apache contribution to Operation Ellamy was full speed ahead and the summer we all thought we would spend at home was taking a very different shape in the Med.

The French wanted the whole Libya operation complete by mid-July, which would give their government something to cheer about on 14 July during *La Fête Nationale*. But victory, or any approximation of it, looked a long way off when viewed from an Apache cockpit. Despite working a more aggressive, and far less constrained, helicopter operation alongside the NATO action, the French had not changed the stalemate in Brega, where they had concentrated. Helicopters had not proved a quick fix, and the impact of our combined work from Brega to Al Khums was yet to be translated into a rebel advance. We needed to persevere, to keep up the momentum and strike pro-Gad across his front line and in his depth. More importantly, we had to remain undamaged ourselves. The quandary NATO now faced was how to keep up the pressure of helicopter strikes but keep this risky platform from being shot down itself. With the regime positively searching for ways to bring us down, the risk-versus-reward calculation was precarious.

On 19 June Gaddafi announced a bounty for any NATO aircraft shot down. For 32 Brigade an Apache was their most likely prize. We were well and truly in the frame for a massed ambush somewhere near Zlitan. On 21 June a new US Navy remotely piloted helicopter drone, known as Fire Scout, crashed near Zlitan. Libyan State TV showed images of wrecked helicopter parts and jubilant pro-Gad demonstrators claiming to have shot down an Apache. The hourglass had turned; we needed luck as well as judgement to bring us safely though the campaign.

# Chapter 8

# The Raid on Brega

With the bounty promised to anyone who shot down a helicopter, surface-to-air missiles and anything else that could hit us were now massing on the coast and the risk-versus-reward calculation was changing. We didn't notice. The two SA-24 shoots had scared us, but our defensive equipment and our tactics had worked. This made us braver. They had thrown their best at us and we had killed them in reply. In fact, we had, unwittingly, normalized the threat. Right from the first mission, getting brassed up by big weapons was just what happened. The Apache was designed to deal with this, and we were happy to be there, but unfortunately we were being hampered by the risk aversion of our operational heritage. When the missiles started coming at us it was a matter of duty and common sense to stand and fight and kill. Taking on the most lethal of Gaddafi's weapons was expected with each mission. The bounty, the change in their MO and the warnings made no difference. The rapid immersion in violence had changed us. I had lost my understanding of what normal was. Launching every mission with a high chance of dying had replaced normal.

After the high octane SA-24 rampage of Zlitan the worry-beads in Italy wanted to move us away from that area. It was all quite sensible. An increased threat from a weapon system that would surely bring us down, a bounty on our demise and an enemy determined to see us die were all big concerns. We had to come up with new ways of keeping Gaddafi guessing. Nick Stevens and I scoped all sorts of options, including feet-wet day raids and long periods on alert on deck ready to react to any opportunity target. None were taken. We just needed to take the heat out of the threat, and that meant moving away. Twenty days after the first mission we returned to Brega.

An elite battalion from 32 Brigade had moved from Zlitan to reinforce the town, which was now completely militarized. 'Elite' in pro-Gad terms meant SA-24, triple-A, superior training and absolute loyalty to the regime. A new location, yes, but the same pro-Gad would

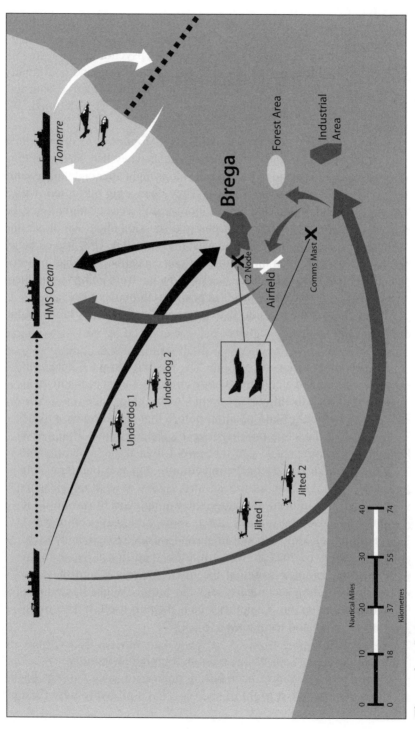

*The raid on Brega*

be firing at us. The risk was unchanged, but we didn't care. We knew we were good for the fight. Zlitan, Brega or Tripoli, we were good to go wherever the targets were. In terms of combat psychology we were still excited and willing to take risks. It was exhilarating, and continually getting away with our lives had reinforced our collective courage. Rushing in low-level against more of the same was welcomed. We relished it.

I flew to the French amphibious vessel, *Tonnerre*, to discuss their experiences of Brega and share ours of Zlitan. They had been operating close to the front line and flying several patrols night after night to the same target area with tremendous success. They were a big outfit, too, with a large planning staff dedicated to aviation as well as a squadron twice the size of ours. We had an open, brotherly discussion about the threat, the firing points, the pro-Gad MO and what to do about it. They had certainly shaken Brega and given the regime serious concerns. They had battered the enemy relentlessly for three weeks. Now we were going to join them in a combined raid to strike pro-Gad positions throughout Brega.

When the outline mission pack came in I called Chris James at the CAOC who explained the plan:

It's probably a four-aircraft job. The jets will drop a C2 node in a warehouse and a communications mast just west of the town at H hour. That's the important event – everything hinges on it. You need to be getting into position before that. The French will be going in at the same time right up by the front line. That's east by a few kilometres so you'll be over Libya at the same time but we have agreed a deconfliction line to stop you bumping into each other. As soon as the jet strike goes in you are clear to proceed. If you need to change the timings you'll have to do it early because these guys have some seriously complicated refuelling schedules to coordinate and we need to tell the French. There are two areas for you to strike. The first is close to an industrial complex south of the town, an area where they are routinely hiding technicals; and the airport might have some action going on too. The other area is the port itself. It is teeming with pro-Gad and technicals.

'Sounds like at least a four-aircraft job,' I replied, hopefully.

'Yes. The French have been hitting them hard since the start of the month, since that first night of the op. That's probably why they've moved in this battalion from 32 Brigade. You know what this means. It's likely to be strong out there . . . they'll have a real go at you.'

We knew it. Pro-Gad would be pleased with his Fire Scout shoot-down. They would believe the regime propaganda that it was an Apache. And they would be bold about taking us on. Lots of them, with triple-A and SA-24. A proper shoot-down would be a big boost for the regime. Conversely, a massive kicking from four Apaches would do away with their confidence and wreck morale.

'Okay. We'll be on our guard and ready for it. Surprise and firepower will shape the plan. Anything else?'

'There are reports of an SA-6 about twenty miles to the south. We don't know if it is just the radar or if it has missiles too. It occasionally gets turned on and then quickly goes off, before the jets get a chance to strike it. You'll have to treat it as hostile if you get a tag.'

An SA-6. This was new. After the phone call was done I flicked back through my notebook and saw that I'd written 'SA-6?' back in May, along with 'SA-24 probably' and 'SA-everything shoulder launched probably'. I called across the flip-flop to Charlie Tollbrooke, 'Charlie, SA-6, refresh me would you old boy.' The hum of industry in the flip-flop instantly ceased. All the aircrew stopped their planning and looked at me and then at Charlie.

Charlie had the facts in his head right away: 'SA-6. Okay, SA-6. Well, known as "Gainful". It has a radar mounted on a vehicle and the missiles are on separate vehicles, so the missiles and the radar are always separate and difficult to find. It is a particularly deadly helicopter hunter and very simple.'

Simple technology means cheap to build, which in turn means mass-produced. Mass-produced Soviet technology today means available to any state with a little spare change. Libya, as it happened, had a lot of cash.

With nine aircrew listening, Charlie continued, 'The system usually has four missile vehicles carrying three missiles each. The radar is called "Straight Flush" and it has a load of radar and optical sensors that find and track the target. If it is on and we are in range, it will find us. Once the radar people are tracking a target they hand it over to the missile people. The missile people then press the go button and a missile or missiles go for the target.'

He paused. 'Are we expecting SA-6 on the next mission?' he asked.

All eyes on me now.

I looked at the team, then at my notebook, then back at Charlie. 'In the south, yes. And since Staff Blackwell and I are going to the south and you and Mr Hall are coming with us, then very yes. Yes we are.'

'Okay . . . this is a really nasty system. SA-6 can be brought to readiness from being hidden and shut down in under ten minutes. Once ready, a well-drilled crew can have a missile off the rail and winging its way towards you in around ten seconds. That makes it something you want to look out for. Of course we won't see it, but the first indication we'll get is a voice alarm announcing "SA-6 Searching", or worse, "SA-6 Tracking" if it's a good crew remaining undetected until the last second.'

I interrupted. 'The assumption is that anything big like this that's still around this long after the No Fly Zone began is a survivor. A talented survivor.'

Charlie concluded, 'If you get either of those Searching or Tracking tags in the cockpit you have seconds to get the chaff out and get away. Seconds . . . this is a match for anything that flies.' He took a red pen and wrote on the whiteboard:

Source: Wiki. SA-6. Finds U @ 50 miles. Launches @ U @ 15 miles. Missile goes @ Mach 2 – 2.8. Duck, dive, run. Chaff! Chaff! Chaff!

He signed it off with a smiley face.

Unusually, we had two days to plan the raid. Down in the flip-flop we examined the satellite images and the maps. The plan was going to need precision timing and sufficient flexibility to adjust those times if things changed on the night. I needed two patrols of two aircraft each, one to go deep into the desert and hook round to the southern targets and the other to stay feet-wet and hit the port. I opted for the southern patrol and took callsign 'Jilted'. Nick was point man for the port and took on callsign 'Underdog'.

My route would not be complex but it was long, and this meant fuel would be tight and delays could be costly. The usual 30 nautical mile sea track would be followed by 30 nautical miles over the desert to a holding point about 5 miles from the first target area. The aim was to get to the holding point one minute before the fast jet strike went in west of the town. That way we would not waste fuel waiting, and the surprise of emerging out of the desert from the south would be intact. Underdog could afford to leave *Ocean* after us and make the straight 30 nautical mile sea track to a feet-wet holding point. Arriving one minute before the bombs went in gave us precious time to select our first targets. At the moment the bombs struck the warehouse and the radio mast we would launch our first missiles. Then the real fight would begin.

At the point where I considered the fight to be over, or at a specified fuel state, I would call our departure and each patrol would turn north and track the 20 nautical miles to the pre-arranged recovery point. This meant we would need 900lb of fuel to get us back on deck with our minimum landing fuel. That night we privately agreed to make the decision to head for Mother at 1,200lb. Mark Hall and John Blackwell had planned this 'for the wife and kids . . . just in case'. An extra 300lb of reserve fuel, that's almost 15 minutes of flying or 30 nautical miles, our whole return sea track and then some. These were wise heads, tuned to the hazards of combat at sea.

The time on target was agreed with the CAOC and everyone went about their planning. We organized the planning across all ten of the aircrew; no one was spare and we still had daily maintenance to complete in order to get the aircraft ready for the mission. In the afternoons two of the crews would conduct the air testing, ensuring the guns were still accurate, the engines perfectly tuned, the radios all working and the flares and the radar faultless. The rest planned. In the evenings we all continued the planning until the small hours, and then bed. I insisted that we all stay in night mode so that we would be at our best between 8.00 p.m. and 4.00 a.m. – the time bracket for all our missions in Libya. This meant sleeping from 5.00 or 6.00 a.m. until 1.00 or 2.00 p.m. The rest of *Ocean* continued in Defence Watches, eight hours on, eight hours off, as they had since mid-May. Some people, particularly the Commodore's team and key personalities on the ship's company, were 'one of one', with no 'oppo', and had to work long days without a break, even when alongside. The CO was one of those. He would start shaping the mission after breakfast, work through the day building the plan, be part of the mission brief, follow the progress once the patrol had launched, manage the guntape debrief and mission review and finally get to bed between 2.00 and 5.00 a.m.

For the Brega raid we had the 'No Go' items all ready and Underdog had a drone assigned. Everything was in place: targets seen; plans of attack designed (a coordinated attack at the same time as the French went in); times agreed and rehearsed; fuel and weapons loaded. Risk was studied. We called it 'medium'. It was a 'Go'.

On 24 June *Ocean* was back in combat mode. In the early evening watches had changed over, fresh eyes were on station. Eight aircrew were alone with their thoughts. It was an early strike that night, back in time for the midnight meal. I was excited and anxious as usual. Wherever I was in the ship I felt alone and on the edge of death. When I ate I was alone in my head; when I stepped out on to the quarterdeck in the tranquil sunset I was willing the fight to come on. I wanted to get going and get on with it. And I was afraid.

After the final checks and authorization were complete I signed for the aircraft, walked out on to the flight deck and climbed into the front seat of the front Apache. The deck was full. Four fully armed Apaches, each with a five-man team of ground crew soldiers, two engineers and a marshaller, sat lashed to the 600ft of flat top. CJ's team had provided exactly what we needed, with nothing spare. Any technical problems now would see a patrol cancelled. There must have been forty people on deck all aiming to get those aircraft into the sky.

I strapped in, noted we were heading north into wind, and spoke to John Blackwell: 'On in the front. All good?'

'Problems with the whole missile warning system, boss. Engineer is on his way.'

'Okay. Any others?'

'Yes, the radios seem a bit weak. Same engineer will take a look.'

We had a whole load of 'greeny' problems – electrical issues. The aircraft had woken up all grumpy. The wise head of the electrical specialists tapped on the window, plugged his headset into the wing stub and said, 'You'll have to do a full shut-down and restart. See if that clears it.'

John Blackwell re-set the systems and closed down the aircraft. I noted the time; we needed to be off in 15 minutes to make the time on target. I tore a sheet of paper from my kneeboard pad and wrote 'Rolex 20. New TOT 2120Z'. With a completely silent flight deck, all radars and radios off or in listening mode, we used a runner to get messages to and from the Operations Room.

While the Rolex was being negotiated John and I rebooted the aircraft and the engineer diagnosed and fixed the faults to see us safe into battle. All the while *Ocean* was still heading north.

After twenty minutes of frantic work by the engineers we were ready to go. My patrol launched into the black. The delay and northerly course for launch had put us an additional 17 nautical miles from our intended launch point. I quickly calculated the time needed to get to the holding point. The southerly track with a tailwind would help, we could cut a corner here and there and just make it on time. We'd have a bit less time on target, but all things being equal we'd be back on deck in under two hours.

This assumption would later bring John Blackwell, Mark Hall, Charlie Tollbrooke and me within a hairsbreadth of crashing into the sea.

'Head one-seven-zero. One hundred, one hundred, buster.' Head just left of south, both aircraft at 100ft, maximum speed. We were racing into Libya again. Maximum power, maximum fuel burn, let's get there!

We settled into formation, John keeping our aircraft on course, setting the track for Mark and Charlie on the wing. I scanned with the radar and the FLIR, left and right, left and right, until the coast came into view.

'Actioning gun.' The familiar thud and clunk as the 30mm cannon under the nose jolted to life. Now the 30mm followed my scan . . . left and right, left and right, wherever my eyes settled the sensors searched. Both aircraft rattled across the beach, not a man or a building in sight. No vehicles, no trees. No wires. Just the desert. A height of 100ft was perfect. My hands felt light and quick on the sight controls and I had a good feeling. Anxiety gone, back in Libya, combat coming.

I cut a corner off the route to hit our timings and Charlie followed. We spread the formation so that we were abreast, about 1,000m apart, low-level and quick. We raced onwards. I spotted a building ahead and John brought us wide. Mark Hall spotted it too and looked in with his infrared sight.

'Two men . . . one lying down . . . the other . . . the other's . . . waving! He's waving!' Mark reported. A new sort of welcome, that did not involve a firearm or a missile! The two men were beside a low building and what looked like a fuel truck. Perhaps they were smugglers, or just going about their daily business. Whatever it was, they were right in the middle of a war and two attack helicopters had just raced past in the darkness. They were clearly not pro-Gad.

Eight minutes later we arrived at the holding point. Bang on H-hour. As we flew through our final waypoint the glow and ripple of bombs rupturing the night took my left eye for a second as my right eye interrogated the infrared image of the industrial complex to the front.

'Nothing seen!' I called to Mark.

'Me neither.'

With nothing on the target I checked around the woodland that skirted the northern side.

'Looking north . . . technicals.'

'Weapons! Weapons on the rear, engaging, Hellfire!' I shouted across the net.

'In constraints . . . good to f . . .'

John Blackwell guided me from the rear seat. I could see from the symbology in my right eye that he was ready and as he said the 'f' of 'fire' I fired a Hellfire missile.

We were close in and I could see the weapon system was similar to the one Big Shippers and Jay had taken on the previous week. There was a man on the back, at the weapon, square on to me. My Hellfire impacted midway along the pickup truck, eviscerating the man and sending his mangled torso spinning rapidly in a cartwheel, to land 100m to the right of the vehicle.

Pandemonium erupted on the ground. Pro-Gad emerged from everywhere, it seemed. John pulled away. 'My eyes off target,' he called as we broke away.

'On . . .', called Charlie, as he and Mark opened up with the 30mm on the scores of pro-Gad rushing in and out of the wooded area.

'Okay, let's come back around,' I directed John. 'This is where they are. Lots of other vehicle heat signatures in the woods.'

'Wilco . . .', he answered, just as white light and dark in a head-breaking strobe rattled around us. 'MY GUN! MY GUN!' he screamed. 'TRIPLE-A!'

We had flown right over the top of a triple-A gun that had very cleverly remained hidden on my initial visual sweep of the industrial complex. Now it had engaged us, and John was looking right at it out of his right-hand canopy window. With one flick of his right thumb on the cyclic control he actioned the gun and slaved it to his right eye, then immediately pulled the trigger. Nothing happened. I still had the missile system actioned and this prevented the gun from working. The angle was so tight. The weapon processor knew that the gun could engage our own missile if I had fired one, and it therefore prevented the gun from firing. In the moment we had forgotten about this. The triple-A site was a just a few hundred metres from us and almost underneath. John fought the useless trigger while saving our lives with his flying.

'I can't get it!! I can't get it!!' he shouted.

'Triple-A . . . me . . . now!' was all I could manage on the net to Mark and Charlie.

John banked our aircraft hard to the right and weaved a tight corkscrew profile to evade the triple-A, as Mark and Charlie ripped the site up with their 30mm. John and I dipped low into the desert and then swung hard back around on to the target area. We intended to join Mark and Charlie in taking apart the ambush, but just as quickly as triple-A had put us on the defensive I got a more urgent warning.

'SA6, tracking.' It was the distinctive voice of the calm American lady.

'SA6! CHAFF! GET DOWN!' I called, my left eye interpreting the situational display indicating an SA6 to the south. It was out of range of my Hellfire, but I was very much in range of its radar. John immediately descended and brought the aircraft into a precision turn, releasing chaff as he did so.

I burst-transmitted to Mark, 'SA6 . . . south!'

'Nothing seen, tipping in on the triple-A now,' came the reply. Mark and Charlie were in the clear and they couldn't see a missile in the air. They concentrated on the triple-A site.

I could see on my situational display in the cockpit that the SA-6 had us locked. In the hierarchy of danger this outdid the triple-A, and John reacted with the manoeuvre we had practised off the coast of Cyprus only four weeks before. His flying needed to be absolutely accurate, and fast. We had to get low, break lock and evade.

I talked to John as we raced earthward: 'Chaff! . . . 100ft . . . chaff!'

The American lady interrupted: 'ALTITUDE LOW! ALTITUDE LOW! ALTITUDE LOW!', as we raced through the 100ft setting. I immediately silenced the alarm.

'Cancelled. Keep going. 80ft . . . chaff! 60ft . . . chaff! Keep going . . . broken lock! 50ft, level there . . . continue this heading . . . new height warning set at 25ft.'

He had done it, evaded the triple-A and broken lock with the SA-6 all inside a minute. John and I were lucky to be alive. But pro-Gad had been ready for us. He was bristling. We'd killed the immediate threat; now it was best to leave the rest to talk about it.

To Mark: 'Broken lock with SA6. Very low-level, heading west. I have you visual.'

Mark got on the net: 'Triple-A destroyed. At least three men . . . looks like there might be more. Can't quite see where they all went.'

'That'll do for that,' I transmitted. 'Good work. Let's move away. I have you visual. Head two-eight-zero. One hundred, one hundred.'

My patrol broke away from the southern target area and headed west to reposition closer to Brega itself. Our next target was the now disused airport south-west of Brega. We turned north to get our sights into the area. Looking north at the town with my left eye I could see streaks of fire racing skywards and similar hitting the ground. Nick Stevens and the Underdog patrol were engaged in a fight for their lives.

Three miles north of Brega port, Nick was trying to identify targets with the help of the Pred. To the south he could see the triple-A and tracer fire whipping the sky around my target areas. Having launched fifteen minutes later than us, he arrived to find Brega on full alert. Unknown to both patrols was the fact that surprise was never ours at all. The Rolex, endorsed by the CAOC, was not passed on to, not understood by or ignored by the French, who stuck to the original timings and woke the whole town up as they launched their assault to the east. In the CAOC Chris James watched helplessly as the huge aircraft-tracking screen displayed helicopter icons lift and depart the *Tonnerre* after he requested they delay by twenty minutes. In the Ops Room in *Ocean*, Big Shippers could see the same data feed. The timeline unravelled before we got off the deck. Whatever the Apaches did that night, pro-Gad was awake and waiting. Risk, originally assessed as 'medium', was at the red end of 'high' before we'd lifted, and Underdog were about to experience their share of the pain.

Brega was writhing with violence and throwing it skyward. To stay out of pro-Gad range Underdog needed the Pred to give him targets, but the drone was slow and seemed confused over where to look. Realizing he needed to join the fight to take some of the heat and attention away from us, Nick rapidly took control, giving coordinates and descriptions of target areas to the Pred and directing his target search. Pred looked and reported 'nothing seen'. He tried again, and again the Pred reported negative. In the front seat of the lead aircraft Nick was utterly frustrated. Brega was full of targets and Jilted was clearly in trouble to the south, but Pred-man just sounded bored. Time, which was never on Nick's side, was now critical. He had to get right into Brega, find targets himself and change the battle.

Checking his map and target imagery, he made a quick plan and burst a transmission to Reuben Sands on the wing: 'We've got to do this for ourselves. Close in for FLIR find, same targets as briefed.'

Reuben and JB knew what this meant – the Pred was not the de-risker the 'Go' brief had said it was, just as time was not the provider of surprise – and they had to make up the difference.

Little Shippers nudged the cyclic forward and he and Nick closed in on the maelstrom. Searching a few hundred metres to the west of the port, Nick immediately began identifying armed pro-Gad soldiers rushing between defensive positions. Triple-A systems were being readied and technicals were Mad-Maxing all round the town. The targets were there, right there, in plain sight. And so was he.

Within a minute of closing the coastline, a bright orange flash captured his right eye in the same nano-second as the American lady in the wing calmly announced, 'Missile launch, ten o'clock.'

In his cockpit JB saw it too; at the same time as the flares began punching out of his patrol commander's aircraft he screamed, 'Missile in the air!' across the mission net.

Both aircraft went into the pandemonium of self-preservation. While the rear-seaters controlled the height and speed to deceive the missile, the flares fired out and away to seduce the savvy seeker head, while both front-seaters looked into the launch point. Everyone stopped breathing and willed themselves smaller, twisting in the five-point harnesses anchored to the armoured seats, shoulders hunched and jaws clenched tight shut.

The missile arced towards Nick and Little Shippers. In the two and a half seconds since launch it had covered two kilometres and was now just one second from its target. The seeker head had done its job and ignored the flares; all was looking good for pro-Gad.

In that final second no one spoke; there wasn't time. Everything had been done, they had all dedicated those last three seconds wholly to their survival, the American lady had done her best, too, and they weren't giving up. Then a last set of flares spat out and glided away, leading the missile with them. JB saw it pass within 20m of the patrol. In that final second, when all four pilots braced for impact, the MANPAD missed.

JB and Little Shippers pulled their aircraft hard to the left and pointed directly at the launch point, closing quickly.

Alive and in disbelief, Nick went on the offensive. A quick glance back at the launch point, a flick of the thumb and, squeezing the laser trigger, he stored the coordinates and transmitted to Reuben, 'The launch point tallies with the suspicious activity at the supposed artillery site, stand by for QBOs.'

Reuben was already in position: 'No need. On your left, ready to go, eyes on the target, Hellfire in 20 seconds.'

Their response was accurate and lethal, but the patrol remained very much on edge. The enemy could hide, then pop out of buildings to take a shot when it suited them. The combat indicator of a hurrying man crouching and pointing next to a coastal bunker now drew the eye. Thousands of hours observing people move in Afghanistan had made all four pilots highly attuned to what was normal and what was suspicious. A few more minutes of searching passed, then came the confirmation needed to engage. Another man emerged from the bunker carrying a long tubular object and ran towards the crouching man. Bunker man threw the long tube on to his right shoulder and pointed it in the direction of the patrol. They were head-to-head with a MANPAD team. Underdog was once more just seconds away from being shot down, but this time it was the Apache that got the missile off first.

Nick spoke: 'Good target. Me shooter, you looker, I'll break right. Firing now.'

One Hellfire, two hundred rounds of 30mm, and forty-five seconds later the MANPAD team were dead, their weapon systems burning with a white intensity, sending high explosive debris across the harbour. Pro-Gad was on the run. Nick had taken control of the fight. His patrol had narrowly escaped death twice and now they were engaging a panicking enemy ground force whose most potent weapon had just failed.

Underdog had to exploit this opportunity, and once again the Pred was asked to help. But again the response came, 'nothing seen'. He hadn't seen the MANPAD launch or the response and hadn't attempted to assist in the aftermath. Back in the Ops Room in *Ocean* Big Shippers could see via the tracking data feed that the Pred was ten miles out over the Med and had no chance of seeing into the port. Nick didn't know this and reasonably assumed that everyone on the net was as interested as he was in staying alive and fighting. The combat dynamics had been reduced to the primordial fact that it is the soldier beside you, in the same danger as you, who fights as hard as you. The out-of-range observer, with no emotional investment or sensation of fear, can enjoy the option of disinterest, and tonight he took it. Underdog was on his own.

Two miles to the south-west, Jilted raced toward the airfield. I could see vehicles moving in and out of the town and Underdog's Hellfire thrashing the harbour targets. Brega was full of pro-Gad all rushing to respond to our attack.

The airfield itself was quiet. We scanned and ran in a couple of times, but there was nothing much to see. I was concerned about another triple-A ambush and the SA-6 to the south and didn't want to hang around for any nasty surprises. On my second run-in against the airfield I noticed our fuel was at the agreed 1,200lbs required to return to *Ocean*.

'Bingo. My lead. One hundred, one hundred.' I actioned the gun and John turned the aircraft north-west towards the wild, empty beach, searching amongst the dunes and bushes for heat; but nothing stirred. And then the sea.

Once we were clear of the beach and safely over the Med I called, 'Two hundred, two hundred,' clicked the navigation route on to the recovery point and listened in to the radio. This was procedural work now. *Ocean* and the Apaches knew the recovery point, and it was now about arriving at the right height and speed to conduct the always nervous final circuit to land. With ten nautical miles to run I called *Ocean*: 'Jilted, inbound, five minutes.'

Nothing came back.

'Jilted, inbound, five minutes,' I repeated. Still nothing. I remembered the weak radios from earlier and continued.

After a couple of miles, again, 'Jilted, inbound, five minutes'. Again, nothing.

I transmitted to Mark, 'Nothing seen or heard, can you try . . .'

He had a go, but got the same silence.

I tried once more, the tension in my voice making it a little tense: 'Jilted, inbound, five minutes.'

'Jilted, send SITREP.'

Result! *Ocean* was on comms! A relief, but we were now at the recovery point, right on the coordinates and I could not see a ship. Anywhere.

'Wilco. Just need a steer. I'm getting nervous about this. Have you got me on radar?'

'Negative. Wait . . . radar still coming on . . .'

'I need a steer, currently at the recovery point.' I was at 200ft over the sea, 20 miles from Libya with 30 miles of fuel left and beginning to feel alone again. The fear was with me.

'Head three-five-zero. Twenty miles,' came the calm voice of the Ops Room.

'Wilco'. Twenty miles! I immediately got on the net to Nick and called his patrol back: 'Knock it off. Mother twenty miles north of recovery point. Return now.'

Back in Brega, Underdog patrol were taking turns as looker and shooter. The patrol destroyed two triple-A systems in the harbour area, one as it was being towed by a technical. My urgent call was received as they considered eating into their spare fuel to chase more manoeuvring triple-A systems.

Little Shippers was quick with his calculations of fuel burn, best speed and power settings to remain airborne and reach the now very northerly Mother.

Nick turned his patrol north. 'Copied. Rounds complete. Tracking for Mother.'

Ahead, in my patrol, we flew on. I still had control but was nearing the end of calm. Searching left and right with the infrared, I finally found the ship.

'Yes! Got it!' I called out to John. 'Head three-five-five, there she is!'

'That's the best the news I have ever heard . . .' he replied. But as he spoke I realized I was wrong. My heart settled low in my chest with dismay. I was wrong.

'Sorry, mate. It's a cloud. Continue on course.' As I spoke a caution alarm sounded and my right-hand MPD showed a graphic of both fuel tanks indicating low. 'Just low fuel, but we knew that,' I joked, not able to mask my concern. 'Continue.'

This was serious. Very, very serious. I felt the fear surging and settling, surging and settling. With no more than ten minutes of fuel left I decided to brief the deliberate ditching procedure. It had to be discussed now, while we still had control, before the panic, before the water and the dark and the violence of eight tonnes of Apache going into the sea.

'You will fly and jettison the remaining Hellfire and then bring it into a low hover. I'll explode the canopy. I will then take control. You'll get out. I'll move it away, trim it and then I'll get out. Okay?'

It was feeble. I felt breathless and weak as I spoke. How could we have got into such a state? We had survived the triple-A and the SA-6 and fought a battle and now, out over the sea, we might perish because we couldn't find the ship and our fuel was about to run out.

'Understood,' replied John. 'At endurance speed now.' He was flying at the lowest power setting he could to keep us in the air, as I searched with increasing desperation for *Ocean*.

The infrared sight relayed an endless steady green nothing until, with just a few minutes of fuel left, I found the heat of *Ocean* white amongst the sea and sky.

'My line of sight, left, *Ocean*!' I called to John and then on the radio, 'Mother visual, joining on long finals.'

Pointing my FLIR at the heat spot, I stored her coordinates and sent the data to Underdog. This gave Nick and his team the most accurate steer available. Meanwhile, John Blackwell flew directly at our gradually defining one chance of a safe landing. I hurried through our before-landing checks as *Ocean* slowly took on the shape of a ship. With each second our fuel reduced. Pound by pound we were getting ever lighter and ever closer to ditching. I thought back to the early days in 2010, finding *Ark Royal* pitching alarmingly in the dark off the north coast of Scotland, and the tension in the cockpit, hands tight on the controls, as Mark Hall and I laboured into a slow and untidy landing in poor weather at night. That was eight months ago and we had all practised dozens of night landings since then. This landing, on *Ocean* at war, had to be fast and accurate. Otherwise we might all die.

In Flyco, Wings peered out of the aft-facing window as his controller issued our joining instructions: 'Jilted One you are number one for Two Spot, Jilted Two is number two for One Spot. Both aircraft cleared to land. Confirm weapons safe.'

We usually landed one at a time, and the second aircraft was only allowed to begin its approach once the first was safely on deck and all weapons systems triple checked for disarming and safety. There was no time for this now. We had minutes of fuel left and Wings could see the danger. He knew the risk right now was one Apache ditching as it ran out of fuel waiting for clearance to land while the other Apache safed its weapons. Wings had the flight deck ready, the ship on a flying course and the officer of the watch listening intently to his concerns.

A mile off *Ocean*'s stern John Blackwell steadied our aircraft at 400ft and 60 knots at the top of our final approach.

'We're cleared in, good lights, continue,' I called, seeing the glide path indication lights beckoning us from the flight deck.

'Yep, good lights. Right eye difficult, but good lights,' he replied. Having been looking through the infrared projected into his right eye for the past two hours, he was now struggling to see the normal lights necessary to guide the aircraft on to the flight deck. While we had been searching for *Ocean* he had not been able to settle his eyes off the infrared in time to land. This meant his right eye had been staring at a bright green image all night, and his retina would take at least ten minutes to get back to seeing in colour again. With his right retina peering as though through a misty, brown-stained haze and his left eye good, John was steering us for the ship. My sight was no different. I flicked the infrared on and off as we made our approach, to check we were still on the right course. Between us we had two good left eyes and two poor right eyes. Just enough. There was only going to be enough fuel for one shot at the approach and landing. Any delay could be fatal for us and for Mark and Charlie. John shot the approach.

'Good glide slope, good speed, good rate of descent . . .' I called the numbers as he flew, visually matching the aspect of the flight deck with what he knew he needed to see in order to get alongside safely.

'One mile . . . 200ft . . . 50 knots . . . all good, continue . . .' We descended. 'Quarter of a mile, 100ft, 40 knots . . . 80ft, 70, hold height.'

John now had the flight deck visual. Wings had thrown on all the lights. There was no need for secrecy now. 'I can see the marshaller on Two Spot. All good. Moving over the deck now.' He brought us alongside in the 70ft hover, checked his visual references and with about two minutes of useable fuel in the tanks manoeuvred us sideways to the right, over the deck and planted the aircraft on its spot.

I immediately transmitted, 'Jilted One on, weapons safe.'

Flyco replied, 'Deck is safe, Jilted Two cleared to land.'

Charlie had already begun his approach when Flyco cleared him in. Forty seconds later they roared past us, barely paused to hover alongside and landed with a bounce on the spot to our front.

'Good landing, mate. Really good landing, no debrief points,' I said to John, mimicking the sort of dialogue an instructor would give during a check ride.

'Thank you. If it felt a little hurried it's because I suddenly remembered I'd left the iron on.' His humour had returned.

'All good, lots to talk about, but first I need a little lie-down. On the flight deck!'

The relief of being on deck was replacing the adrenaline of the mission. The reality of our situation was making me shake. As soon as John stopped the rotors I got out. Hauling all my ammunition and weapons with me, I jumped down on to the flight deck. I knelt, ostensibly to unload my Sig and Carbine, this action masking my relief and the surge of weakness that comes with knowing that I'd just got away with my life twice in combat and once more over the sea. Had I been alone I would have wept. I wasn't, so I stood up and walked inside the ship, just as both Underdog aircraft approached to land.

I went through the airlock, turned left and stood in the engineering compartment. The Crew Chief was sitting behind the counter. He pushed the folder towards me: 'Everything all right, Boss? Any damage?'

'Took a bunch of triple-A and tracer was everywhere, needs a good look over. Flies nicely though, shoots straight and finds ships in the dark and everything,' I replied and signed the aircraft into the folder. My handwriting was barely legible and I was unable to add two numbers together. My head was unable to compute the simple task of signing the aircraft in. I was full. And I was scared.

I pushed the folder back across the counter, turned right and walked further into the ship. As I rounded the first corner the ship's Captain stopped me. 'Something went wrong. We are conducting an investigation. We'll have the answers by the time you turn to tomorrow.' This was straight-out leadership. He was waiting to talk to me and he wanted to be the man on point to tell me what would happen next. I thanked him, saying all was well in the end and that it had been a powerful mission land-side.

I went further into the ship and the next person I saw was the Commodore. He reiterated the Captain's comments. More leadership. These were the senior men who sat in the Operations Room during every mission. On this particular night several unrelated actions had combined to place *Ocean* 20 miles north of the usual recovery point 20 miles from the coast. In the final analysis I had been responsible for the initial deviation: because I had persevered with fixing the faults on the aircraft when we started the engines, the ship had maintained its northerly flying course, taking her and us further from Libya. The ship was expecting me to take off; instead I was diagnosing and fixing faults. While we were airborne, a SKASaC had landed and conducted a changeover of crews. All the while, *Ocean* was heading north, away from Libya. Then, with all done, she headed south-east for the recovery point. As she did so an engine failed. Consequently, she was on half speed and more than twice as far from the recovery point as she should have been. *Ocean* was not going to make it in time for our planned recovery. Her radar was also switched off to remain undetectable. When I called up on the radio she couldn't see me to give me an accurate heading to fly to find her. When I said I was 'nervous' they pulled out all the stops to find us, but in the end we had to fly the distance to find her. These unrelated incidents combined to bring us to the point of ditching into the sea.

The raid on Brega was a defining mission for us. We had made a complex plan with a time on target coordinated with jet strikes and the French aviation attack. CJ's team had given us all five fully mission-capable aircraft and we'd flown four of them in two separate patrols. We had struck hard against a well fortified and well armed enemy. They had fought back aggressively. We had survived SA-6, SA-24, triple-A and all sorts of assault rifle and PKM rounds. And we had won. Then we had dealt with a self-inflicted emergency in finding *Ocean* and getting back on deck. This was the mission where everything happened. We met the full range of the threat, defeated it and struck our targets. During planning we thought the mission would sit somewhere around the 'medium risk' mark, but in reality it was off the end of the scale, well beyond 'high'. In not accepting the Rolex the French had gone in ahead of us and blown the fragile element of surprise. In having a bad night the Pred had failed to keep Underdog out of range and give him targets. If these factors had been in the original plan it would have been a definite 'No Go'. But in dealing with all this we had shown that we could handle much more than the CAOC was willing to send us against. We were braver than ever. The squadron didn't need to be shackled with a list of 'No Go' items designed to boost confidence in the easy chairs. But they decided that we had 'got away with it'. We were lucky to have survived such a night, and the whole mission served to validate the need for a gradually lengthening list of comfort blankets. The decision men chose pessimism. Back in *Ocean*, the bar was open and we were quietly talking about the toughest mission army aviation had flown in years. But no one else mentioned it. It didn't make the media. There was no flag-waving or congratulations. A jet could bomb a ship tied up in a harbour from 25,000ft and it was all over the telly. We raided Brega with the 100ft low height warner sounding, striking many moving targets, evading sophisticated weapons and dealing a severe blow to Gaddafi's military effort in the east. And the only people who knew about it were the team who shaped it, those who flew it and those who survived on the ground.

*Chapter 9*

# The Turning of the Tide

June 2011 was a brutal time. By the end of the month we were on edge, tired and anxious. I wondered when our luck would run out; we all knew a crew was going to get shot down if the operation continued in the way it had unfolded thus far. The squadron was in a routine, just as the ship's company was in a continual cycle of defence watches – everyone stuck in the big grey battleship. The excitement of a novel operation, its risk and drama, had been replaced by a will-we-won't-we routine of planned and cancelled missions, interspaced with the occasional actual launch. The CAOC was cancelling more than we flew, and we were becoming very grumpy at our lot. The psychology of this was hard on us. We planned, got ready, mentally prepared to face the gauntlet again, went through pre-flight rituals, morphine and guns and strapped into the aircraft on deck; then the mission was often cancelled minutes before the launch time.

On the ground, small moments of progress occurred as the front lines around Misrata and Brega moved in favour of the rebels, now loosely organized as the Free Libyan Forces (FLF). We had contributed to this, but the big breakthrough had not happened. The regime and the FLF still faced each other across no-man's-land, and the coast west of Tripoli was firmly in Gaddafi's hands.

To compound my grumpiness I was aware of some scathing comments from the UK concerning our reaction to the SA-24 shots. Our Mission Reports had made readers back home unhappy and some were questioning our methods. One missive – an outright criticism of how we had approached the operation – made particularly painful reading. But I didn't recognize any of the signatories – no helicopter pilots there, I thought – and we were justifiably indignant, given that we were the only people who had survived an SA-24 shot in the history of military aviation.

We were given defined speeds and heights to fly at, precise timings not to exceed at targets and specific direction to run away if we were shot at. This had fast-jet fingerprints all over it. Printed in four pages of well edited, crisp English was a desk-bound opinion on how not to get shot. This was old-school risk aversion. I could imagine the meeting: experts in missiles, one or two jet pilots, some agenda-driven cynics and a sorrowful staff officer charged with formulating their groupthink.

But we kept away from the debate and the CO went into bat. Some engaged in predictable finger-waving and tutting, but others were more reasonable – they needed to understand how it was. The team in *Ocean* and the CAOC sent it all back and told them we were in a war and they needed to be constructive and helpful; after all, that was the point of serving on the staff. Trials were conducted, data was analysed and evidence was produced; and after a brief clearing of the throat and some staring at the shoes their thesis got repackaged and sent back to us.

Video conferences were held, and while the aircrew slept the risk-holders talked it through. When the critics offered up their opinions the CO asked them what they could do to help. I watched from the sidelines and was pleased that we had a central team who were trying to keep us safe and were managing to persuade the 'experts' to do something useful about it. We were in a new type of combat, helicopter pilots weaving to avoid hitting houses and wires while being shot at. We Apache aircrew and the close team, the people who had lived those criticised missions, knew the threat, how to cope and how to keep going.

The London wailing and gnashing of teeth was the backdrop to our own very real angst at the start of July. On our last mission in June, John and I evaded an SA-5 radar lock-on. SA-5 is designed to shoot down high altitude bomber aeroplanes. Its missiles are huge, 10m long, Mach 7 monsters, but there weren't any of those left; the jets had dealt with them right at the start of the campaign. But we knew the radar was out there, and although there were no missiles associated with it, we still had to evade it because the radar operator could guide other weapon systems on to our position. The SA-5 was, in effect, a highly accurate early warning device for whatever pro-Gad wanted to aim and shoot at us. With the American lady in the wing telling me all sorts of bad news about the SA-5, we had to break the lock and get away. We were horribly exposed, over the sea about 500m from the shore, had nowhere to hide and had to trust the chaff shredding in the tail rotor as we manoeuvred and descended to evade.

Chaff and turn, chaff and turn, descending all the while. Chaffing and evading – there is no more tantalising experience of fear and control than conducting the deliberate degree-perfect angle of bank turn, descending to almost nothing, watching the crests of gentle waves settle to smooth sea massive in your infrared right eye, while firing chaff into the tail rotor to escape the lock-on of Gaddafi's air defence radar systems. Wild and chaotic, but controlled. Controlled, because otherwise you will be shot or you will crash. Anything other than pinpoint accuracy, black of night over the sea and hell unleashed just beyond the beach, will leave you dead. One-nil to Gaddafi and Campaign Catastrophe for Cameron. Dead British soldiers entombed in shot-up and ditched helicopter swaying with the tide on the seabed. Pinpoint accuracy and lethal aggression in the fight. That is how we kept ourselves alive, and no amount of advice from the distantly concerned in London on how to do it better and run away was going to persuade us otherwise.

The fear I had experienced in June had started to gnaw away at my tolerance of criticism. I took it as a personal attack by people who did not appreciate the fight we were in. The criticism seemed to rest on a theoretical matching of Apache and missile-seeker. But we knew of no one else who had been shot at by these systems, so naturally assumed we knew best.

I knew I had the best team available to succeed in this fight. I believed that their combined advice was all we needed, because they had experienced the fight at first hand; they were our Apache experts, both at sea and over Libya. They were highly experienced combat operators. In their own discrete fields they were also experts in the kind of knowledge and skills we collectively needed to stay ahead of the regime. The 'punch-in, sit-down, pontificate, punch-out' staff opinion was not needed where we were. We ten knew best. On reflection, our attitude to the advice we were given could have been more conciliatory. Running away was, perhaps, the right thing to do. But it didn't feel right, particularly as we had been successful in prosecuting everything that had shot at us. Part of our response was based on confidence and self-belief and part was meeting staff hostility with the operator's sense of higher knowledge.

In any case, I was experiencing another frustration from the UK that bewildered and angered me – the denial of the Operational Allowance.

We had expected to receive the Operational Allowance: a sum of money paid daily, we thought, to recognize the sacrifice of our people on operations. We were wrong. The allowance, we were told, was about proximity to risk, not commitment to an operation. As such, HMS *Ocean* was deemed physically too far away from Libya to attract the money for those who remained inside the vessel. Only people who got within twelve nautical miles of Libya would get the pay, and then only on the days they made the journey.

If the men and women in *Ocean* had been conducting clerical work in the fortified centre of Camp Bastion in Afghanistan they would have received the allowance. But our soldiers, sailors, marines and airmen in *Ocean* got nothing, not a penny. It was a baffling, parsimonious and divisive decision. Hard-working men and women committed to an operation with little notice and much uncertainty saw the irony in their plight and concluded they were not valued. My mother mentioned the folly in writing to her MP. The MP for Gosport since 2010, a large naval constituency, wrote back expressing her sympathy and reassured her constituent that she would write to the Defence Secretary on the matter, adding that we were doing essential work in support of RAF pilots. Mum responded, pointing out that we were soldiers and sailors at sea supporting Royal Navy and Army pilots in demanding circumstances and that our experience of risk and rigour was valid and ought to be better appreciated. She also made the point was that HMS *Ocean* was not an Italian hotel.

First admonished by the experts and then trivialized by the bean-counters, our morale took a dive. From the most junior soldier to the squadron headquarters we felt alone in a dangerous place with only criticism, pressure and zero appreciation of our work from outside. The CAOC understood it, the Commodore, the Captain, the ship's company and the CO with us in *Ocean* understood it, and we most definitely knew it. But it seemed this understanding was limited to us and it had not percolated to London. The irony was that, despite everyone watching us, we were alone.

After the bad news about the Operational Allowance, but insisting on no let-up in our output, we looked to the CAOC for our next turn of the wheel.

To take us away from Zlitan, Jack and Chris in the CAOC proposed a new area to the west of Tripoli, and we were happy to take up the offer. They had argued hard to get us into a raiding strategy by which we could sting pro-Gad in one place, move hundreds of miles up the coast, then take him on in a new place the next night. This was more relevant to 'cognitive effect' and it kept us away from pattern-setting in one place, in which case we would surely be shot down. This was safe regime territory full of smuggling routes from Tunisia further to the west and it provided Gaddafi with all the lines he needed to keep the FLF tied up in the Nafusa mountains to the south. The capital was his, even though NATO restricted regime movement. Despite this, the familiar face of the regime, Moussa Ibrahim, regularly issued statements from Tripoli proclaiming impending victory and denouncing NATO.

Where Zlitan and Al Khums offered local depth to Khamis, the area west of Tripoli was his father's and their combined existential and strategic depth. This was where 80 per cent of their fuel was coming from and it was running out, with an estimated three months' supply remaining. The regime had to control the capital and the roads west to Tunisia. Oil, fuel and weapons filled those arteries and gave sustenance to the man who saw himself as both a Nasser-like Arab nationalist and a uniter of Africa.

Raised in the desert during Italian colonial rule, Muammar Gaddafi grew up to loathe Europe and develop an extraordinary sense of his own heritage and entitlement. His ideas and his zeal were infectious. He joined the army, continued to recruit support for a utopian Arab Libya at the centre of Africa and in 1969, at the age of twenty-seven, overthrew King Idris in a bloodless coup. Wealth redistribution, expunging foreign influence and consolidation of power were his priorities. The ludicrous three-part counterblast to liberal democracy, *Al-Kitab al-Akhdar* (The Green Book), followed, and he slipped from revolutionary to eccentric sponsor of much of what ailed the West. Insisting that democracy and capitalism were evil lies and that his skewed version of social revolution be taught weekly in all schools, Gaddafi set about educating Libya from the top and at its grass roots simultaneously. He centralized power, stamped on political dissent, amassed huge wealth and filled the prisons. His sponsorship of terrorism in the 1980s, killing British, American and French citizens in large numbers, set him apart as a uniquely detested leader internationally. However, despite his continued sense of regional importance, the 1990s and early 2000s saw him being brought back from international isolation. Steps towards resolving the Lockerbie criminal trial and the payment of compensation to victims' families were accompanied by an easing of sanctions. The final big-ticket move was his buying of the 'if you have weapons of mass destruction we will come and get you' message on the banner carried by Rumsfeld and Bush as they rattled into Iraq in 2003. Gaddafi had some and he didn't want to get invaded, so he handed them over to Blair and everyone had a big hug. Now, eight years later, NATO leaders were over the happiness of tea in a tent and a dismantled nuclear programme. Gaddafi had killed hundreds through his sponsorship of terrorism, he was promising carnage to his own people, and now it was time to unseat him. By July 2011 both the rebels and the regime had everything to gain, and the civil war showed no sign of easing. The wicked colonel had to protect what he had left while squeezing the FLF on all fronts.

In Tripoli the well-groomed and melodiously articulate Moussa Ibrahim continued to court the captive media and control the narrative. The regime's line was consistent: NATO is a foreign invader after our oil, the rebels are sponsored by NATO and are not true Libyans, and we are winning – these were the central themes. Ibrahim held daily press conferences in the Rixos Hotel and churned out the story with unfailing passion. His face was always on the 24-hour news feed in the operations compartment in HMS *Ocean* – his personal message to us was that he wanted to resolve our differences over a cup of tea. Every now and then he also called us murderers.

The surreal narrative of conflict, in which we were part of the plot, was being played out all around us. Walking from the flip-flop to the Go/No Go brief took me past the big telly and whoever was on CNN, Sky, ITN, BBC or Al Jazeera. Occasionally it was Sarkozy or Cameron, but more often it was Ibrahim. Launching into combat with the political rhetoric of all sides fresh in my mind lent an unexpected psychological edge to the operation. The physical and emotional overload of June had a profound effect on us all. Every aspect of our work was scrutinized, it seemed, by both our own people and the regime.

After Brega we were all ready for a change. More of 32 Brigade was not how we wanted the summer to unfold, and Chris James had just the tonic to soothe our nerves. Having given Khamis a bloody nose in Brega and around Misrata and Zlitan, he recommended that we go west to his barracks and knock out the rear party. Anything military that could be used to reinforce combat effort on the front line was a target, as long as it was not parked up and clearly out of commission. Khamis had attempted to hide several T-72 Main Battle Tanks and other armoured vehicles in the forest behind the barracks. And, unknown to us, he had scouts and radar systems on the beach waiting to spot a maritime landing or helicopter assault. The proposition was perfect: go to Khamis' house and smash it up while he's out. The message would be impossible to ignore – helicopters are rampaging around the country, you can't take them down and now they are targeting your safe places. There is nowhere to hide.

Chris and the team had cleared several targets to be struck over two or three nights in quick succession. The effect of this would be to make the regime look behind themselves as well as at the front line, and to deliver the message that if you go to work and threaten Libyan civilians NATO will come and get you, wherever you are.

The first week in July was set for the raids. More VCPs were on the list, and while the intelligence people finalized their assessments and the legal people gave their view, we got ready to visit the Al Maya barracks.

We had no interest in the barracks itself, or anything inside its perimeter. What NATO's reconnaissance aircraft had detected was the gradual movement of machines of war, Main Battle Tanks and Armoured Personnel Carriers, into the wooded area outside the barracks. Khamis either wanted to hide his reserve firepower or he was getting ready to bring it east to Zlitan or south to the Nafusa Mountains. NATO wanted to dissuade him from either option, and we drew up plans to come in low off the sea and add Hellfire to his problems.

On the afternoon of the raid the CAOC confirmed up to nine armoured vehicles and Main Battle Tanks dispersed in what looked like an olive grove just to the south of the barracks. The satellite image made it look simple – come in from the north, confirm the picture on the FLIR, fire and leave. It looked like Khamis had taken the vehicles out of the back gate and stuffed them in the woods. They were only 700m from the low tide mark and in fairly thin woods. We wouldn't need to get over the land. Feet-wet, all good.

John Blackwell and I got the plan together along with Mark Hall and Charlie Tollbrooke. There wasn't much to do. We knew where *Ocean* would launch and then recover us, then it was a straightforward low-level sea transit and strike. All done in an hour, maximum safety – resolving the risk and reward equation back to where we wanted it.

When it came to the Go/No Go brief I was calm, a welcome change. No feet-dry, triple-A, MANPADS or radar threat to worry me. Just the sanctuary of the sea and a long-range shoot.

After all the pain of the surface-to-air missile assessments and the 'how to do it better' memos, and the actual MANPADS, triple-A and chaffing to escape the radars, John and I were happy to take on a mission with apparently simple targets outside an empty barracks miles away from the front line. The pre-mission brief was short, an easy discussion with well-honed crews, air and ground. CJ had the flight deck furnished with spare aircraft and the 56th Rescue tough guys were primed and ready. All set, back in an hour.

The timeline ticked, and *Ocean* sent us south once more. I checked in with Matrix:

'Prodigy launched as fragged.'

'Prodigy, clear to proceed, stand by for words,' came the reply. Matrix had news. 'We have a radar threat on your target, assessed as live. Appears to be active-search out to sea. This is your priority, stand by for coordinates.'

At 18,000ft above the Al Maya Barracks a Pred had spotted something on the coastline. Almost 900 miles away in the CAOC the team were working out what it was and what it meant. Matrix, at 36,000ft somewhere over the Med, was the go-between. My patrol of two Apaches raced in towards the new target at wave-top height with an estimated time of arrival of just under ten minutes.

Matrix passed the coordinates; I plotted them into my Tactical Situation Display on my left-hand MPD and data-burst the information to Mark and Charlie. The radar was directly in front of the barracks on the rocky coastline, right on our track.

'New target, check data. I'll confirm with Nomad, but when the time comes it will be my lead, me shooter, you looker, then re-set for the original strike.' I altered the plan and we continued south.

Matrix pushed us to our own strike frequency and I made contact with Nomad, the Pred. As ever, all was calm in Nevada: 'Prodigy, armoured targets south in the trees, radar truck on the coast. Lasing now for your sight.'

Nomad fired his laser, I switched my FLIR to the laser search mode and it began hunting for his laser code. Within half a second the FLIR was pointing at the coordinates Matrix had given me. Tucked into a sand berm 200m to the north of the barracks and elevated above the high tide mark, sat the target. A heavy truck with a search-radar mounted above had a clear view north out to sea. The truck was warm, its engine warmer, the radar was ready. The target was corroborated. Good to go.

The radar must have been switched off; nothing was showing on my Tactical Situation Display, and if anything was emitting out there the American lady in the wing would be telling us all about it in her disarmingly calm and precise voice. So in we went, John Blackwell holding the aircraft steady as I let the laser return a positive guidance for the Hellfire. The shot was easy, and the truck and radar disintegrated into shrapnel and fire, killing and ejecting the pro-Gad operator out of its side. His white-hot body was thrown sideways, coming to a rest 30m from the truck. As John banked the aircraft right to pull away from the explosion three arcs of tracer fire weaved around us and Mark Hall came on the net.

'Tracer left! You're under fire! I'm tipping in.'

Five pro-Gad scouts, AKs in hand, had watched us and engaged when we were closest to the beach. Mark and Charlie dealt with all five, posting a Hellfire neatly among them and following up with the gun.

With the distraction of the radar dealt with and, coincidentally, having dismantled the scouting screen, we were free to run in on the T-72s. I could clearly see the barracks and the wooded area, but I was unable to see through the trees. We ran in straight from the north, then tried it again running in from the west right along the beach, dangerously exposing ourselves, to try a different angle. Nothing worked; we couldn't see a single defined target. There were heat spots, but the trees obscured their identity. The 'olive grove' in the reconnaissance images was in fact a forest.

I called to Mark, 'No joy, can't see the targets. Regroup feet-wet.'

We needed to get away from the barracks and make a new plan, having now flown in three times and given away the surprise.

Mark came back: 'Try Nomad, see if he'll buddy-lase it for us.'

The theory was that we could fire our Hellfire and the Pred could guide it into the target with his laser. We just needed to be careful that the missile-seeker was locked on, then Nomad owned the rest. Nomad was directly above the barracks, way up high, and he could see everything; we were low-level and were never going to get the right line of sight.

I got on the net to Nomad: 'How about your laser, my missile? If you can, could you get permission for the strike too?'

We had never practised this, it hadn't been briefed or authorized. I had no idea if it would work.

Nomad was quick to respond: 'Prodigy, yes CAOC say it is a go; we have permission. You have my code, call for laser on and count down to missile release. I'll do the rest.'

A man in Nevada, who was probably coming to the end of his shift, about to head home, pick up the kids and some groceries, was now about to guide a load of Hellfire into some tanks on the other side of the planet.

Mark and Charlie went in first and we followed. Four minutes later, four T-72 Main Battle Tanks were burning, out of action in the woods. We turned north and were back on the flight deck an hour and a half after we'd left.

The next couple of weeks saw us running in on several VCPs, disrupting the regime's grip on the main roads west of Tripoli. We launched a four-ship mission to break up control of the roads in and out of Zuwara and Az-Zawiyah. Nine Hellfire and 200 rounds of 30mm cleared the VCPs. A week later the regime had rebuilt them. Smelling an ambush, we launched again, this time coming in from the desert. Jay and Big Shippers noticed heavy weapons all pointing out to sea – it certainly looked like a 'come-on' designed to lure us back – but together with JB and Reuben they put eleven Hellfire and 500 rounds of 30mm into the VCPs and weapon systems. Savvy planning had brought the patrol in from an unexpected direction and rapid high-tempo firing thrashed the ambush before it could be sprung. The regime didn't go for a third rebuild.

On the same day I received a letter from the Guild of Air Pilots and Air Navigators informing me that 656 Squadron Group had been awarded the Master's Commendation for their development of the Apache's maritime capability. Recognition while at war! This was great news. Now renamed the Honourable Company of Air Pilots, the Guild are global sponsors of everything aviation and are held in the highest esteem by aviation professionals. To receive an award from them was indeed a top honour. I knew who'd written the citation and went to thank the CO.

We were back on the up. No one had launched a surface-to-air missile at us for two weeks and the FLIR image was conclusive – pro-Gad wanted to run away and live. Each time an Apache crossed the coast the scouting screen ran for cover. Finally, at the six-week point, the message was getting through – don't fight us, because we'll fight you back harder and we'll win.

*Chapter 10*

# The Week of the 27

In mid-July we went back to the Zlitan area. This time we weren't going to mix it with BM21s, ZSU 23-4s or the troops on the front line. This time we were going to break the back of the brigade by convincing Khamis that there was nowhere safe to rest, store equipment or manoeuvre in depth. This time we would strike his support areas, where 32 Brigade was spread 20 miles in depth from Al Khums to Zlitan with large numbers of vehicles and troops using requisitioned buildings as well as government premises. Their task was to re-supply, reinforce and rotate with troops on the front line, a further 15 miles to the east. These troops were busy fighting the rebels and besieging Misrata. Pro-Gad had shelled, burned and razed the city, terrorizing her population with artillery and direct fighting since February. The FLF had edged the front line west towards Zlitan, but pro-Gad could still dominate the area. Our task was to disrupt pro-Gad and, in doing so, create opportunities for the rebels.

The first mission was to destroy a set of buildings just five miles west of Zlitan. They were only two miles south of the beach. On the map it looked straightforward – come in off the sea, identify the targets, strike, return to Mother. We would probably only need to be feet-dry for a matter of minutes. The reality proved not to be so simple. The ground between the target area and the coast looked good for a SAMbush. There were also other areas of military interest which could become targets for future missions. We didn't want to be circling above this, inadvertently telegraphing our future intent or inviting a fight. Flying around conducting attack profiles seemed unnecessarily risky. If we had to fly in that area we would want to do so only once, low and fast, gun actioned, ready to defend ourselves. So we chose a long navigation track, entering 30 miles to the north, flying inland and then sweeping south and east before taking on the target from the south. This unexpected approach would give the impression we had come from far inland. Of course this came with its own risk. Would we give ourselves away with a long land track? Would we be engaged on the beach on the way in? The long land track gave no choice but to undertake the short escape route back to Mother via the low, fast, gun-actioned dash through SAMbush territory at the end of the mission. We would be low on ammunition and fuel, leaving very little margin for the fight and survival. Being behind enemy lines, possibly battle-damaged and low on essentials, is a difficult plan to sign up to. But as we considered the options it was clear that the land track, attack from the south and dash offered the best chance of success for this mission, as well as following our modus operandi of surprise and firepower.

Mark and John had recommended the route to me, highlighting the pros and cons. The launch was a long way north of the target and we would arrive at the coast near Al Khums, where Gaddafi's SF were based. There would be a long land track through the hinterland and across the desert. Fuel would be tight, but surprise would be on our side. Shooting from the south gave us the best chance of a quick and devastating attack. We discussed the various points of entry and exit as well as the likely threats on each leg of the route.

These were two experienced operators with well over 1,000 hours flying in Afghanistan between them. More important than that, they were crafty, independent thinkers. I could expect them to consider all the possibilities and present a plan that embraced the unorthodox while making the most of the aircraft's capabilities. To continue to survive and win on this operation we had to be agile planners. A well considered plan would help us cope with the combat reality. This gave us the best chance of making the right decisions on the spot in those chaotic combat moments when risks become real and the enemy makes a determined attempt on your life. Surprise, speed, firepower and darkness were top of our planning needs. With a team like this, all I had to concentrate on was the target set and how to attack it.

On mission day, when it came to reviewing the route in the afternoon we spent a long time poring over the satellite imagery of the land track. Maps of Libya were adequate around the cities, but not so accurate in the hinterland or the desert. Among the hazards we had to be sure of were the various wires, electrical and telephone. Almost all of Libya's industrial infrastructure was on the coast, and that meant massive, high-tension, helicopter-catching wires were everywhere but seldom marked on the map. We would be flying low-level at night, and those wires presented a very real threat to our flight safety. Adding that to the fact that we would spend almost the entire sortie over enemy territory at around 100ft, I knew I had careful planning and risk-mitigation to consider.

I looked at the route: fly right past Gaddafi's SF base; a long low-level transit, lower than the wires, past miles of industrial complexes; push south-east into the desert and then swing up from the south to strike the targets; then a dash at full tilt over two miles of perfect SAMbush country with little fuel and perhaps just a round or two of ammunition left; finally, go and find *Ocean* somewhere in the darkness at sea. After seven weeks of missions over Libya this was accepted as a normal night out. It was a 'yes' from me.

When it came to the mission brief, Doug and his team had already loaded our Hellfire and 30mm. The 5th crew had proved the systems in each aircraft, *Ocean* was ploughing onwards to the launch point and the weather looked good. It was now a matter of getting a 'Go' out of the CAOC, a 'Go' from the Commodore and any last-minute discussions with the CO. I highlighted the risks and indicated where aircraft could escape to the left and right of track if things unravelled. I showed the team where we could break off the mission and turn for home. I discussed the likely enemy response at every phase – his weapons, how he might use them and how we would respond. Finally, I detailed the target, dividing up responsibilities between the two aircraft, describing which weapons were to be used and in what order. We checked our understanding of radio frequencies, heights and speeds to be flown, attack headings and the sequence of firing.

Finally, we confirmed with each pilot what his actions would be if the worst was to happen over either sea or land – a forced landing due to mechanical malfunction or enemy fire. The 56th Rescue crews, callsign 'Jolly', were always keen to listen to this part, and their mission commander would note all routes, radio frequencies and likely escape and rendezvous points. They would sit in the Operations Room throughout the mission, ready to launch when needed. In rehearsals and exercises, which they continually conducted, the Jollys proved they could get two HH60s packed with PJs[7] and medical kit off the deck and on mission within seven minutes of being notified in the Operations Room. From the day they arrived on board we flew reassured that determined, courageous and experienced combat operators stood ready to come and get us if the call was made.

There was a lot activity in the target area that night. The usual fast air missions were going in all around the country, but there was also naval gunfire to the east of Zlitan, not too far away from our target. As part of her mission, HMS *Liverpool* would be firing illumination rounds that hang in the sky under parachutes, turning dark into light for miles around. Acknowledging our need for darkness and their need for light, our missions were scheduled to take place at different times – mine some twenty minutes after the naval gunfire was complete.

At the conclusion of the mission brief, we heard it was a 'Go' from the CAOC – targets good, support aircraft on task.

And then the ritual begins: the transition from planner and risk-mitigator to man about to rush into the fight and pull the trigger again. I would lean on the railings of the quarterdeck in the early evening light with a cup of tea. It was always too hot at the start and the wrong side of cool at the end, and every time I would tip away the dregs and watch the falling liquid separate out into mist and settle in the ship's wake as we ploughed steadily forward to our launch point. This was my least favourite time in the day. I was always nervous. Waiting was difficult.

With the tea done, I'd head for my cabin and close the door behind me. There I'd sanitize my clothing, removing badges of rank and identity, ensuring my escape map was in my pocket, that I had a tourniquet in my upper arm pocket and another one in my thigh pocket. No money, no wallet, no photos, no letters, nothing that made me anything other than just a man in a military uniform. The last thing I'd do was touch a photograph of my girls. It was summer where they were too. Summer and smiles and hats and dresses, sitting on a picnic rug on the lawn in the garden, dog asleep on the right-hand side – K had sent me out a collage of happiness. I would turn away and swallow down the fear.

Then I was ready. On leaving my cabin I had made the transition. We sometimes refer to this as being in your 'mission bubble'. We get used to it from our earliest sorties on the Army Pilots' Course. Aircrew need their own space for mental preparation. They need to organize their thoughts and rehearse in their mind how they wish the sortie to go. On the Pilots' Course test sorties are always nervous affairs, and those who complete the course and then complete the equally demanding Apache Conversion Course know very well the pressure of testing sorties and develop their own individual coping mechanisms to deal with that pressure. Once in a Regiment, there are six-monthly check rides and periodic sorties with Aviation Standards to keep you going. My coping ritual was a product of that evolution, but it now had the additional concern of the very real prospect of perishing within the next two hours.

My next stop was back in the flip-flop. Signatures were exchanged for a Sig Saur 9mm pistol, a 5.56mm L22 A2 Carbine assault rifle and two morphine syrettes. The morphine was placed next to each tourniquet in their respective pockets, my logic being that come the moment of injury and the need for self-aid I would have some chance of locating a tourniquet and some morphine if they were kept together. John had already passed this stage on his way to signing out the aircraft, conducting the walk-round and flashing up the systems.

I had one more moment of professional consideration. About an hour before launching each mission the Commodore held a Go/No Go Brief. The mission, the Rules of Engagement, the threat, the ship's systems and the weather were all discussed, and the last word prior to the Commodore's decision would be the view from his Policy Adviser, a sharp mind from the Civil Service with a direct line into the top of Downing Street. He would give an informed opinion as to where this mission sat in the strategic political context of the whole operation and advise how the intended course of action contributed to that political end and how it was compliant with the ministerial submission that bounded our activity.

It was declared a 'Go'. All we had to do now was fly it!

That final Go/No Go Brief was the last dispassionate check of our planning. I would stand to the rear or to one side, as discreetly as possible, aware that people would be looking at me but not wanting to be seen. I would be nervous, because now I wanted to get on with it: get in the aircraft, listen to the radios, build a picture in my mind, test and check the systems, count down, launch, go and get the task done, avoid coming unstuck. I always did my best to look quiet, appear a picture of focused professionalism. But a closer look would have noticed that my toes were folding and unfolding in my boots, my teeth were slowly grinding together; I was out there, my mind was rehearsing the fight, my body was readying to deal with the fear and all I wanted to do was get out and get on with it.

With a final 'Go' from the Commodore, the command team from the ship and the battle staff would take their places in the Operations Room. I would check that nothing had changed, the target was still valid, there was no new information and the Rules of Engagement were still good. Then I'd grab my kit and walk to the flight deck.

It's a long walk through passageways and up ladders to get from the Operations Room to aircrew lockers and out on to the flight deck. On my way I would pick up my go-bag – a shoulder bag full of ammunition for the Sig and the Carbine, some water and other survival items I might need should I end up on the ground in Libya. Evidence from combat experiences of aircraft landing or crashing in a hostile environment is that what is attached to the pilot will leave the aircraft with him; what is not may well get left behind in the chaos of the moment. Aircrew wear a load-carrying vest which houses some survival equipment, a radio, a GPS, a rescue strop; it also holds our body armour. On to this I attached my own breakout knife, my Sig and as much ammunition for the Sig and Carbine as I could find room for. My final port of call was the engineering space, where the REME quietly managed the paperwork and coordination of engineering in a darkened environment. John had already signed for the aircraft and I could hear it running on the auxiliary power unit on the flight deck outside. I would check the paperwork, make an appreciation of the aircraft weight and centre of gravity, its engine performance estimates and its weapon calibration, and note any engineering limitations. A brief word of thanks to the crew chief, then in went my in-ear protection, on went my flydanner[8] followed by my helmet, and I was off through the airlock and out on to the dark, hot flight deck. Typically, the senior ground crew sergeant was on hand overseeing our arming and refuelling on the darkened deck. He would also shake my hand and say, 'Have a good one, boss' as I stepped up to the aircraft. I'd nod, smile, count the remaining lashings holding the aircraft to the flight deck, have a quick check of the missiles and then climb inside the front seat. The front seat of the front aircraft; there is nowhere else to command an Apache squadron from.

Once in the cockpit, straps on, helmet-mounted display over the right eye, door shut, air conditioning taking the edge off the humidity, everything was better.

'On in the front . . .' I was plugged in and able to talk and hear through the intercom.

'Got you, sir,' from John in the rear.

'All good on the wing,' the Arming and Landing Point Commander added.

'Any dramas with the aircraft?' For these missions everything had to be in full working order; we could not carry any faults with us.

From John: 'All good, just weapons checks to go.'

'Okay, ready weapon ops checks.'

We cycled through each weapon, with the Arming and Landing Point Commander confirming the gun moved as it should. Each missile was interrogated and confirmed to be responding correctly. After that there was nothing else to do, just wait, listen in to the various mission frequencies that were being flown by the jets and keep to our timings.

'Forty minutes to launch.'

From John: 'Roger. All ready for engines when you are.'

I would count down to the last ten minutes. Everything went on a timeline, there was no need to use the radios or a runner. Up in Flyco, Wings knew the timings; on the bridge, the Officer of the Watch knew the timings; down in the Operations Room, the team knew the timings. The ship would turn on to a flying course, and with eight minutes to launch we started the engines. Engine One, then Engine Two, auxiliary power off. I could see my wingman doing the same just a few feet in front of me, his tail-rotor uncomfortably close to my eyes. Perfectly synchronised activity, no words exchanged, perhaps fifty individuals within the ship all performing a function to deliver us to these final few minutes.

John: 'Ready pre-take off checks.'

I'd go through a list of challenge and response and together we'd set the aircraft ready for launch.

Me: 'Lashings.'

The team outside untied the lashings that secured us to the deck. I counted each lashing, gave a brief flash of my torch and then looked at the marshaller. He looked up and down the flight deck then pointed at me with both marshalling wands and gave us the signal to lift.

John: 'Lifting.'

Me: 'All good. FMC is in, my canopy jettison, your stores jettison.'

This was our final brief on how we'd deal with an engine failure on take-off. When the aircraft is just a few feet above the flight deck all feels safe, but then the handling pilot moves the tremendous 8-tonne beast to port and we go from 5ft above a deck to 70ft above the sea in a hover. The engines would be working hard; if one was to fail this is when it would happen. As soon as we were clear of the flight deck John pitched the nose gently forward and we gained speed as we climbed to circuit height. The second aircraft went through the same procedure, with Mark in the front and Charlie at the controls. This was accurate flying, following a strict procedure of rehearsed heights and speeds close to the sea at night, no lights. The second aircraft had the harder job. They had to catch up, settle into the correct formation position and 'call in'. This highly perishable skill has to be practised regularly. Regardless of how good or how experienced a pilot you are, low-level formation flying is demanding stuff, and doing it over the sea at night with no lights adds an extra dose of nerves.

Mark called, 'In'. He could see me and had settled into the pre-arranged formation.

Me: 'One hundred, one hundred, head two-two-zero.' This signalled that I was happy with the formation and that it was time to descend to low level, 100ft, and begin our run into Libya. It was time to charge on into the black. As we did so I made a call to the airborne command and control platform, callsign Matrix, 'Matrix, this is Prodigy formation, launching as fragged.'

From 36,000ft somewhere over the Med a calm Southern States voice in Matrix replied, 'Prodigy you are sweet, sweet, continue as fragged.'

Then, a moment later, the calm southern accent again, 'Prodigy, Matrix, there is still some naval gunfire putting up Starburst in your sector, you need to hold short at this time . . .'

Me: 'His timings are a little out, when will the naval gunfire stop?'

Matrix: 'Just checking that now . . .'

We had a long way to go to get to the coast, and a longer track over the desert to hook round and attack from the south. We didn't have the fuel for self-inflicted delays right at the start of the sortie. I got on the radio to the Operations Room in *Ocean*: 'NGS on-going. They're firing Starburst in the target area. Need it to stop so I can proceed.'

Operations Room: 'Sorting it now . . .' A brief pause. 'Sorted, no more NGS.' Someone had spoken to *Liverpool*. She'd overstayed her timings to engage a final target and was in her combat moment. I would have done the same myself. And I would have received the same persuasive telephone call telling me to stop! *Liverpool* and *Ocean* both JCHATted the cessation of NGS, and Matrix called me to continue on our way.

Thirty nautical miles of sea-track at 100ft – I was willing the coast to get under us. Soon the familiar desolate shoreline came into sight. There was not much of a beach and the ground rose steeply in the form of small cliffs to a height of about 30ft above the breaking waves. We spread the formation wide to confuse Gaddafi's scouts and raced across the rocky beach into the hinterland.

Then, quickly on the inter-aircraft net, Mark's low northern drawl: 'Being observed, two men, all the right profile, suppressing with 30 mil.'

He fired twenty rounds of 30mm cannon in the vicinity of two insomniacs who appeared to be hiding in the cover of a collection of partly built houses. Watching helicopters from cover; in enemy SF territory; just after midnight – this amounted to compellingly suspicious activity. Mark had seen them watching the skies as we went feet-dry; it added up to the typical precursor to a MANPAD launch. We had expected some interest. With the 30mm landing close by and the message clear, the two scouts leapt, split up and ran for cover.

Mark: 'They're on the run, no further engagement, continuing.'

Once clear of the coast we settled on our south-easterly course and kept as low as we could. I had the gun actioned, my left trigger finger close to the trigger guard, my right trigger finger by the laser. The FLIR was slaved to my right eye simultaneously looking out for where the next shot would be coming from, as well as all for wires, masts, pylons, buildings and the like that interfere with helicopters.

With 90 per cent of the population living on the coast, and all the industrial infrastructure of the state there too, there were thousands of pylons, high-tension wires and masts not plotted on our maps. We were flying low, much lower than the wires. Over my left eye I had a single NVG. NVG is an image intensifier, it needs some ambient light to function and it takes that light to present you with a green video image. What you see is what is actually in front of your eye. Over my right eye I had our Apache infrared sight projected from the FLIR mounted on the nose of the aircraft. What you see with this is actually 3ft in front of you and 2ft below you, where the camera is mounted. Infrared doesn't care how dark it is, it looks for differences in temperature, however minute, and the FLIR converts that heat difference into a video image. So you have two separate images from two separate sources using different parts of the electromagnetic spectrum. My brain does its best to fuse the images to make one visual scene. All the time I am aware that the FLIR image is the one that my sight and my gun is using, the NVG image is just to find objects that the infrared doesn't pick out.

Wires were my biggest concern. The Apache has wire cutters positioned around the fuselage, but those huge high-tension electricity wires will still cause a lot of damage, like a 100mph baseball bat striking the windscreen. This would more than likely result in the aircraft going down in a very untidy way and two rather ruffled soldiers tabbing their way to a rendezvous for an HH60 'Jolly' pick-up. I never got an answer to my 'what would we do if we had to leave an aircraft on the ground in Libya?' question. Would someone come along and 'deny' it? Or would we leave it for Gaddafi to play with on telly? Either way, someone senior would be embarrassed, and I was sure they would let me know all about it. Bumping into wires had all sorts of pain associated with it.

Using the two video images gave us the best chance to see them, but it is a difficult brain- and eye-straining skill. Our risk here was about flying low enough to survive an unscheduled fight while also being able to see obstacles in time to quickly climb, cross and then descend again. We train for this at home and conduct sortie after sortie of low-level flying at night to give us the skills necessary to do it in combat. It is a fine balance, back in Suffolk, to keep aircrew operationally fit in all their flying skills while not upsetting the communities we live in. Occasionally we get complaints, very occasionally someone will try and blind us with a high-powered torch or a hand-held laser. However annoying the noise of a helicopter passing low-level at night may be, flying thus is an essential skill, and this particular evening four Apache pilots were using every ounce of that critical training to keep them alive behind enemy lines over Gaddafi-controlled Libya.

'Wires! 400m, 12 o'clock. Go to 200ft.'

John: 'Got them, climbing . . .'

'Not on the map, those ones. Continue at 200ft.'

John: 'Wilco.'

We continued over undulating terrain between 100 and 200ft, the gun moving with my head, eyes searching near, middle and far, left to right, FLIR flicking from white hot to black hot to change the view and break out the threat, be it man with MANPAD or just lethal wires.

'Map says wires in 700m.'

John: 'Not visual yet.'

'Hold 120ft, looking . . .' Then, 'Got them, left eye, 300m. Climb!' I had found them on NVG first.

John: 'Climbing . . .'

'Hold 200ft, wires in 500m, now good on black hot FLIR right eye.' Now FLIR was helping, I mentally merged the NVG and infrared images.

John: 'Visual, all good . . . quite a late one, that.'

Doing over 100 knots we crossed the wires, held our height, crossed another set not on the map, banked right into the desert, descended and began setting up for the target. Charlie and Mark kept formation, searching for their own threats and matching us for height and speed. For the most part all was going according to plan. So far it had been an average night out over Libya.

With five miles to go we went into our pre-planned attack profile. Our target was a collection of storage buildings used by 32 Brigade to house soldiers and equipment. The aerial reconnaissance reports showed they were very active, and it looked a good Apache target set. We were authorized to hit specific buildings while leaving others untouched –

typical of the discriminatory method of modern targeting. This is important from both a legal perspective and a moral one – we were interested in unseating 32 Brigade, not adding to the woes of the civilian population they were threatening. A neat Hellfire strike would do the job and contain the damage.

Our long transit was almost complete. We picked up the distinctive dried meander of the *wadi* that would lead us to the target and I flicked from gun to missiles, defence to offence. Now we were on the attack. I switched to the Bowman radio to coordinate the attack; this way it was possible for *Ocean* to listen in if she was close enough.

'Running in, targets identified, no changes, continue,' I transmitted.

The patrol split. John kept us heading straight for the target area, while Charlie and Mark flew momentarily east and then banked hard back toward the targets. We had now set up a coordinated strike, in which each aircraft attacked the target set, near simultaneously, from a different heading. This allowed us to get two different views of the same target, very useful when making sure no civilians were in the area, and also offered fewer places for the enemy to hide.

Mark fired first. I was counting down to my own shot when I saw one of my targets demolished by the familiar force of a Hellfire, followed by the destruction of another.

'You're taking my targets?!' It was half question, half incredulous observation.

'Yes, sorry, tumbleweed, better now . . .', he replied. In Mark Hall country that's as good as an apology gets. With no time to discuss manners I accepted, and we agreed who had what from the remaining targets and pressed on with the attack. Together we fired ten Hellfire in just four minutes – buildings destroyed, no movement within the wreckage. Outside, Gaddafi's soldiers were rushing about in the vicinity of other buildings. Maximum effect, much chaos and the sound of the Apache rushing overhead.

We left the scurrying, panicked soldiers – they needed to tell their seniors and their friends that the Apache had been and done this, much as their colleagues had been doing for the last seven weeks up and down the country. None of them had a go at us. With such a weight of fire coming in on them in a small area, usually two or three Hellfire at a time, only one or two seconds separating each impact, it must have seemed like the world was ending. Cognitive effect builds its own momentum.

On the way out Mark put another Hellfire into the VCP guarding the site. That was our final target for the night. I gave a quick burst on the radio, in part to tell *Ocean* we were on our way, in part to collect the team and head for home.

'All targets destroyed, one hundred, one hundred, head three-five-zero.'

Gun actioned, scanning for trouble, we made the mad low-level dash north up the *wadi* to the coast and then the search for Mother. No one stirred, not a shot came our way. Silence and the Apache was all that followed the roar of ten Hellfire that night. The plan had worked, audacious as it was. Crafty minds had kept us ahead of Khamis. That and ten Hellfire in four minutes.

\*

There were three more missions like that during a single week in late July, all to locations being used by 32 Brigade to run their operations. Some of the targets were buildings, others no more than large sheds or storage containers. Two of the missions were coordinated strikes with Royal Air Force Typhoon and Tornado aircraft. These missions were put together by the CAOC with precise detail, down to what sort of weapon would be used for each target, what the attack heading would be and the order in which the targets were to be hit. In normal Apache operations we prefer more freedom to decide our way of working; but it was their air war for the most part, their big fast planes sitting up there five miles above us, and such a prescriptive method removed a lot of risk.

The idea was simple: disrupt 32 Brigade, create chaos, do it repeatedly and make a lot of noise with 500lb Paveway IV from the fast jets and the much smaller Hellfire from the Apache. And once the dust settles, all that is heard, if anyone can still hear, are rotor-blades as the Apaches tip in for another attack. Keep building that momentum, keep getting in their heads: you can't stop us and we will keep on fighting you until you stop threatening the civilian population. You have no place to hide.

The fourth mission that week destroyed an ammunition and weapons storage facility just behind the front line. The targets, ten in total, were all within a walled compound just off the beach. We could stay feet-wet for this one, a straightforward run, shoot, watch the fast air weapons, say what we saw and get back to *Ocean*. Total simplicity, with all the coordination done in the CAOC and just the final details completed between me and the jet mission lead on the telephone that afternoon. I felt rather good about my gunnery as I controlled three Hellfire in the air at once, their discrete explosions delivering the precise effect I wanted. Then I called clear and watched the awesome sight of a Paveway IV obliterate the adjacent buildings. Big and clever, I thought – but I won't tell them that! One target remained. I glanced at the map and the reconnaissance photo. It was a storage container, a huge air-conditioned metal box the size of a bus, allocated to Nick and Little Shippers.

'Just your last target to go.'

Nick: 'Yes . . . left it after the first run in. You still want me to have a go?'

'Yes, I'll watch you in. I have you visual.'

'Wilco.'

In went a November Hellfire, and the storage container separated into millions of pieces as the ammunition inside went off. The explosion was enormous! The sound, after the initial Hellfire strikes and the Paveways, must have been incredible and heard, with the other strikes, all the way across the front line, giving heart to the rebels and the fear to 32 Brigade.

'That's the one!'

Nick: 'Yep, that'll do it!'

'All good, returning to Mother.'

The total mission time was 45 minutes. We'd fired six Hellfire and observed the Paveway IVs take down their targets from way up at 25,000ft; and all that was heard between the explosions was the rhythmic thunder of our rotor-blades. Simple, safe enough, hard-hitting and back on deck in less than an hour. No missions were planned for the next few days. This deserved a beer.

In four missions a pair of Apaches had flown just twelve hours and fired twenty-seven Hellfire. We'd struck targets across the full depth of Khamis Gaddafi's outfit and inflicted irrecoverable damage to his capability. We'd done so alongside HMS *Liverpool* and in concert with Typhoon and Tornado. And, of course, there were also several thousand Free Libyans on the ground doing the hard fighting. This combination of platforms and weapons created more problems than Khamis could deal with, left huge holes in his front line and saw the rebels begin to advance.

Back on *Ocean* we were in good spirits; it had been a very successful week. I wondered, privately, what it would take to get this operation completed. Brega was key, so was Zlitan, but the biggest prize was

Tripoli. Only the rebels could make the difference on the ground, but with such a large and sustained aerial effort from NATO, it seemed to me that the tipping point was coming. The stalemate of April, May and June would give way in favour of the rebels and the newly recognized National Transitional Council (NTC), and the race for Tripoli would begin. While pacing the flip-flop or the Operations Room I kept my mind on the tactical detail of how we might be part of that, but in the wardroom we all discussed what forces would be unleashed in the final reckoning and how Gaddafi himself might try to defend his last bastion. A protracted urban battle with huge loss of life, displaced persons, destroyed infrastructure and arrested state functionality has no winner. In such a scenario the state is ruined from the inside out as the dictator clings to power and robs what he can from the remains. At the same time, the fighters tear each other apart to gain irrelevant advantage, and in every street and under all the rubble lie the civilian victims who had no choice but to stay and watch the whole shameful disaster unfold. This is what NATO sought to avoid in Benghazi when the jets first flew in late March. Keeping Tripoli from a similar fate must have been in their minds now.

There was talk of Gaddafi being given refuge in Venezuela, but also of his determination to remain in Libya. The NTC appeared keen to kill or capture him and his sons and inner circle. This made a fight-to-the-last-man scenario more likely. But perhaps if the rebels could gain the advantage in Brega, Zlitan and the Nafusa mountains to the south of Tripoli, all at the same time, then the tipping point might arrive sooner. The rebels could then advance across all three fronts.[9] Gaddafi would not be able to contain them. Defections and desertions would increase. No one would be available to defend Tripoli. Those who could do so would take off their uniforms and leave their posts. Conscripts would run back to their families. Support for Gaddafi out of fear of his internal intelligence apparatus would disappear. Libyans could stand up for themselves in ever greater numbers as they calculated that the security forces of the state would not reach them. This was the scenario NATO needed. On the telly, the usual talking heads peddled their expertise – some spoke of the stalemate continuing for another six months, others said this thing could go big pretty soon. In HMS *Ocean* we wanted a little bit more, but not too much. We felt we were winning our own small battle but we were also very alert to the dangers we faced, and those weren't going away. By 3 August we had been at sea for 100 days. So much for a six-week exercise!

# Chapter 11

# The Rebel in the Mountains

With combat in Brega and Zlitan we had fought on two of the three Libyan front lines. The third appeared too far inland to risk helicopters. Keeping to the coastal options kept the decision men happy: short missions with minimum vulnerable time. But the taking of risk is about the balance of reward, and we were constantly analysing this risk-and-reward calculation. The layering of jets and drones and the timeliness of target fidelity were all part of trimming away that risk, real or otherwise.

The easiest thing to do was not fly at all. This would keep Gaddafi guessing, but without action was ultimately toothless. If we had to fly, the safest way was to remain feet-wet over the sea and launch Hellfire from as far away as possible to remain outside the triple-A and MANPAD range. But this required targets right on the coast, almost on the beach. Beach fighting was not big in Libya, so we had to go inland. This was where we entertained the most risk. But getting tangled up with the best of 32 Brigade and coming out on top had proved we could operate inland and that the cautious approach to risk could be reconsidered.

Intelligence assessments made a long way from us that shaped planning ideas in NATO had begun to point to the third front, the Nafusa mountains. Here the same stalemate existed as everywhere else. When intelligence is presented to the front-line combat operator, he can question it, he can ask where it came from and he can try and analyse it himself. None of this is ever met with anything other than a patient stare from the Intelligence Officer. The work is done. The information has been gathered, considered, analysed and distilled into options. These options are then considered by the decision men, and a plan is made. The plan is then given to the combat operator. We are expected to get on with it; the asking questions part is not in our gift. Our part was in providing a plan that satisfied the risk warriors, then manning up, guns and night sky, and charging again into the barrage. And now intelligence suggested that the third front would break out first. It was closest to Tripoli but it needed a catalyst, and helicopters could help.

The analysis was clear: Colonel El-Moktar Firnana, the rebel commander south-west of Tripoli, wanted more from NATO. He wanted to unlock the third front line as the quickest and most likely route to Tripoli. Intelligence analysts had asserted only the previous month that the rebels in the mountains would remain there. They were tribal, it was their home, they had won it back and they had no interest in advancing on Tripoli. Now that view had changed completely.

Talk of a deep strike into the mountains began in early July, but these were just exploratory discussions. We were used to coastal strikes, and the Brega raid had made the CAOC apprehensive about sending us a long way overland. But the information kept coming in. During a slow off-mission day in a quiet flip-flop, with most crews in rest or flying maintenance sorties, the Commodore's Intelligence Officer bundled down the chain ladder and pointed at Nick.

He always wore a half quizzical grin, perfect for man in his line of work. 'How do you fancy unlocking a war?' A fair ask, given that it had gone on long enough, we were probably running out of luck and a rapid win was what we were in it for.

Nick was quick to reply: 'But what would we do afterwards? We'd probably just get sent to fight somewhere else, or worse, get sent home. Some of us would have to get proper jobs, meet our families and everything!'

'Fair one. However, if you were tempted, the commander of the rebel forces down in the Nafusa Mountains appears to have been admiring your work. Word in the mountains is that if that area gets some Apache attention they might break out. His troops will be in Green Square in two weeks.'

'Wow, that's quite a bold shout. Which mountains again?'

The intelligence man pointed at our map. 'About 50 miles south-west of Tripoli . . . he's a big hitter, this guy, and the source is good. This might happen. Just have a think in case the CAOC throw it at you as a fastball, you know, fuel, weapons, routes in and out, all that risk mitigation stuff too.'

It was a curious heads-up. Someone had placed an idea in someone else's head; it turned into half a plan, then made its way to us. This was compelling, completely new. The mountains were a long way inland and the whole land track would be over consolidated pro-Gad territory. No change to any other land mission, but here it was right over Tripoli's surrounds and certain to be rough all the way. If the rebels thought they were likely to break out from the Nafusa mountains, then Gaddafi might have noticed it too. If Khamis had told his Dad that he'd been well and truly knocked in Zlitan and Brega by helicopters flying low, apparently ignoring his MANPADS and triple-A and smashing his soldiers, then it was likely the regime would guess we would be used on the third front. They would be expecting us.

But nothing came of it. It all went quiet. The chance flashed and then went out altogether. Throughout July we flew coastal missions to Zlitan and west of Tripoli. Several other missions were suggested, planned, briefed and subsequently cancelled when no targets could be verified prior to launch. Our frustration increased. After the blooding of June we were certainly overconfident, and the CAOC were right to clip us when we suggested wilder alternatives, but it was clear we could do more and succeed. Coastal or inland? It was all about risk versus reward, time and need. July wasn't the time, and we had all but run out of lives in Brega in late June. The need now was for us not to come unstuck – keep the Apache in the campaign for all the reasons it was introduced, but not put it in too much danger. The fanfare was over, the media had gone home, we'd got away with our lives but come close to losing 80 per cent of the squadron's combat power and aircrew over Brega; brutal war was now our firm reality.

The CAOC didn't want to send us to the mountains. Our task was to deal with 32 Brigade and not get knocked down. So we got on with the 32 Brigade gauntlet in Zlitan and the coast west of Tripoli.

By the end of July we had flown twenty missions into Libya. Along the way, over those two months, ten more had been cancelled. From the outset the CAOC was clear – they would not allow us to launch unless they were certain we had a valid target to strike. All ten of those cancellations resulted from target uncertainty. A rate of five per month was acceptable and it demonstrated to us that we were being given serious consideration in the CAOC. But it also demonstrated that reconnaissance or other 'find' assets were in short supply. These are the frustrations of resource-finite operations. The lower flying rate didn't change the tempo for our soldiers and engineers. They still had to provide mission-ready aircraft every day, right up to the late night mission cancellation. They endured a monotony of hard work throughout the day, only to see unflown aircraft returned to the hangar late at night. To their credit, not one mission or sortie was lost due to lack of aircraft readiness. They gave us exactly what we needed to fly every day and night of the embarkation; and they went unrewarded with any Operational Allowance.

With 'finding' the target out of our control, we were becoming frustrated with the cancellations. We wanted a new place to strike, a new interest to give us the assets we needed for the decision to let us launch. Nick wanted to see what the mountains were like.

By the end of July there was change in our team in the CAOC. Chris James had returned to the UK to take up a new post in the Ministry of Defence and Glen Parker had come out from the School of Army Aviation to replace him. Glen was another deeply experienced Army flyer. He had bounded through the ranks from private soldier to major and had been a helicopter instructor for the last fifteen years, with operational experience in every theatre of conflict the British Army had been to in the past twenty-five years. Six of our ten aircrew had flown with him or alongside him in Afghanistan the previous winter. He knew the Apache and operations but he was about to endure the shock of capture that only a combat operator can suffer when catapulted headlong into a staff job! PowerPoint, email and telephones were not his usual weapons, nor was he used to tolerating the egos of men in flying suits who sit behind desks. After a brief period of orientation, during which he witnessed three of our mission cancellations, he set about finding new Apache targets in a fast jet community. He settled on the mountains . . .

After the week of the 27 we had a period of maintenance aboard *Ocean*. We were also in the boredom phase and to stay sharp we got on with everything weapons. With no missions planned for five days we recalibrated the 30mm guns in the air and also fired our own personal weapons from the quarterdeck. Mark Hall gathered the aircrew and went over our guntape, pointing out the best and worst of the footage with lessons on how to improve. We conducted our six-monthly personal fitness tests and got our Operational Record up to date. The flip-flop was busy, but it wasn't mission planning, it was administration. We wondered if we had run out of opportunities.

Glen Parker scheduled a call from the CAOC and broke the silence. It was Nick's turn to command the mission and at the given time he picked up the phone, with the rest of the aircrew coincidentally in the stiflingly hot flip-flop.

I sat close to the phone and listened in to the conversation.

Glen dispensed with the polite chitchat: 'Stop sunbathing and listen in. Do you remember that possible mission to the Nafusa Mountains mentioned last month?'

Nick nodded and said 'Yes' while pointing to the mountains on our map. His indication to the rest of us caused an audible cessation in work. Weapon cleaning, report writing and morphine counting stopped, and the aircrew moved in close to hear the conversation.

'Well, the FLF commander is still there, and an Apache mission is being discussed here on the floorplate as an option. That is if you think it's still feasible?' He knew it was feasible and was taunting Nick.

'What's the target set?' Nick replied. 'More importantly, it's a long way and our time at the target will be limited, so who will be cueing us on?'

'Sadly, same detail as before. You're unlikely to get a Pred, still all booked up on other tasks in Tripoli. However, the Int guys are confident that the area's been a stalemate for several weeks, and the front line is well defined. Target sets will be much the same, checkpoints and technicals, however there are known to be a few Armoured Fighting Vehicles still operating in that region.'

Glen thus gave him a little hope, although we all thought it might come to nothing without the Pred. We had heard similar before, so we accepted it but didn't expect much to develop. Our best hope was that because we hadn't operated there before, Gaddafi's forces were likely to have remained in the same locations for extended periods. Where NATO aircraft had operated in the same area for more than a couple of days Gaddafi's troops had become cautious and would move checkpoints frequently in order to thwart the targeting cycle.

Nick's call was background noise now in the flip-flop. All eyes were on the maps, the numbers and the weapons load. Nick talked the detail with Glen; the rest of us ran the plan.

Little Shippers brought up the maps on the mission planning system and began drawing planning lines – cigarette packet calculations in modern wiggly-amp ways. He was looking for places to cross the beach, how to find the right approach and identify the wires, the best escapes, emergency landing places and water sources. From this he could give a time estimate to the target, time available at the target and the fuel we would need to get home to Mother. Little Shippers was faultless with numbers – time, fuel and aircraft performance were his specialities.

'Feasible' could only come from the CAOC. If they could get something to validate the target so their rules on launching us were satisfied, then we would be good to go. The chances of launching were entirely down to how much the CAOC wanted us to fly.

With the phone call done, Nick briefed us:

Possibly two missions on different nights. Just a pair of aircraft for each. One lot of targets here near this town [he pointed at Bi'r al Ghanam, just 45 miles south-west of Tripoli and clearly on the main road between the capital and the mountains]. The other is here at this random desert road junction and the airfield nearby. It's being used as some sort of staging point sending troops down to the front line. [He now pointed to Okba airfield, deeper into the desert]. Mission one on the night of the 4th. Mission two the following night or perhaps a couple of nights later, depending on how the first one goes. The initial target packs should come through tonight or tomorrow. The reconnaissance photos are quite old, but it's all we have to plan with. Once we've come up with the outline route and timings we should have more recent imagery. They are apparently going to do some overflights with photo-pods tomorrow.

'Pred?' I asked. 'I mean, on the mission night.'

'No, 'fraid not. Jets, either F-16 or Tornado, are being allocated.'

'Great, so we're on our own again then.' John Blackwell injected some humour. 'Bit like in Brega when the triple-A and SA-6 were lashing about and nothing came from on high to make a difference . . .'

Jay cut him off: 'Well, you're not really on your own, John. See, you and the boss are together, in the Ops Room on the radio. You're not on the mission, either of them, look at the schedule!'

Everyone laughed, apart from John and I. I looked at the schedule. Jay was right.

John was cut down to size: 'Right, I'll go and make the tea then, just as soon as I've finished counting the morphine and polishing your boots!' He accepted his place. Eight aircrew kept laughing and John and I waited for them to stop. We would sit these missions out. Everyone had done so before and now it was our turn.

Nick had three days to plan. The target areas were given, but the target imagery was weeks old. He held on to the promise of better pictures and spent his time working the route in and the route out. Target packs would always grow as reconnaissance sorties confirmed the viability of the target. When a target area was being considered the NATO Targeting Board would take interest and demand more information. More reconnaissance was flown, better images were obtained and analysed and weapon types were recommended. Eventually, the Targeting Board would agree to the target and allocate it to a particular aircraft type. Often late in the afternoon of the mission the Targeting Board would say 'yes' or 'no' to our target for that night. To us this meant 'fly' or 'cancel'.

If the mountains were a genuine target area the old imagery would have to be updated. However, this target pack didn't develop. Nothing much had happened in the area for weeks, and it was not receiving much NATO interest. With this scant level of understanding a similar mission along the coastline around Zlitan or Tripoli would have been dismissed early or cancelled on the day. However, as we had never been there before, we had surprise on our side that de-risked the mission just enough to get a green light. The senior men decided the risk was worth the reward. In the background Glen had worked hard to convince them and he knew this would open up a whole new range of options for us. So, while we had very little detail apart from coordinates and an outline description of a collection of vehicle checkpoints, the mission was gaining traction. It looked like a 'Go'.

With a day to go, Nick agreed the launch point and the recovery point with the ship's Ops team. He selected the ingress point and a separate egress point on the coast, a key vulnerability for us. Little Shippers and JB spent hours scrutinizing the satellite imagery looking for wires and other hazards over all 50 nautical miles to the target and the 50 nautical miles back. Adding the 50 nautical miles of sea transit meant they would have little time for diversions or unscheduled fights if they were to have maximum effect at the target end. They also knew that if they turned for Mother with little ammunition and fuel left, the run home could be a ragged gauntlet.

Bi'r al Ghanam is the first significant settlement after a northerly descent from the mountains on to the low desert plain. An army on the march had two options: head north to the coastal city of Az-Zawiyah and then east along the coast to Tripoli; or straight north-east to the capital. Owning the town and the road meant control of the region. Our target checkpoints were strung out along the main road that ran north-east towards Tripoli. This road was considered to be a key strongpoint for pro-Gad. It prevented the FLF getting out of the mountains and it enabled easy re-supply to help keep them pinned down. Disrupting that strength might help open a gap in the pro-Gad defence and just might encourage the FLF to exploit an opportunity to advance.

Although the mission would be long, it was planned in our now standard way. Take-off and low-level sea transit, up to 30 nautical miles of it. Cross the coast, guns ready. Race into the desert and cover 50 nautical miles still at low-level, lower than the wires, to the target. Arrive, observe, decide shoot or no shoot. Three separate strikes. Break off. Another 50 nautical miles, again lower than the wires, cross the coast, low on fuel with guns ready, and then out into the black to find *Ocean* 20 nautical miles north in the Med. Seven phases, each briefed in minute detail. They knew their heights, speeds, times, approach angles, weapon choices and trigger pulls. They also knew how they might undo heat-seeking surface-to-air missiles, triple-A and anything else pro-Gad might throw into the sky.

It was a typically aggressive plan: strike the most heavily defended area first with surprise intact, then see what was left. Depending on the weather conditions and the flight profile, the enemy would likely hear them during their run in to the first target. Pro-Gad might get as much as 40 seconds of prior warning if he was listening hard and was able to break out and interpret the low thunder of the Apache on its attack run. The first Hellfire impact would confirm any doubts. After that, the meticulously briefed and rehearsed plan was just a set of ideas Nick could shape into hasty orders for subsequent strikes.

The first and second sites were within a few miles of each other, so surprise would be lost at the first trigger pull. This was about rapid target confirmation followed by maximum firepower. Nick wanted to minimize the attack runs to get as much firepower as possible down on the target with minimum time between trigger pulls. He would have to locate, identify and prosecute as many of the enemy as possible, ideally all in one run. The CO and Jack Davis had been meticulous in their discussions with the CAOC lawyer – the ROE were good to go, pro-Gad owned the space and no one else was there. If it looked military, it was a valid target.

So the evening arrived. The plan was briefed. It was agreed. It was low to medium risk – good for all. Even without any new imagery it was a 'Go' from the CAOC and the Commodore. Aircraft ready, *Ocean* in position. They were set.

I went up to the briefing room and signed the flight authorization. Nick and Reuben countersigned, picked up their personal weapons and ammunition and disappeared out through the airlock on to the flight deck. While they were starting up the systems an intelligence update came over the net from Matrix suggesting that there might be a ZSU 23-4 in the target area.

Nick thought, 'Result!' I thought, 'Risk!' It wasn't enough to change the plan; they had considered the chances of something like this happening and how they would respond. The dispassionate risk appreciation had been done. It was still a 'Go'. I settled in the Ops Room, John Blackwell beside me, radio headset on, text JCHAT streaming on the screen in front of us. I laid out the mission timeline and a printout of the map and plotted the potential ZSU 23-4. It was right on the first target. Still a 'Go'.

Up on the flight deck both aircraft were online, engines up, and without a word or a signal they lifted one after the other exactly according to the timeline and disappeared into the low-level night transit south to Libya. I could read on the JCHAT that they'd checked in with Matrix and were on their way. Within ten minutes they were out of radio range of *Ocean* and I expected to hear nothing more until their in-flight hot report was given on their way back over the sea an hour and a half later. The clues as to what might be happening at the target end would be lines on the JCHAT if they spoke to Matrix and he, in turn, reported to the CAOC and us at sea. For the first time as the squadron commander I felt totally without control. I sat back and glanced at the timeline. At the top of the A3 page the crew names were shown: Nick and Little Shippers as Valkyrie One, Reuben and JB as Valkyrie Two. I quickly totalled up their combined experience. Valkyrie One: 4,400 flying hours, 400 deck landings, 2 years in Afghanistan in the Apache. Valkyrie Two: 7,600 flying hours, 250 deck landings, 2 years in Afghanistan in the Apache. They could win in any fight, and I had nothing to worry about; but I still wanted to know how they were at every stage of the mission.

*Chapter 12*

# Opening up the Third Front

Out over the Med the patrol neared the coast all bright and promising hostility. Choosing the crossing point for this mission had been difficult. There were no good places and the missions west of Tripoli in July had used up the best places to enter and leave. Any soldier knows that pattern-setting encourages ambushes. The pro-Gad experience of attack helicopters had so far been a very negative one for them. But we knew and they knew that one, just one, helicopter shot down would be a big win for the regime. We also knew that MANPADS will eventually get through, either by luck or through sheer number of missiles in the air. There would be a bonus, possibly even a shiny new technical, to the man who brought down an Apache. Good news for the regime on the 'cognitive effect' front, bad news for us. The Zlitan double and the Brega experience made us respect this threat, but it also gave us confidence that we could survive even the most sophisticated MANPADS. Tonight the patrol had to cross the coast close to built-up areas and over wires, gun actioned and searching for the threat with the FLIR.

The two aircraft crossed the coast simultaneously, guns slaved to FLIR, FLIR slaved to the right eye of the front-seaters. Where they looked the sight and gun aimed, picking out any suspicious heat spots among the dunes, trees and buildings. Their speed and height meant they only had a few seconds to interrogate any potential target. In the rear seat the handling pilot had his right thumb on top of the counter-measure dispensing button, ready to push out chaff and flares if the American lady in the wing gave the bad news. They wanted to keep low, but the massive electricity pylons and high-tension cables strung between forced them up and over, presenting a perfect shot to anyone with an AK or a PKM. As soon as the wires were beneath them they dived down, weaving and banking to break up their flight profile and make targeting harder. The advantage of a moonless night was temporarily lost among the streetlights and headlights, and they were agonisingly exposed to a quick-minded pro-Gad soldier. Both front-seaters were rapidly searching

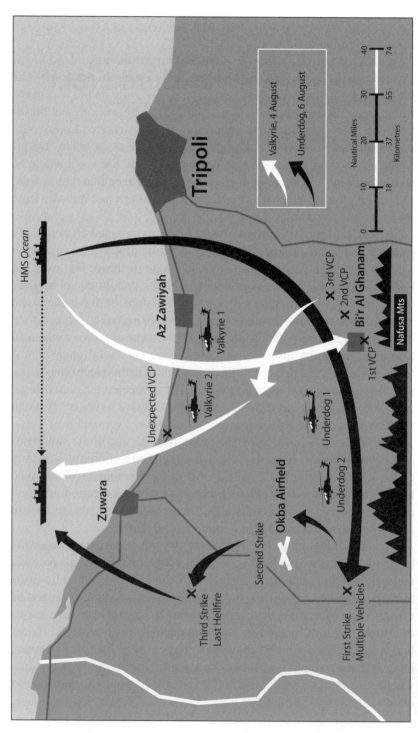

*The final two missions south-west of Tripoli*

for weapons on vehicles, men moving suspiciously or a flag identifying a checkpoint; but no incoming came.

Within a couple of miles the industrial infrastructure and the towns gave way to the hinterland and then the great expanse of the desert. The patrol had got through the first obstacle and was now on the way to the target. Back on the coast, pro-Gad would surely be working out that at least two helicopters had just come from the sea, departed to the south and would have to come back north and cross the coast again. Troops on the ground would be alert and waiting, troops to the south would be notified of what was coming: another Apache patrol behind regime lines and roaring towards their target, Hellfire and 30mm just minutes from release.

In the Ops Room back on *Ocean* I noted the estimated 16 minutes to the coast and the additional 27 minutes across the desert to the first target were just about up. No news so far was a good thing. Out over the Libyan desert, Nick had slaved his FLIR to the pre-stored coordinates of the first vehicle checkpoint on the road linking Bi'r al Ghanam with Tripoli. He glanced out through the canopy with his naked left eye, then through a single Night Vision Goggle with the same eye, then exchanged the binocular rivalry in favour of his right eye via the infrared sight. A few seconds of this two-eyed, three-elements-of-the-electromagnetic-spectrum scrutiny and he had thoroughly interrogated the entire target area. All was just as he anticipated from studying hours of map and satellite imagery.

The lights of the town glowed against the backdrop of the mountains just beyond. Steep, jagged and black against the midnight sky, they concealed thousands of FLF and Colonel El-Moktar Firnana. This would be the first time the mountain rebels had heard attack aviation. It would also be a new experience for Gaddafi's men blocking the road to Tripoli.

Nick broke the silence: 'Two minutes, call ready.'

He was setting up for the first attack run. In his mind he recalled the target imagery: a hastily built checkpoint with armed technicals pointing down the road in either direction. He searched the target area for clues to recognize the target. This situational awareness building would be central to his decision to shoot. The target had to be right, just as described, for him to engage. He needed to have reasonable certainty that it was indeed a pro-Gad military target. Recognizing the target, gaining an appreciation of the reality on the ground and then deciding whether to attack or not was his responsibility; he was the mission commander.

He also needed it to be fast.

Reuben replied, 'Ready. Breaking right.'

JB banked their aircraft away from Valkyrie One and set up on a new heading to give a different visual perspective on the target. They ran in as planned, bang on time, but neither aircraft could see a valid target.

Nick called, 'No target, breaking off,' and Little Shippers took them away to the north with Valkyrie Two covering their extraction.

Nothing was on the target area, no ZSU 23-4, not a single movement. Nick asked jet man if his Litening pod could see anything. 'Negative,' came the reply. Nothing. No movement, no people. This was unnerving and it did not tally with the targeting imagery taken three weeks before. Pro-Gad survivors were lying low, perhaps they'd heard the Apache coming, or got a message from the coast. After five months of NATO aerial strikes those who were still in business suppressing the uprising were the survivors. They had adapted their techniques and were still alive.

Nick transmitted, 'Nothing here, no point in hanging about, fuel says it's time to move on. My lead.'

The second target was a checkpoint at the crossroads where the main route to Tripoli and the road directly north to the refinery town of Az-Zawiyah met, a critical confluence vital to Gaddafi's defence of the coastal oil towns and the capital. This had to be occupied permanently. As briefed just three hours earlier, it was Reuben who would be first on target two, and as soon as the checkpoint came into view he immediately began his attack run. This time the imagery resembled almost perfectly what he saw through the FLIR. In his right eye in glorious green shades of temperature sat the checkpoint in the right place, the technicals with weapons mounted on the rear, the flagpoles and flag. Then the ultimate confirmation: troops with weapons manning the checkpoint and the roads leading in and out.

'Target is good, multiple technicals and soldiers,' Reuben relayed to Nick.

'Visual. On your left, ready.' Nick confirmed he was looking at the same targets.

Reuben was already on the 30mm cannon and had fired the first 20-round burst, each of the rounds detonating as it struck the checkpoint, vehicles and road junction. Even if a round landed near rather than directly on a target, the fragmentation sprayed out with an effect similar to a high explosive grenade. He pulled the trigger again and again, methodically adjusting the fall of shot and working his way from one target to another.

The effect was immediate. Nick, as the looker, watched the 30mm arcing into the checkpoint in curved flight then exploding on impact. Twenty rapid high explosive detonations in a small space, all within two seconds, destroyed a technical. Then, just five seconds later, more rounds whipped in, another two-second twenty-point explosion wrecking the next vehicle. Pro-Gad vehicles and equipment erupted in fire and the ambushed soldiers sprinted from the scene, abandoning the checkpoint.

Nick finely focused his FLIR and methodically searched the checkpoint. There was no need for him to add to the hell on the ground. The checkpoint was out of action. Two vehicles were burning and their weapon operators were dead. Pro-Gad soldiers were in disarray and no one was attempting to fire into the sky – a sure sign that they knew such an action would be fatal. Nick had no need or wish to pull the trigger just because targets remained. The area was not obliterated, it hadn't been bombed into the Stone Age; it had simply been rendered non-operational. Better still, twenty to thirty pro-Gad were now out of work and unlikely to return.

Both aircraft watched as men ran out into the desert. These soldiers were about to spread the word – 'the Apache came to the mountains and we had no chance'. Desertion was a genuine option for these men and it was gathering momentum across the country. The gentle nudge of eighty rounds of 30mm was all the persuasion they needed.

With panic around the fire on the ground, Nick took the patrol out over the desert to the west and set up to run in on the final target, another checkpoint. The previous attack would have been audible to the men manning it, but they could not have known what had happened. Thundering guns and explosions, all over in less than a minute, was all they knew. Helicopters, probably, but confusion would be in every mind.

The third checkpoint guarded the junction between the main road to Tripoli and the road leading east to Garyān. It was surrounded by desert, there was nothing else there and it was isolated and vulnerable. Keeping the patrol far enough away not to be heard, Nick slaved his infrared sight to the coordinates, zoomed into the maximum magnification and immediately recognized the distinctive junction, the low, thin trees and a barrier across the road. He stepped out a field of view, decreasing the magnification, and watched a heavy truck approach from the north. It drew up to the barrier and stopped. An armed man emerged from a shack beside the road and stepped up to the driver's side. The soldier and the truck driver appeared to talk. The soldier pointed in the direction of checkpoint two and then at the mountains. Nick concluded they were trying to make sense of the confusion. After a minute the soldier opened the barrier and the truck rolled onward towards the front line.

Nick wanted a clean target, no visitors, and he took a few more seconds to search the rest of the checkpoint. It was lightly defended by sand berms driven into piles by a digger. Decent enough protection in a land battle, but no match for the Hellfire and 30mm that was about to come from the sky. Unseen and unheard, they made their final preparations for the attack. This time Nick was the shooter and Reuben was the looker.

With missiles ready, their seeker heads searching for his laser code, they banked in unison hard to the right, rolled out on an easterly heading, and Nick settled his sights on the lead technical behind a defensive berm. Still out of sound range, he breathed out slowly, paused, checked his missile had locked on to his laser, which in turn pointed directly at the technical, and spoke to Little Shippers: 'All good, firing.' His left index finger lifted the trigger guard and squeezed the thick, clunky trigger.

A quarter of a second later a roar and fire signalled the departure of a Hellfire missile from the right-hand side of his aircraft. The heat haze from the rocket motor obscured his infrared vision for a brief second and the 20lb warhead, boosted by a powerful solid fuel rocket motor, climbed before curving down to meet the terminal end of the laser energy on the technical. Nick kept his eye focused on the infrared image with his laser pointing at the target. In the rear seat Little Shippers allowed his left eye to watch the arc of the missile against the black night, first climbing, then apparently straightening, heading for the ground and hammering into the target. The Hellfire hit smack in the middle of the vehicle at the front of the flatbed, shredding the weapon mounted on the rear and ripping the cabin apart. A ferocious explosion was the giveaway sign of more ammunition inside going up with the missile impact. The whole truck burned intensely. Isolated checkpoint three was being destroyed.

'Too much obscuration from the fire, breaking off. Your target,' Nick called, and Little Shippers banked left, away from the attack, and invited Reuben to take on the shooter role.

He was already in position and ready to fire. Within 20 seconds the checkpoint building and another technical erupted in fire as thousands of white-hot Hellfire fragments smashed them beyond recognition. There was nothing left. The checkpoint had been totally dismantled in one pass lasting less than 30 seconds. Vehicles burned and the shack was reduced to splinters, a burning hole left where it once stood. At the first explosion the barrier soldier had run up one of the sand berms and he was rolling down the other side as the second technical was engaged. The berm had saved him, absorbing the Hellfire fragments and the shock wave. He rolled to the bottom of the sand bank, got up, then stumbled to the ground. Immediately he got to his knees and, once back on his feet, sprinted north. After about 20 seconds he slowed, stopped and dived headlong on to the ground, then curled up with his knees against his chest and held his head in his arms as if he was bracing and protecting himself. He was expecting to die.

Nick had no wish to kill him. This man was the bearer of the message, part of the cognitive effect, and Nick led the patrol away: 'Done. Regroup at the western holding point. My lead, one-hundred, one-hundred.'

With enough fuel and still plenty of ammunition left, they turned for home, contemplating another daunting coastal crossing. The easy desert transit went quickly. Flat, empty nothing was soon broken up by lights, roads, buildings and the hinterland. With 30mm guns actioned, infrared over right eye and all systems slaved to the trigger, the patrol spread their formation wide and hunted for hostility among the compounds, ditches, roads and trees.

With the coast in sight both front-seaters' eyes were drawn to a long slow stream of traffic ending at a military checkpoint just a couple of miles to their left. This was the road to Zuwara in the west and Az-Zawiyah and Tripoli to the east, a critical artery and a pro-Gad supply route. The regime had to control it, and that made them vulnerable.

With his right-hand trigger Nick sent out a pulse of laser energy that returned the bearing, distance and precise coordinates of the checkpoint. His right thumb tracked the target with the infrared, keeping it steady on the checkpoint, while with his left hand he stored the information in his target database.

Pressing the transmit switch on the floor with his left foot, he spoke to Reuben in Valkyrie Two: 'Checkpoint left nine o'clock two miles, stand by for data.'

Two seconds later, Reuben's onboard modem told him a new data package had arrived.

'Seen. Good data. Ready your QBOs.' Reuben now had the tactical picture and was ready to react.

Nick took the patrol out over the sea to relative safety while he made his plan of attack. They had passed the checkpoint close enough for the pro-Gad soldiers to hear them and start running. The recent experience of checkpoints along the same road only a few weeks before would have struck fear through their hearts. The pattern was well established: a checkpoint was set up, however surreptitiously; NATO would identify it and helicopters would be heard; seconds later, the checkpoint was destroyed. Manning a military checkpoint was both boring and dangerous work.

This checkpoint was outside Nick's target area and he needed NATO permission to strike an opportunity target. He got on the net to Matrix and described what he could see. Within seconds the answer came: 'You are clear to attack. Report BDA.'

Nick hit the transmit switch again: 'QBOs. Me shooter, you looker, trail left, break right. Attack heading one-nine-zero. Hellfire to gun, first trigger pull at 4,000m. Turning in now.'

Reuben read back the message to confirm his understanding as JB manoeuvred their Apache to keep the lead aircraft in sight just ahead. He had to watch the target to observe the strike and assist if required; they also had to watch out for any incoming fire in return, effectively becoming the guardian for the patrol.

It was a straight, uncomplicated shoot. The checkpoint soldiers had made a poor attempt to hide themselves and their vehicles among some trees near the road. In taking the patrol out to sea Nick had gone out of audible range, making the soldiers on the ground think they had hidden successfully. But by not joining the traffic they had differentiated themselves, displayed their weapons and underlined their legitimacy as a target. The two or three minutes all this had taken had also been enough for the traffic to move on, leaving a clear, unambiguous target free of any civilians. Hiding among trees may have given sufficient cover to avoid a high-up jet strike, but the low-flying Apache could see beneath the branches, right into the hiding place. There was no cover, and hell was about to thunder in off the sea.

Little Shippers counted down the range: 'All steady . . . in constraints . . . five hundred to go. Missile will come off the left side.' His calm tone was intended to reduce the adrenaline that accompanies shooting.

In the front seat Nick was absorbing the forty or so pieces of symbology in his right eye telling him the Hellfire was ready and locked-on and his laser was functioning correctly, and giving him every detail he would ever need about the aircraft's height, speed, power and heading. He could tell where Little Shippers was looking, where the other aircraft was in relation to him, where the target was and where the coast was. He had to select which information was immediately important. He knew the target was his priority. Reuben and JB would do everything he needed from the wing aircraft, and Little Shippers would deal with their own positioning and aircraft management. Now Nick just had to select the target and decide whether it was good to shoot or not.

He could see which vehicles were manned and which were empty. Selecting the empty vehicle furthest from the pro-Gad soldiers, he actioned a Hellfire missile with his left thumb and pulled the trigger with his index finger. The missile roared away from the aircraft and obliterated the vehicle.

Nick paused. He could have launched two more missiles in quick succession and controlled all three in the air at once. But this would have given no chance to pro-Gad on the ground, and he didn't need them to die. He needed to deny their vehicles, their weapons and their equipment, but he wanted them to have a chance to run for their lives. And they did so with impressive speed. Ten soldiers threw away their AKs and leapt over each other to put distance between themselves and the checkpoint. Three more missiles followed into the technicals at the now abandoned checkpoint. Four vehicles gone, no loss of life, checkpoint scrubbed and more pro-Gad out of work. Job done. The patrol turned north and headed for *Ocean*.

Back in the Ops Room the JCHAT feed that had been idle for 90 minutes streamed a SITREP:

Valkyrie.  7xHellfire,  540x30mm.  Targets  destroyed. 6xTechnicals, 1xbuilding, multiple mil pers. Zero CD. Zero civcas. Outbound. ETA 10mins.[10]

Another result, and they were on their way back. *Ocean* got into position to receive the aircraft, and a couple of minutes later Nick came over the net: 'Valkyrie inbound, Mother visual. Weapons safe.'

I remained in the Ops Room until the roar of both aircraft could be heard on the flight deck. The front-seaters would be getting out of the aircraft very soon and making their way down to the flip-flop. My next job was to debrief the patrol, review the guntape and draft the MISREP. John and I took the maps and the timeline and headed off to the flip-flop. We descended the chain ladder into the planning compartment and saw Nick already in and signing in his personal weapons and morphine.

John was straight in with the baiting: 'Sir, seven Hellfire and no ZSU 23-4? What happened, did you miss it?'

'Didn't see it, must have been switched off and hiding,' Nick offered, knowing he was about to be mauled.

John turned to me. 'See, if we'd been on it that ZSU would have been done right with the first trigger pull, no problem.' He looked at Nick. 'So, just me and the boss with the ZSU kill then. Shame, I thought you were going to join our exclusive club. Never mind.' Then, with an even more sarcastic inflection: 'Come on, load up your guntape and let's see what a pick-up truck looks like when a Hellfire hits it . . . again.'

Nick, damp through with the sweat of another combat mission and long low-level sea track, could only chuckle and sit down to write the MISREP.

His narrative was the now prescriptive retelling of the facts – heights and speeds, headings and missile launches, coordinates and target effect. Checkpoints and technicals again, but they were significant. If the regime controlled the roads the FLF would be held back. If we knocked the checkpoints out, fear of loitering attack helicopters would encourage more desertions, the roads would be clear and the FLF could move. The no-show from the ZSU 23-4 was good news; being surprised by one of those could have presented a very different outcome. We reviewed the guntape and finished the MISREP.

From an initial five addressees, we now had to send our MISREP to over thirty people, and our Ops team had to work through until breakfast to edit and upload the guntape footage. Every other day a new email would arrive from someone in London demanding to get early sight of the MISREP 'so I can brief my boss'. I knew that by the time I got to my cabin, tired and grateful that we'd got through another mission without coming unstuck, officers in London would be opening their email, reading the MISREP and viewing the footage.

The scrutiny was intense, much of it necessary and useful. Some of it, however, was just access to information. Occasionally, contextless questions were generated that made our days longer than they needed to be and made me wonder if these people really knew where we were and what we were doing. Ignoring the CAOC, they would reach right into the ship to question us. Bypassing those who knew our work, they made the electronic leap of thousands of miles to ask 'Why did you fly there?' or 'Why did you shoot that?' Often such missives were double- or triple-sent over a period of hours, if the initial email was not answered immediately. Of course, by the time the London latte had cooled enough to drink and the email was sent, I was asleep in my cabin. The question-generator didn't know that, and the third email would usually arrive with highlighted demands for his second-guessing by about lunchtime. Which was also, as it happened, the time that I would get out of bed.

Back at the sharp end of the war, the FLF had watched the mission going in. Pro-Gad did desert, and a gaping hole opened just where the regime needed to be strong. Colonel El-Moktar Firnana took his opportunity, and the following day Libyan rebels began to advance north, taking ground previously held by Gaddafi. A tentatively planned Apache strike against more checkpoints was aborted late that night due to uncertainty over who was where on the ground. We chalked up another cancellation, but the irony was that the success of our first strike on the third front was putting us out of business.

## Chapter 13

# Okba and the 99th Hellfire

With the roads out of the mountains now contested and the utility of the Apache proven, Glen Parker settled on the Okba airfield staging ground for a mission. If Okba was put out of commission the FLF could advance out of the mountains on two or three routes, take the north coast and move on Tripoli. Opening up more than one avenue meant the regime would be spread too thinly to hold back the FLF. With Az-Zawiyah under threat they would probably withdraw to defensive positions around the town. Once that fell, their final option would be to defend the regime in Tripoli itself. NATO now needed to open those routes north and north-east while still attempting to kill the regime from the top down. For our part, we were firmly on the front line creating opportunities for the FLF to advance.

Two days after the first raid we sent another patrol towards the mountains, this time further inland than we had ever gone. The target was Okba airfield and a checkpoint nearby. Although the aircraft and the surface-to-air missile battery that once operated from there had been destroyed, pro-Gad were still using the area as a staging post for soldiers to gather and then set off for the front line. It was their last safe place before meeting the FLF. Our task was to take it from them, removing their safety and destroying as much equipment as possible. If this worked it would create a gap in the front line where no pro-Gad could show up. The FLF could then move forward, the next stop being the coast and then Az-Zawiyah. If we failed, the FLF would have to fight their way up a single road and through the desert to reach the coast. This would cost lives, take weeks and could ultimately be repelled if the regime were clever enough. This was an opportunity, a tipping point, the chance for the FLF to get the momentum they needed to make a rush on Tripoli.

The plan was almost identical to the earlier raid. Nick was the patrol commander. He and Charlie Tollbrooke took the callsign Underdog One. Big Shippers and Jay Lewis, in the wing aircraft, joined them as Underdog Two. But Okba was a long way inland. More time low-level over Libya meant more opportunities for pro-Gad to have a go. We still needed to keep *Ocean* over the horizon and inconspicuous, so they had to accept the distance and resolve to keep enough ammunition in reserve in case they got into a fight on the return leg. The long transit also meant that there was little time on target. This, in turn, meant that decisions to shoot and re-engage would have to be quick and precise. We considered whether fitting additional fuel tanks would be useful but rejected the idea once Little Shippers calculated the extra weight this added. Extra weight meant less Hellfire. Less Hellfire was the wrong answer.

The CAOC said it was a 'Go' even without a Pred on the mission. We had fast jets with Litening Pods and laser-guided missiles able to dash between Tripoli and us in a matter of minutes. If we got into trouble they were to lend a hand, and if we needed to find a tricky target they might look down and guide us on. That was the plan, anyway, and it all looked good on the slide they sent through. But we doubted whether a jet was going to help in a SAMbush; he couldn't do so unless his pod could see into the future, which, with all the wiggly amps in the world, it couldn't. Still, we were winning with every mission and this was going to be no different.

Nick briefed his plan. It was simple: arrive, observe, decide shoot or no shoot, move on and repeat at the next target. At the final 'Go/No Go' brief the Intelligence Officer told us of an increase in pro-Gad activity on the coast and reinforcements moving south from Zuwara towards the mountains. A column of eight vehicles had been reported in the target area. There might be more targets than we had ammunition for, but it was too late to spin up two more aircraft and make a four-ship; Nick would have to judge his ammunition expenditure.

Again, John and I were in the Ops Room, timeline and map laid out on the desk, JCHAT glowing and the 56th Rescue Squadron hanging around waiting for a shoot-down to dive into. At the given time the aircraft lifted and ducked low into the night. Within a few seconds the howl of their engines had faded and *Ocean* turned south-west, heading for the recovery point.

The radios and the JCHAT remained silent for the next two hours. *Ocean* cut a tight circuit at the recovery point and the Ops Room got restless, then anxious. Two hours was just about on the fuel limit; a few more minutes and they would be burning into their minimum fuel for landing.

At the two hour and five minute point the radio burst into Nick's request to join and land. Wings was up in Flyco with his senior controller. 'Cleared straight in,' came the reply. I did a quick fuel calculation in my head: they should be right on their minimum, a minute or two more and we could be listening to an emergency. No need. The aircraft landed in turn, and five minutes later Nick and Big Shippers were in the flip-flop, guntape ready on screens set up side by side.

I climbed down into the flip-flop. Big Shippers looked up at the chain ladder: 'Sorry we're late, bit of a bob and a weave on the egress. Small problem with helicopter hunters on the coast. Shot it, but then thought it wise to give the whole area a wide berth.'

'No holes?'

'None,' Nick put in. 'Techs won't know until they get them into the hangar, but none felt.'

'Fuel okay?'

'To the pound. Spot on, in fact,' Big Shippers answered.

'Good. Now let's see this helicopter hunter thing.' I walked over to the guntape screens.

'Ah, no, not yet,' said Nick. 'First you have to see what eight technicals look like before and after a trigger pull! We were down to ten-round bursts on the gun. We needed all five aircraft out there, it was swarming!'

I sat down in front of two screens, Underdog One's guntape on the left, Underdog Two's on the right, and began to watch the synchronized minute-by-minute playback of an extraordinary mission.

With Nick and Big Shippers filling in the detail of radio calls and in-cockpit communication not heard on the guntape, I tracked the timeline into the first target. What I saw was staggering. Eight vehicles, engines warm, weapons mounted and soldiers nearby, were parked right on the coordinates. The technicals were strung out in an east-west line beside an apparently abandoned set of sheds not far from the road. Underdog One had been looking at the first planned target area when Underdog Two had spotted them just a few hundred metres away. Around twenty pro-Gad soldiers sat 50m to the north of the technicals. As the aircraft closed and the crosshair of the FLIR interrogated the target, the soldiers got up and started walking with purpose, just a little too quickly to be natural, away from the technicals.

Nick described his thoughts: 'That was it for me. They showed technicals and weapons. And that they were trying to put distance between themselves and the technicals completed the picture. That and the AKs you can see each of them carrying! I broke off and gave Underdog Two a laser target handover for the technicals.'

Nick, now too close to go straight into the attack, used his laser to hand over the confirmed targets to his wing aircraft. Jay's FLIR, set to laser search mode, immediately settled on the technicals. The well-trained and experienced crew had anticipated Nick's demands and were ready to take on the technicals.

Big Shippers took up the story: 'It was difficult commanding from the back seat. There were so many targets we could have got three missiles off right away and steered each into a different technical, but I could see there were still some pro-Gad hiding in the folds of ground near the centre of the group. Jay was searching every technical for the best one to engage first. The one on the left looked empty so we went for that one, giving the poor sods a chance to change their minds.'

From the symbology on the guntape I could see Underdog Two was ready to fire, laser pulsing and missile seeker-head locked on. I watched the first Hellfire go in. The missile left the right-hand rail of the aircraft, briefly leaving some heat shimmer on the video image, then tracked for the concentration of laser energy on the first technical. It hit dead centre of the flatbed, just where a weapon, probably a ZU-23-2, was mounted. The technical was destroyed in a huge explosion, indicating more ammunition had gone up with the Hellfire hit. Jay's sight then moved four technicals to the right before moving back to the left. There were still some pro-Gad trying to hide, lying down close to the right-hand vehicles, while others were crawling away close by. Jay brought the sight back left to the technical next along from the now intensely burning first target. Continuing to engage from the left would allow the pro-Gad further right to get up their courage and start running.

The second Hellfire ripped the next technical apart, detonating its ammunition. This was confirmation for the crawlers; they got up and ran for their lives. Jay checked the third technical and observed a soldier get up and run away to the right, before pulling the trigger for a third time and sending another Hellfire in. He was now too close for more Hellfire and needed to save some for the next target. Changing the FLIR polarity from white-hot to black-hot, he flicked his left thumb up to de-action the missile and bring his gun online. With the aircraft fast closing on his breakaway point, he sent four 20-round bursts of 30mm into the two central technicals. Switching back to white-hot FLIR, he sent another 100 rounds on five bursts into three more technicals, with Big Shippers guiding the aircraft on a left break.

The whole engagement, from first Hellfire hitting the left-hand technical to the last 30mm hitting the eighth technical to its right, took

1 minute 35 seconds. Eight technicals destroyed or damaged, no one dead and up to twenty-five pro-Gad out of work in just over a minute and a half. And Underdog hadn't even got to their main target yet! This sequence was declassified the following day by the Ministry of Defence under the 'defenceheadquarters' tag and released to the media as an example of our activity that night. It can be seen on YouTube; just google 'Apache Libya'.[11]

I turned the page over on Nick's briefing pack and looked at the route to Okba, the primary target for the mission. Nick and Big Shippers clicked forward the infrared guntape and played part two of their night over Libya.

Okba airfield had been a regime airbase for decades. Well away from the bustle of the coast and the attention of Tripoli, it sat untouched in the desert. One road linked it north with Zuwara, 35 miles away, and the Nafusa Mountains, another 40 miles to the south. When the civil war began its accidental importance emerged, as a natural pro-Gad supply and staging post. Just as quickly, the third front line formed in the tribal areas of the mountains and NATO began searching for targets. Okba had been watched for months. It was active and gaining a reputation as an important part of Gaddafi's southern operation. Occasional overflights had brought back photographs; analysts pored over them and concluded it was an active military area, no civilians, all activity nefarious and good to strike.

Only five miles north-east of the burning technicals, the regime operators at Okba would have heard the chaos coming from the sky, so the Apaches had to get there quickly and make fast decisions to maintain their momentum.

Now Underdog One and Two were banking hard round to the right, levelling out on their pre-briefed attack heading, infrared sights slaved to the Okba coordinates. Nick had two minutes to run, barely enough time to race through the pages on his MPDs, check his fuel state and weapons configuration and read the map. This was where meticulous planning, briefing and rehearsal took over. All four pilots knew what to do next. They'd all planned it, walked the map, the headings and the heights, briefed it and answered questions to check their understanding; now they were living it out second by second over Libya. NVG over the left eye, infrared zoomed in close over the right, both front-seaters went hunting for targets and threats.

From five miles out Okba looked quiet: no movement, just scores of silent buildings on an apparently disused desert airfield. They flew past the destroyed surface-to-air missile site to the south-west of the airfield, checking it was out of action, and settled their sights on the airfield itself.

Nick fast-forwarded the tape, describing his decision to move in close: 'I wanted the standoff range to maintain surprise and use the jet to suggest areas of interest, but they saw nothing. I asked the jets if they could see any movement, any targets, but they came back with a negative. "Nothing seen down there," was his phrase. We decided to take a look anyway.'

Okba airfield stood lonely and apparently empty, its parallel east-west runways unused in months and its aircraft apron on the north side completely bare. About 100m north of the runways stood the distinctive pentagonal compound with Hardened Aircraft Shelters (HASs) forming spokes from its hub. The HASs were out of use, destroyed by delayed-fused 2,000lb bombs from miles up right at the start of the campaign. Since then the airfield had had no air utility and the place had been left to get hot and gather sand. But pro-Gad was using it to store equipment and rest soldiers prior to sending them south to the Nafusa Mountains. It was their safe place to make plans, gather weapons and set off to attack the FLF and civilians in the mountains.

'See those five HASs.' Nick pointed at the screen. 'There's a heat source in a second . . .'

And gradually I could see an emerging heat spot glowing white against cooler black temperatures and moving across the ground to the west of the pentagon. I wanted to see more, and as if anticipating this the FLIR zoomed in closer to identify the mover. The white-hot glow grew and took shape: a man, hunched over, carried something long and heavy across both arms. He moved quickly in a straight line and stopped suddenly in the open where a mark on the ground, about 10m long and a metre wide, crossed his path. Then it was as if he was enveloped into the mark – his body appeared to be swallowed and only his head remained visible.

'Trench system,' said Nick. 'Look here and here, there's loads of them.' He pointed out similar marks around the airfield on Jay and Big Shipper's guntape. 'They've run out from the buildings and positioned themselves in trenches, and that is probably a MANPAD he's just dropped off. They must have heard the commotion to the south-west. I reckon they were getting ready to defend the airfield.'

With the preceding target just five miles away, the sound of the Hellfire and 30mm ripping up eight technicals would have carried easily in the desert night. Any pro-Gad in Okba would be ready and waiting, expecting the Apache to visit. The movement on the ground looked like classic pre-launch anti-helicopter work. Zlitan twice, and the Brega mission, had told us that much.

Nick sent in a Hellfire and instantly changed the picture. Then 30mm followed up the Hellfire and the manned trench ceased to be a threat.

As Underdog One broke away to the left Jay and Big Shippers, who had been searching for targets in the same area, were cleared in to the attack.

Jay destroyed a pair of warm-engined military trucks near the trench system and, shifting his sights further north still by another 100m, settled on a communications node with its satellite dishes and antennas pointing north-east towards Tripoli. With one Hellfire and now low on ammunition, he switched to the minimum 10-round, one-second bursts and added 60 rounds of 30mm in a 30-second onslaught that cut Okba off from the rest of Libya. Now it was isolated, and on fire. The place where from where the regime thought it could mount attacks into the mountains was broken and in disarray.

The inter-aircraft radios were cackling with information about target coordinates, pro-Gad runners, weapons systems being moved and vehicles moving and hiding. But it had already been a long mission, ammunition was running out and both aircraft were low on fuel for the long, hostile transit back to the coast and beyond.

Between the two aircraft they picked off four more vehicles, sending pro-Gad once again racing into the desert, useless without his weapons. With just two laser-guided Hellfire and sixty 30mm left, Jay and Big Shippers noticed their fuel was now at 'bingo' – the minimum quantity left to allow a safe return to *Ocean*. It was time to leave, and Nick made the decision to do so. With targets racing around the airfield it seemed ridiculous, but the point had been made and jet man had better things to do over Tripoli; so, cursing the fact that he had just two Apaches in his patrol, Nick directed Charlie and Big Shippers to turn north and begin the low-level transit back to Mother.

Nick and Charlie took the lead, but Charlie was off form, he couldn't keep it straight and level, the aircraft was off heading, its height constantly changing. Being very low-level, this nibbled precariously at the margins for error.

'Sorry, Nick, HMD on the blink. Keeps dropping out. Everything is wonky. Static in the eye, no feeds, symbology off, using the NVG on the left to keep us somewhere decent.'

Charlie was dealing with a Helmet Mounted Display failure. The information being projected into his right eye was intermittent and more of a distraction than an aid to low-level combat flying. In a low threat environment the aircraft could have climbed away from the ground to a safer height and allowed the crew time to rectify the fault. Not here. Not 50 miles inland behind regime lines. They had to stay low and accept that they were down to one set of eyes.

'Okay, got it, I have control.' Nick took the flight controls while Charlie tried to wrestle the technology and set himself up to fly the return leg.

Meanwhile, Nick transmitted to Jay and Big Shippers, 'Heading zero-one-zero, your lead, we're lame duck, HMD failure in rear seat, call passing.'

Big Shippers was straight on the net: 'My lead, passing left-hand side 30 seconds heading zero-one-zero.'

He and Jay now took control of the patrol as it entered its most vulnerable stage. The transit back to the coast was over new ground, 60 nautical miles of it, all pro-Gad. During planning, the satellite imagery looked clear of habitation, and their chosen crossing point to the Med was only a few miles away from the Tunisian border. The patrol had kept to their fuel calculations and they had just enough to get across the desert and then coast out to find *Ocean*. Both aircraft knew they were in the final and uniquely exposed phase of the mission: low on fuel, very low on ammunition, a long time inland and with pro-Gad waiting for them to come back north and cross the coast. If the regime was going to stop an Apache, this was their chance. Tonight the added complication was that only one Apache was fully operational, and it was providing both navigation and defence for both.

In Underdog One Nick was flying, hands on the control, as well as searching for threats, while tracking Jay and Big Shippers, who were able to search and navigate while taking the lead.

They raced at 120 knots low-level across the barren emptiness, scanning all the while. With ten miles to run until the heightened anxiety of crossing the coast, Jay picked up a heat-spot on his FLIR hidden amongst some trees – probably a life-saving observation.

He notified Big Shippers: 'Technical, right 2 o'clock, 2 kilometres. Group of trees. Technical in the centre. Weapons on the rear, dismounts seen. Actioning missile!'

In the rear seat the master of Apache gunnery glanced in at his right-hand MPD displaying Jay's FLIR video image and directed Jay: 'Coming right. It's too close to fence around. Underdog One is

vulnerable. Coming into constraints, you have one shot. Closing fast
. . . good Lock-On Before Launch, missile will come off the left rail
. . . ready.'

Big Shippers had expertly aligned the aircraft to give Jay direct line
of sight through the trees at low height. Three pro-Gad soldiers were
hiding, attempting to keep a tree between them and the aircraft, but they
weren't the target. The threat was on the back of the technical; a large
weapon system, possibly a MANPAD, was mounted on its rear.

On the inter-aircraft radio Jay told Nick what was going on and what
was about to happen: 'Technical at zero-two-zero, less than 2 kilometres,
engaging now.'

Closing on the technical at over 100 knots gave Jay just two seconds
to get his missile in the air; any delay would mean the Hellfire might
not have time to boost away from the Apache and gather the laser energy
to steer itself to the target. Fast-moving, close-in missile firing requires
a deft touch and lightning quick decision-making. Recognizing his
chance would be over in a heartbeat, he pulled the trigger and sent his
sixth Hellfire of the night into the technical. It took less than four
seconds to reach the target. As the missile struck the technical a
concussive wave of energy and shrapnel washed through the trees. Jay
instantly stepped out a field of view on the FLIR and saw the three men,
their backs to the trees between them and the wreckage of their technical.
At less than one kilometre from the mayhem Jay saw three more pro-
Gad out of work.

'Delta Hotel! Technical destroyed head left three-four-zero to avoid.
Slowing to 80 knots for you to catch up.' Big Shippers passed the good
news on to Underdog One.

With the patrol linked up, but still with seven miles to run to the
coast, the danger had not passed. The technical in the trees had got their
collective adrenaline pumping and Underdog Two, still in the lead, had
just one laser-guided Hellfire and a handful of 30mm left. More
concerning was the fuel. Effectively running through the technical,
rather than boxing around it, had saved a few pounds of fuel, but it was
still going to require precision navigation from both *Ocean* and the
Apaches to avoid embarrassment over the sea.

Their final leg took them out over the coast past a narrow eight-mile
long spit of land providing a natural shelter to fishing boats, only a few
miles from the Tunisian border. Jay could see several boats afloat
directly on his flight path. Stepping out to the widest field of view with
the FLIR, he could see small boats left and right too.

'Coming right.' Big Shippers weaved the patrol between the boats, and they left Libya behind. It seemed that early August was the big fishing season in western Libya. They had to treat each boat as a potential threat, keeping low to avoid them. The AWACS up high and SKASaC out at sea fed them a stream of avoiding manoeuvres over the radio. This meant they could not follow a straight line to *Ocean* and consequently edged towards their fuel reserves, eventually landing just as Big Shippers reported – spot on, to the pound.

In the flip-flop all four aircrew looked exhausted. It had been a long night and our longest mission. It was also our most successful in terms of targets struck – only slightly disappointing in that it was not a four-ship.

Doug Reid, doing his ammunition accounting, called across to Jay, 'That was Hellfire 99 for the op so far, Jay.'

Another ten Hellfire could have been used at Okba, but that could wait for another day, we thought. The CO came in to see the debrief and immediately got on the phone to the CAOC to pass on the story. The third front was very much ours to deal with. We'd proved it again. But it had not been easy; it was risky, and the margins for error on the return leg had been very slim. We knew we were mortal, and pro-Gad only needed to be lucky once.

On the ground three scenarios now looked likely. One was that the FLF would turn the broken regime military over. The FLF would then march unhindered into the capital and take control. The second was a long bitter fight north, gaining and losing ground, eventually reaching Az-Zawiyah and Tripoli, where the agony of fighting an urban battle would turn the capital into a Stalingrad. The third, and least likely, scenario was that Gaddafi would realize he was losing and either surrender (very unlikely) or flee along with his inner circle, leaving the regime leaderless. The innumerable dynamics of war eventually yielded an amalgam of all three scenarios, but in early August any one of them looked likely. What was certain on 6 August 2011 was that a gaping hole had opened up, perhaps coincidentally, directly to the south of Okba. Within hours the FLF were on the march north. And pro-Gad were not there to stop them.

*Chapter 14*

# Finishing with War –
# Only Two Average Days

After two weeks of unlaunched deck alerts, tuned to the fight but hearing the 'do not fire' orders from the decision men in the CAOC to jet man in the sky, we knew our work was done. There were no more opportunities without tightly coordinated and dynamic targeting. We needed live eyes on the target to launch and talk us on. With no boots on the ground, the eyes had to be airborne at the same time as us.

We tried it once with a UK Joint Terminal Attack Controller (JTAC) in a maritime patrol aircraft off the coast of Zlitan. The JTAC spent three hours watching tanks and artillery arriving in the vicinity of pro-Gad positions. I was on deck with Reuben and JB as the wing, all systems checked, all ready to go, *Ocean* primed, everyone on their silent timeline. In the aircraft we listened to the Strike net.

JTAC to Matrix: 'Five Main Battle Tanks, three multi-launch rocket systems on trucks. All pointing east towards Zlitan.'

Me to John: 'Yes, in just a minute we'll get the signal to launch . . .'

Matrix: 'Roger.'

JTAC: 'They came from the west, from the pro-Gad lines.'

Me: 'Ready for rotors . . .'

'Roger. We are uncertain of the pattern of life. It is considered an ambiguous situation,' came the view from Italy.

Me: 'What?! He's not making it up!'

JTAC: 'I have been observing for three hours. I understand this pattern of life. This is *my* positive identification. These are pro-Gad targets! What do I need to do to get you to launch AH?' His frustration loaded the transmission.

Me: 'Three hours! Let's launch!'

Matrix: 'AH have been stood down. No target.'

Me: 'What?!'

Silence. Darkness and silence. And, just west of Zlitan, 32 Brigade covered their retreat.

Back on *Ocean* I leant back in my seat, powered down the weapon systems and let my thoughts out: 'That's it. Our work is done. If they won't launch us to that target we won't do any more of this.'

A minute later Doug tapped on the canopy. 'It's a cancel! Stand down, no target!' he yelled through the engine noise.

The targeting decisions made in the CAOC had been very sound in the preceding months. Now, with the front lines broken out and fighting springing up in new areas hourly, understanding the ground truth had changed. They could no longer huddle round reconnaissance photographs, reflect on legal advice and spend an afternoon arriving at a decision. The situation on the ground was changing quickly and the established method of target decision-making was no longer valid. The comfort of time had gone, and along with it went the certainty of being right. The decision men in the CAOC could either delegate or say 'no'. They said 'no' and thus regained certainty.

What was once a clear picture of pro-Gad, front line and FLF was now one large contested space. Targets identified by reconnaissance in the morning had moved by midday, got engaged in fights, were abandoned, deserted or destroyed. The regime and the rebels had the same equipment, and there was no way of telling who was who except, perhaps, by spending time observing what they were doing. To launch strikes into this risked ruining the now tentative opportunity of success. NATO, who for months had stared at an impasse, was trying to make sense of the rebel advance and needed to put the brakes on air strikes until the hundreds of men in flying suits watching screens and holding meetings understood the ground.

Off the coast of Zlitan the maritime patrol aircraft continued its observation. The JTAC was a soldier and he'd spent more than a decade understanding ground in combat, intuitively knowing the difference between normal and hostile. He could see and understand. He hadn't thrashed past at 500 knots and taken a photograph – a fraction of a second – for someone else to analyse. He was watching, and had been watching for hours. And he was there, in the present. He understood the pattern of life and he knew he was right. Pro-Gad was on the move; Khamis had lost Misrata and was knocking over Zlitan on his way back west. The JTAC, in a maritime patrol aircraft, was witnessing and relaying the whole retreat.

We could launch. He could talk us on. He knew the situation on the ground. We had sixteen Hellfire between us and well over a thousand rounds of 30mm. The last fighting forces of 32 Brigade could be stopped and the regime could be presented with another problem as they searched for an escape from the growing rebel advance. But there was a residual risk – 'maybe, just maybe, the tanks and artillery now bombarding civilian Zlitan could be FLF'. It was easier to say 'no', whatever the reality, however absurd the 'no' was at the time. It was their civil war after all.

With the FLF on the march and pro-Gad increasingly in disarray, NATO sensed it was time to shelve risk. No need to launch vulnerable helicopters when jets could burn holes in the sky with invulnerable abandon; and there was not even any need for those jets to be given authority to launch their weapons. The stalemate was over and the tipping point had arrived. The risk-versus-reward calculation for NATO was now about securing a quick clean exit, reputation protected and enhanced, with no unnecessary damage – even if that meant not shooting targets that would have been taken on the previous week.

Nine deck alert missions in twelve nights had resulted in no target and no launch; almost half of our cancellations had occurred in the two weeks after the rebel advance. That so many missions were cancelled would later be considered a statistic somehow underpinning failure, an easy number for the naysayers to embrace. Someone totalled up our combat flying hours and inaccurately worked out how long it would take to fly the same in 24/7 Helmand, then adding their own easy-chair opinion that our total was equivalent to just a couple of days' work for the Apache in Afghanistan.

Facile comparisons with gold-plated Helmand were disappointing. Our work in Helmand had gone on since 656 was first across the line five years earlier; in Libya, however, we were involved in a new and unprecedented operation given to us with just six days' notice. To compare the high profile security presence of a counter-insurgency campaign with the high intensity fight of air to ground combat misinterprets the character of both types of conflict.

On Operation Ellamy we flew to targets to shoot them, not to reassure them, escort them or watch over them. We were direct and clinical, and we were not in the business of waiting around. We shot our way into Libya, shot the targets and shot our way out again, all the while being shot at ourselves. To strike all our targets, and survive that hell from the ground, could only be done with minimum exposure. To do it with a small team and only five aircraft, given all the layers of constraint and scrutiny, and to base the entire enterprise from a ship – this was exceptional. To paint that achievement as a negative is bizarre.

I defy those commentators to fly hundreds of hours a week over such a hostile place and see if they come back! Libya in the summer of 2011 was not a place to accumulate flying hours day and night, it was a place to be survived. Libya was precision fighting with specific targets for the Apache. A comparison of hours flown in Libya with hours flown in Helmand was meaningless.

These comments were not made in isolation; there seemed to be an undercurrent of misinformation in some corners of Defence. Some curious opinions were offered: 'they needed their hands held by the jets' and 'they were in the way' were popular comments among some who weren't there. These might seem fair when considered from the viewpoint of jet man, but from where we flew, approximately 24,900ft beneath him, it did not feel like our hands were held. The jets were packaged with us to mitigate risk. But a jet wasn't going to stop PKM man or SA-24 man or triple-A man, the three biggest threats to our lives. They weren't going to spot the wires or stop us crashing into the sea while chaffing away from a radar lock-on. Each time those events occurred we dealt with them ourselves. The jets never shot a target for us, nor did they ever find one for us. In that final mission, when the patrol almost ran out of ammunition, jet man said he couldn't see anything 'down there'.

I suspect the jets were as bored by this task as we were frustrated with its insistence. They were happily launching big munitions with great accuracy from miles out, until we came along and made everything complicated. This blurred our worth among colleagues in Gioia del Colle, the airbase in southern Italy from which most UK fast jet sorties were launched. When Apache missions flew, the jets were there in case something really big got up and launched; then perhaps, after the first helicopter was downed, they could engage the missile site. But the reality of our missions bore out the truth that it is the shoulder-launched missile, the triple-A and the man with the machine gun that can damage helicopters. In combat in Libya, we discovered, the only thing that looked after an Apache was another Apache.

A much more credible blend of jet and helicopter came with the combined missions, packages where we simultaneously attacked the same target area – as we did in that week in late July. These were a fast, lethal and accurate use of composite jet and helicopter power. They dealt with risk and targets all at once, and left pro-Gad vulnerable to attack by the rebels. But these represented less than a quarter of our missions. The rest, when we went to our own targets, required jets to 'hold our hands', whatever that meant.

Spending the summer and autumn at sea gave us no exposure to the critics; it also allowed them to mount their narrative unchallenged. By the time we came ashore we had two reputations: one positive, a story of courage and innovation in a risky place; the other much less so, one of hollow opinion and bad science. We should have been able to brief our experience, show some examples of new methods of using the aircraft, write a report and see what could be taken forward from our evolution of flying the Apache in combat. But division had been established.

Some stayed behind desks on the day of the Post-Operational Report, and I presented our experience to the Attack Helicopter Force with empty seats in the front row. Some even lent their ignorance to journalists. Then the journalists published it, and the real story started to get lost. This is how innovation dies in a vertical hierarchy. This is where we start losing wars that haven't even begun.

An exhaustive 'lessons identified' process was conducted. Reports were written, both secret and open. We filed all our post-mission reports, target packs and trigger pulls. Everything that had been part of our experience was written down, filed and stored as our Operational Record. The truth is there. I lectured at home and abroad, speaking in France, Italy, the USA and Canada. I briefed our own people, too, but those who showed up were the ones who wanted to know.

Much was made about the cost of flying jets from Britain to launch expensive missiles at targets in Libya. Much was also made of the comparison between keeping a ship loitering off the coast of Libya and deploying a squadron, lock-stock, hotels, mini-buses and jets, to Italy. Questions were asked and answered in Parliament, and taxpayers got regular updates on where their money went. In the end, the cost estimates varied from £300 million to £1.25 billion for the whole UK contribution to the operation, depending on how the costs were calculated and attributed. MPs and commentators disputed each other's claims and the House of Commons Defence Committee recorded the lot.[12] They also detailed the sorties flown, aircraft and vessels deployed and numbers of personnel committed to the operation. Cost as the deciding metric in conflict is a peculiarly political obsession. The delicate balance of doing the right thing against how much of the national revenue should be spent can make or fail a government. And it is important to the man watching the news on the telly that he knows his taxes are being spent wisely.

History will often be unkind when finance trumps defence needs. But the fact remains – far-off places with a coast are best reached by sea. The fourth *Ark Royal* and her Buccaneers preserved British Honduras in 1972, and most likely saved the ship and her air capability. The South Atlantic in 1982 repeated the lesson, this time with *Hermes* and *Invincible*. Again, in the early 1990s, the fifth *Ark Royal* launched Harriers over Bosnia, and finally, in 2003, both *Ocean* and *Ark Royal* went to Iraq in the helicopter role. One may conclude that expeditionary maritime power, complete with soldiers, helicopters and jets, is a most versatile way of projecting defence.

But in 2010 savings had to be made, and big-ticket items had to go. We were broke. There was no more money. And when government realized they hadn't quite saved enough, more cuts, mostly to people, followed. The recession, financial sobriety and fiscal responsibility drove thinking across all departments. The economy was the highest priority and nothing would be allowed to imperil its shoring up and recovery. Savings were made in every aspect of public finance.

Sadly, the frugal lens reached the front. Pretend men renting time on operations brought thrifty bywords with them. Emulating the parsimony of the man in 'town' was in fashion. I remember listening to a combat description from Afghanistan where, it was said, a passing officer commented on how expensive it was to fire Hellfire missiles. This story duly made its way around the aviation community and still gets the occasional mention when aircrew review guntape.

So, as the righteous accountant trundled off, leaving soldiers stunned, wise incredulity in mock enquiry broke the silence: 'When a soldier calls for assistance, do I need to tap in the cost of that assistance and ask him if he can afford it? I think not . . .'

And they all went back to work, unchanged. The aircrew had all killed men with Hellfire, expensive Hellfire. They all continued to do so. As the tour went on and more Hellfire were used, no further mention was made of money. Perhaps it fell out of fashion.

Alas, the 2010 Strategic Defence and Security Review did not predict the Arab Spring, the last incarnation of the great *Ark Royal* with her air capability was cast aside and a chip was knocked out of the national deficit. Had this not happened she would probably have sailed for Libya, Harriers embarked, in 2011.

In their place, seven months later, sat *Ocean* and the Apache and much, much higher risk. Had nothing changed in 2010 we might still have ended up in Libya, but the blend would have been different, the options much wider, the fast jet operating costs likely to be lower and the utility of ships with strike assets embarked clearly underlined. In 2011 history's rhythm tapped on and conflict did not acquiesce to the economy.

We briefly discussed the meaning of cost and its importance as *Ocean* made her way to Libya. We joked about the living conditions on board and compared the ship to a hotel more precious aviators would refuse to stay in: 'Pilots sharing cabins! How could I possibly go to work under such circumstances? Soldiers and engineers stacked three bunks high in berths of six; surely there is a publication somewhere outlawing this!' Then 'where's the swimming pool?' brought the biggest laugh.

As for ammunition, we knew the situation on the ground was not going to mirror Helmand, and we would do a lot of firing. Engagements would not be fleeting, they were likely to be numerous, frequent and simultaneous. Our view was not complicated by economic concerns. We had hundreds of Hellfire. There were hundreds of targets. We would shoot until one or the other ran out, or until an accountant told us to stop. Until then we would keep going.

In the end we fired 99 Hellfire, 4,800 rounds of 30mm and 16 rockets on 48 sorties, striking 116 targets. The numbers of chaff and flare fired in self-defence against incoming missiles and radar lock-ons remains secret. There were plenty, and they worked. Our targets ranged from T-72 Main Battle Tanks, the ZSU 23-4, BM21s and buildings to the ubiquitous technicals. In fact, the technicals, all capable of shooting us down with their heavy calibre weapons, made up around half of our total targets. These were the main weapons of the regime, and our work against them certainly made a difference to the rebels and to Libyan civilians.

During June, July and early August NATO flew 3,194[13] strike sorties,[14] of which we flew 48, just 1.5 per cent of the whole NATO operation![15] Total targets struck by the UK over the same period are not available, but the total from 31 March to 31 October was around 640,[16] of which we struck 116, or 18 per cent. If we spread those 640 UK targets evenly across the full seven months approximately 92 were hit each month. The Apache flew for 2.25 months, during which 206 targets were likely to have been engaged, making our 116 targets 56 per cent of the UK effort while we participated. Just numbers, that's all.

If there is any value in this potted maths exercise it is that we flew little, fought a lot and, as you will note if you have read the preceding chapters of this story, got stuck into some vicious fights and got away with our lives. The taxpayer, even the critic, might conclude that this represented value for money!

By deploying seaborne helicopters, both British and French, NATO forced Gaddafi to picket the coast, all 900 miles of it, with scouts and MANPAD teams. This tied up a lot of his might and must have had a degrading psychological effect on those soldiers who spent weeks and months dug in, looking out to sea. After the first few missions, when these defences were tested and breached, the coastal scouts must have suffered from very low morale. The menace of the helicopter, its low-level loiter, the thunder of the blades and the almost personal message its munitions deliver were unique in the campaign. No other asset could have the same psychological impact, but it brought risk with it. The delicate risk-versus-reward estimate for every mission had to be captured, assessed and signed up to by the big hitters on *Ocean* and in the CAOC. It was their responsibility to see us safely through – but it was our place to deliver the plan.

All that was behind us now. We had made the journey from experimental exercise to surprise newcomer in a very hostile warzone. *Ocean* and her sailors had carried us, launched us and welcomed us back. They'd tolerated our mistakes, left the bar open and let us sleep when we needed to. The ship had been our protector and comfort and she kept us going when the world beyond the horizon seemed an awfully bleak and threatening place.

So our work was done. After that final unlaunched deck alert on 21 August we folded away the aircraft, signed in our morphine, Sig Saur pistols, Carbines and ammunition, signed 'not flown' again on the authorization booklet and went to the wardroom. Mark and John were invited in and we emptied the fridge of warm Carling while Sky's Alex Crawford followed the FLF into Tripoli on the telly. Those fighters who had watched Nick and his team strike in the Nafusa mountains just two weeks before had rattled through Zuwara, Sabratah and Az-Zawiyah on the way. There were no more front lines, the civil war had turned completely in favour of the uprising and the regime was in terminal decline.

Gaddafi was on the run. Khamis had been killed, by an Apache, or so the regime said. Moussa Ibrahim was silent, his brother killed, again by an Apache, or so the regime said.[17] The inner circle were running for their lives and the Apache was being cited as their nemesis. Tripoli fell first. Brega and Zlitan came next. There was no place for us in the confusion that followed, and we stayed afloat, an option waiting for politicians to time our redeployment home.

A whole new team had trained to replace us: 664 Squadron spent the summer flying from HMS *Illustrious* back home. They had two tasks – be ready for Libya and be ready for Helmand. By the end of August there was no more need for the Apache, but politicians pondered, and no decision was the best decision, so 664 got on the bus. They came out to *Ocean*. We trained together. We planned. The CAOC hinted at Bani Walid. We did our calculations and the engineers installed extra fuel tanks. We were ready, Hellfire, guns and fuel. They eventually said 'no' again. Then it came. At about half past two one busy Thursday afternoon in late September the Captain piped the end of our Ellamy commitment. We could be home by the weekend. Time to pack, so we did. All ready. Plane booked and *Ocean* made best speed for Crete.

We had one last day of work in the flip-flop, processing all our reports, writing everything down, storing guntape, getting the Operational Record ready. Then a last blast in the wardroom and a signal from the Commodore: 'BZ to the Apache team.'[18]

It was the end of war for us. A man called Dave, plucked from the desert by the SBS in February, tracked down by the Navy, flown out to us, boiler-suited and stained with decades of oil and grime, hammered the tired diesel generators into action and *Ocean* tracked for Crete. The Navigator said 20 hours. We were ready to go home.

We had survived. On that last night, sailing back to Crete, in a quiet moment on the quarterdeck with Wings I remarked, 'When we got into this, we didn't know how it would unfold. After those first three or four missions, I expected someone to come unstuck. Now that we haven't, I can't quite see how we all made it, but this is an enormous relief.'

'Yes it is, isn't it. But it's changed you, all of you. I can see that. This is going to stay with you for a long while. Cracking job though, cracking job.'

## *Chapter 15*

# Six Weeks Later

'Never smile when you pack your bags.' Advice from JB on how to keep a happy marriage in the Army. Going away on operations is a challenge we relish. We are about to do our jobs in an unforgiving environment where all our training will be tested. Going away is exciting for the soldier, but anyone at home watching us pack is in a very different place. We have a sense of mounting excitement; they are faced with the big dark space of monotony, hard work and single parenting, bills, insurance renewals, the school run, work, poorly animals and no reward. No thanks or acknowledgement, they are just expected to get on with it. Meanwhile, we are flying the best helicopter in the world in the most demanding places, with our friends. When we are packing our bags we are already there. In our minds we've left home and made the journey. Those we leave behind have none of that nervous anticipation; they are developing coping mechanisms to fill the space, to deal with the unrewarded hard work. We try and make the most of the final few days together, but we are in separate worlds. We argue. We fall out. We make up. Then the soldier leaves again.

After a while, perhaps a few months, the excitement begins to wane and we yearn for home. At home, life has established a new way to fill the space. Phone calls are matter of fact, seldom private and often finished without saying enough of what we feel. Then we edge towards the end. The tour comes to a close, planned or surprise, and we head home.

HMS *Ocean* came alongside in Chania, Crete on 24 September and the job was done. *Ocean* and the Apaches had completed their part in Operation Ellamy. It was time to go home, and the departure was rapid – no time for ceremony or celebration. I wanted to mark it somehow, but there wasn't time, apart from a quick gathering and my words of praise to the eighty-three men and women who had changed the way we operated and carried us to success.

This composite team, put together in part due to availability and in part because of their skills, could not last beyond the success of the operation. We should have gone our separate ways in June 2011, but extraordinary circumstances in North Africa created an opportunity to test us operationally and kept us together to see it through.

The squadron gathered in the galley. I was sad inside, proud on the outside. I was louder than normal. I told them they'd made history, they'd been brave, they'd defied the odds in combat. I asked them to hold their heads up high but wear it modestly. I warned that sceptics would come their way, sometimes out of envy, sometimes accompanied by malice; but whatever they encountered, good or bad, they knew the truth of their industry and they should be proud. I knew this was it, the last time we would be together. The work was done, and finally they were heading home. Our six-week exercise had stretched to twenty-two weeks of an unscheduled operational tour in a new environment for everyone on the team. No one had done this before; they were the only ones. The Sergeant Major brought everyone to attention; I thanked them all and walked away. This was the end of command. The end of unusual conflict. The end of my team, my unique, complicated and courageous team.

That night a last blast in the wardroom, the rec rooms, the quarterdeck and wherever else blurred into panic packing, printing, copying, shredding and readying. By breakfast on 25 September all were ready to move, packed, Post-Operational Report drafted, guntape secured and all longing for home.

They stood on the quayside and waited for coaches to take them to the airport. A rugby ball was passed about, some lay on their bags in the sun. The smokers smoked. The on-ops smokers smoked. Sunglasses and smiles all round. Phones on ears.

I leant on the quarterdeck with Little Shippers, Charlie, Mark and Doug, our eyes on the homebound team. Our bags weren't packed. We didn't leave. We five, ten of our ground crew and a fresh team of engineers stayed.

On the quayside three coaches arrived, bags were hauled upon shoulders and they were gone.

'Let's go make a plan,' someone said. And we went down to the flip-flop and unrolled a new set of maps. We sailed east the same night, but that's another story.

\*

The rest of the squadron flew home. Those who remained on board followed about a month later, and *Ocean*, having sailed 24,000 nautical miles, eventually came alongside in Plymouth on 9 December. Her 310-strong crew had spent 279 days at sea in 2011 carrying another 300 personnel with them. Just 87 of those days were spent on the line committed to the Libya operation; such is the extent and diversity of the tasks our ships conduct at sea. That year Wings managed 13 helicopters and safely brought back almost 3,000 deck landings; and, if there is another statistic worthy of historical record, it is that the ship's dentist performed 256 fillings!

When December came and HMS *Ocean* neared Plymouth Sound, I flew out to be part of her homecoming, spending the day on board when she came into port. Her crew lined the decks in their best uniform, tugboats blasted water, aircraft flew past and the band of the Royal Marines played loud. It was an emotional return, and the prize for the best shore-side placard went to the brave girl who had written 'Dad I'm Pregnant!' on a four-square-metre declaration.

The task was done. Five attack helicopters had proved their worth at sea. Our engineers had kept them flying. Our soldiers had delivered a deck tempo that meant our pilots kept doing what was asked of them. *Ocean* had kept us going. And we had succeeded. We had hit every target allocated to us. And we had not been hit ourselves, despite the unprecedented incoming fire and sophistication of the weapon systems used against us.

I have often been asked about people – pro-Gaddafi soldiers – 'How many were killed on those missions?' Somehow we have become interested in a body count, that most banal statistic of war. A clean and easy answer is: those who shot at us died. Of course this is not the whole answer. There were many pro-Gaddafi soldiers actively threatening the civilian population. They were on our targets, doing their best to keep Libya as it had been for 41 years. And we stopped them with Hellfire and rockets and 30mm. We killed them as we destroyed their tanks and guns and hiding places. And the ones who didn't die told their friends about it and steadily stopped going to work. Cognitive effect must be demonstrably persuasive. There will never be a body count. I think I know the number, but I'll never tell.

Then there were all the constraints of the targeting process and launch criteria; the layering of jets and drones that make responsible people feel better about our risk; the complexity of the Apache and the technology of its weapons. Given all these factors, this was small, agile, adaptable and comparatively inexpensive contribution to a huge air campaign in support of the tens of thousands of Libyans taking back their freedom. We joined the war when it was at stalemate, with civilians being slain daily and having nowhere to hide. The clear delineation of friend and foe made our missions easy to direct, but also put us in harm's way as soon as we got in sight of the coast. In assisting the FLF breakout and getting pro-Gad on the run we completed our task.

It had certainly been an unexpected adventure and one that carried with it the very real danger of coming unstuck. Those early weeks weaving among the triple-A and bracing for the impact of the SA-24 remain hard subjects for all of us to discuss beyond our small group. I feel the dryness in my mouth, the tension in my voice and the grinding of my teeth when the memory is provoked. The view out of the right-hand window of a missile streaking upwards while the American lady in the wing tells you it's happening and flares are pumping out is ever vivid, has not faded. And the memory of the same missile being taken by the flares and then exploding in a final attempt to complete its task remains bright too.

In those moments the fear was huge. Our vulnerability, the fragility of life measured in seconds and centimetres, the instinct and desperation to survive – all these were acute. We all feared, but somehow death did not choose us. Perishing under the sea or being shot to pieces over the land were our clearest fears. In the moments of combat we all had that clarity and so we fought to kill the man and the weapon that was attacking us. A man who fires a shoulder-launched missile at a helicopter is a trained operator, a skilled soldier. If he misses he will adjust his aim and try again or reassess the shot and do better next time. We knew that. He had to die.

Just as I was afraid for my own life in those brightly lit, chaotic battles, I was seized by fear when I sat in the Operations Room in HMS *Ocean* when not the lead for a mission. There I could only follow the battle as far as the radios would reach and then read the JCHAT to catch a glimpse of information as the patrol commander relayed his actions to Matrix, and Matrix JCHATted it to everyone else.

The sound of two Apaches arriving out of the black, tracked by the ship's radar and night sights and landing after a mission, would bring a palpable sense of relief in the ship. With both on board and the SKASaC safely tied down too, the Officer of the Watch would bring the ship to port and head north to safer waters. Each time I was thankful we were all on board. Each mission reminded me that command was an unceasing responsibility. That whatever happened 'out there' was for me to own. The commander can never delegate that responsibility.

The CO and I wrote citations on each of the aircrew and on some of the engineers and ground crew too. In the end there were a number of commendations of various sorts, a solitary Distinguished Flying Cross and one Mention in Despatches. The CO and I wished for more, but sadly they didn't catch the selector's eye, or if they did, someone filtered them out. The citations are never disclosed and the narrative is kept locked away. This secrecy is hard to explain, and it is sad to think that those people – aircrew, ground crew and engineers we had written on – will never know how much we valued their service. We're not in wars to win medals, and we don't swallow down our fear and go out again to face the incoming just to be seen to be brave. Stepping out into the unknown on the first night, and then into the very real and hostile known every night after that, was worth a Distinguished Flying Cross for every one of those pilots on any one of their missions. Blades turning just feet from the waves to escape the hostility, a crew raging through the incoming to protect another, no one shied away. They flew against the most sophisticated threat British Army pilots have ever faced. And each night when they were fired at, be it with an AK, a PKM, triple-A, ZSU, SA-24 or radar-guided systems, they evaded, weaved and escaped the shots, spun about, faced the enemy, killed him and got on with the task at hand. Every time. They were heroes.

With the job done, we all moved on. Charlie and Jay both got back on the Afghanistan treadmill. They've been back there twice since Libya, now having spent over a year of their lives fighting the Taliban. During the 14 September 2012 Taliban assault on Camp Bastion, Jay was airborne and intervened to prevent insurgents rampaging across the main runway towards the camp. The two young upstarts blooded in Helmand and proven in Libya are now among the most experienced combat operators in the Attack Helicopter Force. All this, and still less than twenty-eight years old.

Doug got promoted. He finally made it to Afghanistan on operations in the last year of that campaign and continues to serve in the Army Air Corps, all ink, short hair and keeping-it-real attitude.

Big Shippers went back to the Royal Navy. He had been in the Apache world for almost eight years, been to Afghanistan four times and had to postpone his return to the Navy in the summer of 2011 to help us through Libya. The irony was that he found himself at sea with the Army, so he extended with us to lend his expertise to the new war.

For four years he was the Army Air Corps' foremost weapons expert, an A2-graded Standards instructor and the cornerstone of how we rewrote rules to make sense of the Apache in this new environment. And the Royal Navy wanted him back. They had a new helicopter to bring into service and Big Shippers needed to be at the front of that project too. We've met up, even flown sorties at sea. It's always the same, on the quarterdeck or in the wardroom.

Reuben Sands and Nick Stevens left the Army, and commercial aviation is the richer for their presence. Bright, ambitious minds making their own luck. Little Shippers considered an offer to become a test pilot, but decided that life out of uniform was best, with marriage, a baby and a big, daunting house renovation. CJ also went. The Cumberland Show produce awards are now dominated by the newcomer who lectures in engineering and keeps a smallholding. She was also Young Woman Engineer of the Year in 2011. These are extraordinary people who made our success in war possible.

All teams end, all good things pass. We all have new tasks, new projects and challenges. In early 2014 I took command of one of our Apache Regiments and set about readying the new team for Afghanistan and everything else.

I wrote the last lines of this small piece of aviation history sitting in the late afternoon sun just a few miles north of the Barry M. Goldwater ranges in Arizona, USA. With the USAF F-16s roaring out north and flying low over Gila Bend Auxiliary Airfield, I contemplated our missions racing hard into and out of Libya, and where our story began. We train in Arizona, grateful guests of the United States, and we learn to fight and survive in the world's best attack helicopter. On this visit JB was in charge of teaching a new cohort of aircrew. Their first Hellfire down range, the new graduates of CTR 16 were already settling into their squadrons and getting ready for Afghanistan and whatever comes next. Jay Lewis was also teaching – his speciality being weapons – and 656 showed up too, refined, agile and setting the pace for everyone else to try and keep up with. Mark Hall was their resident instructor. On that same day, over in Afghanistan, Charlie Tollbrooke was flying as usual and Doug Reid was there too, both of them putting their shoulders to the task. Back in the UK, Little Shippers had taken on a civilian instructional role and was teaching our fledgling Apache pilots, soldiers whom John Blackwell had taught the basics of helicopter flight. John had stopped just short of retirement and was allowed to train as an instructor after all. The careers people recognized that although contributing to another cycle in Afghanistan was what they had demanded, his activities in Libya qualified just as well!

Of the ten who flew Apache strike missions into Libya, six are now instructors, four of them on the Apache. All teams end, but their skills have been reinvested. Meanwhile, in Devonport, the mighty *O* is about to slip and proceed after a long refit. In Portsmouth, HMS *Illustrious* has come alongside for the last time. And up in Rosyth the tremendous 65,000-tonne HMS *Queen Elizabeth* has launched, an exclusive bottle of 25-year-old Bowmore tapped on her hull. All ready for whatever comes next.

It has been three years since the summer of 2011. Enough time has passed for those who lived it to settle into other projects, reflect and lend their memories. I wrote to Nick Stevens when thanking him for organizing our first reunion in 2013:

> Sir,
> You are an excellent operations man. Civilian life suits you, but I declare that you are wasted upon it. An outstanding evening, very much enjoyed.
> On other news – we should write . . .

And so we gathered the team, described the project and resolved to tell our story, from our memories, just as it happened that extraordinary summer.

# Notes

1. A daring mission in January 2007 to recover a fallen Royal Marine in which the Apaches flew with rescuers sitting on the wings of the aircraft
2. Floatation Gear and a Canopy Jettison System safe to use underwater were explored after our experience at sea and are now MoD-funded projects
3. Rules of Engagement
4. Issue 1290,10 June 2011
5. 'Gaddafi Makes Britain a Total Laughing Stock', *Daily Express*, 30 July 2011
6. 'British, French Helicopters Attack Libyan Targets for FirstTime', *Washington Post*, 4 June 2011
7. Pararescuemen
8. A head cover that makes the flying helmet more comfortable
9. Apache missions were launched in all three front lines in Libya (Brega, Zlitan and Nafusa), with our final missions taking place in the Nafusa mountains
10. Brief factual text conversations keep all commanders informed. Here Nick had transmitted to the ABCCC, who had then sent the text on JCHAT. His full message was, 'Callsign Valkyrie has fired 7 Hellfire and 540 30mm destroying 6 armed pickup trucks, 1 building and several Regime soldiers. There was no collateral damage, nor were any civilians injured or killed. We are now returning to HMS *Ocean* where we expect to arrive in 10 minutes'
11. http://www.youtube.com/watch?v=hHlk6Ss6Czo The MoD footage, not edited in chronological order, begins with the strike against the communications node on Okba airfield, then shows the 99th Hellfire strike against a technical, as described in the final quarter of this chapter. The footage then shows the destruction of eight technicals described above. In reality, the action took place as it is described in this chapter, but the footage is the actual guntape from that night
12. House of Commons Defence Committee, Operations in Libya, 9th Report of session, 25 January 2012. http://www.publications.parliament.uk/pa/cm201012/cmselect/cmd fence/950/95007.htm
13. Extrapolated from the NATO daily briefing sheets found at http://www. jfcnaples.nato.int/Unified_Protector/page1915311.aspx
14. Strike sorties are intended to identify and engage appropriate targets, but do not necessarily deploy munitions each time
15. The UK flew a total of 2,100 strike sorties during the entire campaign, with our 48 contributing 2.3 per cent
16. UK Ministry of Defence website https://www.gov.uk/government/ news/deputy-pm-welcomes-home-uk-forces-from-libya-campaign published 3 November 2011
17. It is very difficult to measure 'cognitive effect' – the degree to which the regime feared the Apache. However, when Khamis Gaddafi was allegedly killed on 29 August the regime announced he was killed by an Apache. This was reported by CNN and Sky among others. Hassan Ali Ibrahim, brother of government spokesman, Moussa Ibrahim, was killed in Az-Zawiyah on 18 August. Moussa Ibrahim blamed the Apache once more and again this was widely reported in the international media. Whatever the truth in this, it is clear the regime feared us
18. 'Bravo Zulu' – 'Well done' in Navy parlance. To receive a 'BZ' by Signal from the Commodore was high praise